The Next Global Stage

Challenges and Opportunities in Our Borderless World

W Wharton School Publishing

In the face of accelerating turbulence and change, business leaders and policy makers need new ways of thinking to sustain performance and growth.

Wharton School Publishing offers a trusted source for stimulating ideas from thought leaders who provide new mental models to address changes in strategy, management, and finance. We seek out authors from diverse disciplines with a profound understanding of change and its implications. We offer books and tools that help executives respond to the challenge of change.

Every book and management tool we publish meets quality standards set by The Wharton School of the University of Pennsylvania. Each title is reviewed by the Wharton School Publishing Editorial Board before being given Wharton's seal of approval. This ensures that Wharton publications are timely, relevant, important, conceptually sound or empirically based, and implementable.

To fit our readers' learning preferences, Wharton publications are available in multiple formats, including books, audio, and electronic.

To find out more about our books and management tools, visit us at whartonsp.com and Wharton's executive education site, exceed.wharton.upenn.edu.

UNIVERSITY of PENNSYLVANIA

The Next Global Stage

Challenges and Opportunities in Our Borderless World

Kenichi Ohmae

Library of Congress Number: 2004114830

Vice President, Editor-in-Chief: Tim Moore
Editorial Assistant: Richard Winkler
Development Editor: Russ Hall
Marketing Manager: Martin Litkowski
International Marketing Manager: Tim Galligan
Cover Designer: Chuti Prasertsith
Managing Editor: Gina Kanouse
Senior Project Editor: Sarah Kearns
Copy Editor: Krista Hansing
Senior Indexer: Cheryl Lenser
Compositor: Tolman Creek
Manufacturing Buyer: Dan Uhrig

LL Wharton School Publishing

© 2005 by Pearson Education, Inc.
Publishing as Wharton School Publishing
Upper Saddle River, New Jersey 07458

Wharton School Publishing offers excellent discounts on this book
when ordered in quantity for bulk purchases or special sales. For
more information, please contact U.S. Corporate and Government
Sales, 1-800-382-3419, corpsales@pearsontechgroup.com. For
sales outside the U.S., please contact International Sales at
international@pearsoned.com.

Company and product names mentioned herein are the trademarks or registered
trademarks of their respective owners.

Printed in the United States of America

Sixth Printing: October 2007
This product is printed digitally on demand.

ISBN-10:   0-13-704378-3

ISBN-13:   978-0-13-704378-1

Pearson Education LTD.
Pearson Education Australia PTY, Limited.
Pearson Education Singapore, Pte. Ltd.
Pearson Education North Asia, Ltd.
Pearson Education Canada, Ltd.
Pearson Educatión de Mexico, S.A. de C.V.
Pearson Education—Japan
Pearson Education Malaysia, Pte. Ltd.

To Ron Daniel, who showed me the global stage when I was a young, aspiring consultant.

CONTENTS

ACKNOWLEDGMENTS

First, I would like to thank Stuart Crainer for his invaluable help in developing my script for the global stage.

On the publishing side, Yoram Wind of Wharton has been an inspirational and enthusiastic supporter of the book from the very start. His feedback as the manuscript progressed was invaluable.

At the business end of Wharton Publishing, editor-in-chief Tim Moore provided energy at every turn. Russ Hall fine-tuned the words and Martin Litkowski helped get the message to the world.

At home in Tokyo, I am lucky enough to be surrounded by a group of amazingly bright, enthusiastic, and helpful people. In particular, I would like to record my thanks to Messrs. Taniguchi, Kyou, and Tashiro of the Business Breakthrough Research Institute.

ABOUT THE AUTHOR

Kenichi Ohmae is one of the world's leading business and corporate strategists. Born in 1943, he earned a doctorate in nuclear engineering from the Massachusetts Institute of Technology, and subsequently worked as a senior design engineer for Hitachi. He then joined McKinsey & Company, becoming a senior partner, developing and running the company's Japan operations for a number of years. He gained an unrivaled knowledge and sensitivity to developments in a wide range of business sectors.

Many of his books have been translated into English, including *The Mind of the Strategist* (McGraw-Hill), *Triad Power* (Free Press), *The Borderless World* (Harper Business), *The End of the Nation State* (Free Press), and *The Invisible Continent* (HarperCollins). He is a frequent contributor to many of the world's leading newspapers and news magazines, including *The Wall Street Journal*, *The New York Times*, *Harvard Business Review*, and *Newsweek*. He lectures on entrepreneurship at the Attacker's Business School, which he founded in Japan.

He is the founder and managing director of a number of flourishing businesses in Japan, including Business Breakthrough Television (a 24/7 business channel); Ohmae & Associates; EveryD.com Inc.; Ohmae Business Developments Inc.; and General Services, Inc., a cross-border business process outsourcing company in China.

For Kenichi Ohmae, the world has become truly unified with the advent of telecommunications technology. As a scientist and consultant, Ohmae has always been alive to the role that technology can play in breaking down barriers and the implications this has for business and society. He has developed a number of platforms in areas such as distance education, the home delivery of groceries, and an address book database. These include "Air Campus," which facilitates distance learning, and "Everyday dot-com," which delivers groceries using micro bar codes on the Internet or mobile phones. His advice and unique insights are constantly sought by both government leaders and businessmen.

Introduction————————

Ideas do not emerge perfectly formed. They are awkward amalgams of experience, insight, hopes, and inspiration. They arrive on stage blinking under the bright lights, hesitant, unsure as to the audience's likely reaction. They evolve and develop, alert to changing reactions and circumstances.

I have been rehearsing the arguments that form the backbone of *The Next Global Stage* for more than two decades. My previous books, including *The Borderless World* and *The Invisible Continent*, examined many of the issues I am still exploring. Ideas, as I say, do not emerge in a state of perfection.

In its genesis, *The Next Global Stage* has been shaped by two forces.

First, it bears witness to changing circumstances. Over the last two decades, the world has changed substantially. The economic, political, social, corporate, and personal rules that now apply bear scant relation to those applicable two decades ago. *Different times require a new script.*

The trouble is that, far too often, we find ourselves reading from much of the same tired script. With the expansion of the global economy has come a more unified view of the business world. It is seen as a totality in itself, not constricted by national barriers. This view has been acquired not by the traditional cognitive route of reading textbooks or learned articles. Instead, it has come directly, through exposure to the world, frequent travel, and mixing with the world's business people. Paradoxically, perhaps, this breeds a similarity of outlook. Opinions and perspectives are shared; the type of developments in the political and economic worlds that are held to be important are shared, too. With shared outlooks come shared solutions. But a common view of the world will not produce the unorthodox solutions and responses required by the global stage.

Over the last 30 years, I have traveled to 60 countries as a consultant, speaker, and vacationer. Some countries, such as the United States, I have visited more than 400 times; Korea and Taiwan 200 times each; and Malaysia 100 times. Recently, I have been averaging six visits a year to China and have started a company in Dalian, as well as producing 18 hours of television programs seeking to explain what is really happening there in business and politics. I also spend a lot of time on the Gold Coast in Australia and in Whistler, Canada. Of course, as a Japanese national, I live in Tokyo and travel extensively within Japan.

As you can see, I believe that nothing is more important than actually visiting the place, meeting with companies, and talking to CEOs, employees, and consumers. That is how you develop a feel for what is going on. For some of my visits, I have taken groups of 40–60 Japanese executives so they can witness first-hand regions that are attracting money from the rest of the world. I have taken groups to Ireland to see how cross-border business process outsourcing is reshaping its economy. I have taken them to see Italy's small towns that are thriving on the global stage. We have also visited Scandinavian countries to find out why they have emerged as the world's most competitive nations, and Eastern Europe to see how they may be positioned in the extended 25-member European Union. The group has also visited China and the United States twice, as well as India, Vietnam, Malaysia, Singapore, the Philippines, Korea, and Australia.

The executives who join me on these trips change their views of the world. Even in the days of the Internet and global cable news, walking around, listening, looking, and asking a question is still the best way to learn. Seeing what is happening in the world firsthand changes perspectives. Having witnessed the global stage, executives then begin to read newspapers and watch television with different eyes. Gradually, their views broaden and they feel comfortable in their roles as actors on the global stage. It does not necessarily come easily; new skills are required.

The second defining force behind *The Next Global Stage* is that, over the last 20 years, I have witnessed some of the pioneers of the global economy firsthand.

One of the first business leaders to be sympathetic to the notion of the truly global economy was the former CEO of Smith Kline Beecham, Henry Wendt. He saw cross-border alliances as a potential savior for the American pharmaceuticals industry and recognized that internationally based strategic alliances would become important, if not vital.

Henry realized that there were three dominant markets in the world: the United States, Japan and the Far East, and Europe. No *single* company could deal with and service all these markets effectively, no matter how powerful and dominant it might feel. No corporation could hope to cover a market of 700 million people that had a per-capita GNP income of more than $10,000.

Companies traditionally used a marketing strategy that depended on a sequential penetration of each market, whether it was a region or a country. When you established yourself and your product in market A, then (and only then) you moved on to market B. But Henry Wendt proposed that when you have a good product, you have to adopt a sprinkler model, penetrating various markets *simultaneously*. One way to achieve this is through strategic cross-border alliances.[1]

Henry Wendt entered into negotiations with Beecham, a company with a particularly high reputation in R&D and a strong presence in Europe, and, in time, these negotiations led to a merger. Not only did he opt to go down the merger path, but also, with powerful symbolism, he moved the company's corporate headquarters from Pittsburgh to London.

Henry Wendt had foresight and vision. His notion of cross-border alliances was truly innovative. In those days, such alliances and mergers were difficult because each large company was embedded in its domestic markets. These companies were also under the thumb of their respective domestic governments, with which they were closely linked and closely identified. It is very difficult to abandon your home turf. (Witness the more recent outcry about outsourcing.) For one thing, there may be government resistance (as we have seen in merger talks across Germany and France). There are also media commentators, like mammoths or dinosaurs stuck in a freezing swamp, who describe such moves as unpatriotic and unprincipled. They tend to report on one or other side "winning" in any merger, as with Daimler Chrysler.

In a world where borders were weakening, cross-border alliances were the only way for a company to survive and prosper. In the pharmaceuticals world, drugs were becoming more standardized. The important and potentially profitable compounds and formulas became less distinct. This was accompanied by an astronomical rise in the cost of R&D. New regulations piled on both costs and delays. Yet the amount of money invested in R&D had only an indirect link to the level of success that could be achieved. A company could build up the best-equipped laboratories, staffed with the optimal mixture of experience and youthful brilliance. This never guaranteed success. There was still an element of chance determining whether the right leads would be pursued and the breakthroughs realized.

The dilemma is that when the R&D is successful and a superdrug is born, you might not have adequate sales forces in the key markets of the world. So the amortization of R&D money is less, and, at the same time, you might have to keep expensive people in the field even when you don't have drugs to sell. This is the problem with industries such as pharmaceuticals, where high fixed costs demand size to justify them. That is why you need to seek strategic alliances and sometimes to go one step further to total cross-border mergers. In the mid-1980s, examples were few and far between. But now, we see examples of cross-border alliances and M&As almost daily in banking, airlines, retailing, power generation, automobiles, consumer and business electronics, machinery, and semiconductors.

Size and capitalization did play a part. A medium-size pharmaceuticals company might well spend $1 billion in R&D and have no results, but a larger company might be able to sink $3 billion into R&D. It could afford to miss the target more often and still remain profitable. Cross-border alliances allowed more companies to do this. It was only possible, though, once they saw beyond their home markets. Today, the concept of cross-border alliances is no longer a novelty. Henry's path-breaking role deserves recognition.

Another early pioneer of the global economy was Walter Wriston, former chairman of Citibank. He saw globalization as an imperative not because of management or business theories, but because of technological breakthroughs. He prophesized that competition between banks would no longer be based on banking services, but on acquiring better technology. Effectively, the company able to make decisions quicker, often in the fraction of a nanosecond, would be the winner.

Walter Wriston understood the future shape of banking—and of the global economy. It was to be based in a world without borders; it would float around decisions made in a split second, sometimes by nonhumans. Technology was to be the key to success in banking, so the person at the helm of Citibank had to be technology savvy. But his vision left him in a minority. Twenty years ago, most top bankers were traditionalists. They saw relationships of trust and confidentiality forged among business and governmental hierarchies as the key to success, not technology. Technology was all good, but it was for whiz kids, not bankers.

John Reid, Wriston's handpicked successor as head of Citibank in 1984, was not a product of the traditional East Coast banking establishment. Reid was a technologist. An MIT graduate, he had been working in Citibank on ATM applications and other electronic banking projects. At the time of his appointment, he was virtually unknown within the corporation. Some even greeted his appointment with the question "John Who?."

Walter Wriston defended his decision by saying that it was very hard to teach technology to an established banker, but relatively easy to teach banking to a technology specialist. As for relationships, these would develop over time. Under Reid's stewardship, Citibank became the largest bank in the world. Along the way, he astutely led Citibank through the Latin American financial crisis.

Yet another business leader who was ahead of his time was Akio Morita, co-founder of Sony. The original business was called Tokyo Tsushin Kogyo or Totsuko (TTK). This name, even in its abbreviated form, was too difficult for Western markets. So Morita came up with the four-letter *Sony* to represent the quality of sound from his transistor radios. For Morita, the world was one big market, with few or no barriers. He thought big but was no megalomaniac. He famously advised companies to "Think Globally, Act Locally." This philosophy was christened *glocal* by the Japanese magazine *Nikkei Business* and led to the coining of a new word, *glocalization*.

These visionaries shared many of my views about the then-emerging global economy, explained in such books as *Triad Power* and *The Borderless World*. I was fortunate enough to exchange views with all three of them and many others in the mid-1980s and beyond. However, discussions on the importance of the region-state proved more elusive and troublesome. I had to wait until the developments within China post-1998 to gain any sort of useful practical perspective on this issue.

Some Stage Directions

In *The Next Global Stage*, with these intellectual antecedents in mind, I begin by looking at the state of the world and how we make sense of it. Part I, "The Stage," looks at some of the areas of explosive growth (Chapter 1, "The World Tour") and identifies some of the characteristics of the global economy. It then looks back at the birth point of this new era (Chapter 2, "Opening Night"). This part ends with an examination of the failure of traditional economics—and economists—to make sense of the global economy (Chapter 3, "The End of Economics").

In Part II, "Stage Directions," I examine the major trends emerging on the global stage. In the opening section of Chapter 4, "Playmakers," I explore the development of the nation-state and the dynamics of what I call the region-state, the most useful and potent means of economic organization in the global economy. I go on (in Chapter 5, "Platforms for Progress"), to introduce the idea of platforms, such as the use of English, Windows, branding, and the U.S. dollar, as global means of communication, understanding, and commerce. Finally, I explore what parts of business have to change in line with the emerging economy. These include business systems and processes (Chapter 6, "Out and About") and products, people, and logistics (Chapter 7, "Breaking the Chains").

In Part III, "The Script," I provide analysis of how these changes and trends will impact governments (Chapter 8, "Reinventing Government"), corporations, and individuals (Chapter 9, "The Futures Market"). I look at some of the regions that might be the economic dynamos shaping the world beyond the global stage (Chapter 10, "The Next Stage"). In the final section, I revisit my book, *The Mind of the Strategist*, and think through the need for changes in the frameworks we use in developing corporate strategy on the global stage.

The Next Global Stage makes sense of the world as I see it. Twenty years ago, globalization was a term, a theoretical concept. Now it is a reality. *The Next Global Stage* is part of a process of understanding the new rules that apply in this new world—and often, there aren't rules to adequately explain what we now experience on a daily basis. It is not an endpoint, nor is it a beginning, but I hope it is an important step forward for companies and individuals, as well as regional and national leaders.

Kenichi Ohmae
Tokyo
September 2004

Notes

[1] I explored this theme in *Triad Power: The Coming Shape of Global Competition* (New York: Simon & Schuster, 1985).

THE PLOT————————

We live in a truly networked and interdependent world, united by a global economy. In the past, business and economics were like plays (maybe by the same author) performed in separate theaters to discrete audiences. Their actors and actresses were distinct, and their manner of performance was often influenced by the individual theater's tradition. Now the drama takes place on one enormous global stage. The players on this stage are sometimes in competition for the audience's attention, but movements across the stage are free-flowing, no longer obstructed by obsolete stage furniture. The global stage is in a state of perpetual motion. *The Next Global Stage* provides a script to negotiate your route through the shifting plot lines.

This has been made possible by advances in information technology. Data now passes freely from one side of the world to the other, along fiber-optic cables or satellite transmissions. Information defies barriers, whether physical or political. It is facilitated by the establishment of platforms for streamlining the application of technology to definite tasks. Powerful search engines, such as Google, make it possible to find and combine unrelated pieces of information in the digital labyrinth. In the analog society, discrete pieces of information had to be humanly spliced together to draw out meaning. Now, mind-less robots running through millions of interconnected computers are capable of putting together the synthesized information and implications in a matter of milliseconds. Information from 8 billion Web pages (as of January 2005) is amalgamated to draw a synthesized perspective and knowledge in a split second. In the past, it took a wise man or an experienced journalist to relate one piece of information with another, but now any layperson can find relationships among many seemingly unrelated events and incidents by throwing multiple words into a search engine.

In the past, chemists searched relevant articles in *Chemical Abstract*, an authoritative and massive collection of all the work by chemists around the world. Stock buyers and traders searched key information using Bloomberg, Reuters, Telerate, Nikkei, or other influential sources in their particular country. Now Google or other such search engines are the common portal. Chances are, most of the information—or, at least, the clue to the information—you are looking for exists in digital form. So, mankind has migrated into the borderless and digital world without an official opening ceremony at the new global theater.

The global theater has many world-changing implications, some already being put into effect in countries such as China, Finland, and Ireland. The global economy ignores barriers, but if they are not removed, they cause distortion. The traditional centralized nation-state is another source of friction. It is ill equipped to play a meaningful role on the global stage, whereas its component regions are often the best units for attracting and retaining prosperity. The region-state is the best unit of prosperity on the global stage, but this can be enhanced by coming together informally in larger umbrellas, such as the European Union, which can enhance free trade, consistency of governing laws, and market integration.

The revolution in data-transfer technology has already had an impact on the nature of money and capital movement. Money can flow unrestricted to the areas of highest return. Old notions about corporate value are challenged by the growing influence of multiples and derivatives. A lot of traditional thinking on economics depended on national policy. In countries where outside world influences strongly affect the domestic economy, old economic theories do not hold up.

Consider the two very different economic crises in Argentina over the last decade. The first put the whole country, as well as plenty of outsiders, into a state of panic; the second did not. By the time of the second crisis, most people associated with Argentina, both insiders and outsiders, depended less on its domestic currency, the *new peso*, because most of them had converted their assets into the dollar, a global standard for savings and settlement.

If, as I believe, the global economy is powered by technology, then knowledge is its precious metal. India's strength, for example, can be substantially attributed to the sheer volume of its Ph.Ds in science. Emerging nations can propel economic growth through education. An area no longer has to be endowed with mineral wealth or a large population, or a strong military, to become a major player on the global economic stage. It can acquire its wealth and know-how through investment from the rest of the world beyond its borders. This must no longer be seen as a threat, but as a source of immense opportunities.

Although the global economy presents opportunities, there are also challenges to be faced by government, businesses, and individuals. These can only be met by adopting flexibility and pragmatism.

PART I: THE STAGE

1

THE WORLD TOUR

The Curtain Rises

The Great Hall of the People on Beijing's Tiananmen Square is accustomed to choreography. For more than four decades, the vast auditorium echoed to the well-rehearsed speeches of China's communist rulers, urging their compatriots to yet greater sacrifices in the name of Socialism. Alternatively, it rang with plaudits for its leader, Chairman Mao Zedong, the Great Helmsman, each of whose appearances were greeted by the thunderous ovations of thousands of "parliamentarians" gathered from all corners of China for the spectacle.

The auditorium of the Hall of the People can seat more than 8,000 people. Its dimensions symbolized the place where the unity of the nation was displayed. It was a perfect location for mass culture, such as the staging of "proletarian opera"—as long as this did not interfere with its pre-eminent political role.

Most of the former uses to which the Great Hall was put are now overlooked. They are, at best, oddities from the past, not unlike the giant portrait of Chairman Mao that continues to flutter in a corner of Tiananmen. The Great Hall of the People is still home to the National People's Congress, the Chinese parliament, but the bill of fare of its extracurricular activities has changed radically.

In the autumn of 2003, it hosted performances of the Irish dance spectacle *Riverdance*. The show is based on the Irish tradition of step or tap dancing, and the music, written by Irishman Bill Whelan, blends traditional Irish folk music, Japanese drumming, flamenco, and modern dance rhythms. The 70 strong troupes of Riverdancers were in Beijing in response to a personal invitation made by Premier Zhu Rongji during a visit to the Irish Republic.

Riverdance started out modestly enough. It was an intermission piece in the Eurovision Song Contest staged in Dublin in 1994. The winning song is long forgotten, but *Riverdance* goes from strength to strength. Its success has been global. It has been staged in 27 countries, and it is estimated that a quarter of the planet's population may have seen it through television broadcasts. In spite of the show's phenomenal successes in venues such as Madison Square Garden in New York, Tokyo's International Forum, and Wembley in London, success in China was a dream that had driven the show's organizers for years. The Great Hall of the People was just one stop on a tour of the Far East comprising 46 shows in Malaysia and Hong Kong, as well as China.

The response was amazing (as it had been when *Riverdance* visited Japan); the Chinese media gave blanket coverage to *Riverdance* in the week preceding the first show. Nevertheless, there was nervousness among the cast and organizers as to how a Chinese audience would respond to something so novel and so different. The Chinese are accustomed to large-scale spectacles, but these usually have a very distinct and crude ideological purpose. *Riverdance* makes no such demands on potential audiences.

The worries proved misplaced. Each of the six shows in Beijing was sold out, and two extra matinee performances had to be included. In addition to the Great Hall of the People, the Riverdancers staged a performance at a site on the Great Wall of China.

Riverdance caught my attention because, though it may have deep Irish roots, it is very much an international phenomenon. Its original stars were the American dancers Michael Flatley and Jeanne Butler. Its current lead male dancer, Conor Hayes, is Australian, and the *Riverdance* troupe includes dancers from the United States, Spain, Russia, and Kazakhstan, as well as Ireland. So international is *Riverdance*'s style that it has been rubbished by cultural purists in Ireland.

Much of the financial backing for *Riverdance* came from the United States, but the experience and excitement generated by it flows around the world, recognizing nothing so puny as a national border. The audiences who witnessed the *Riverdance* spectacle in Beijing reacted with more genuine enthusiasm than to any of the clichés that fell from the lips of the Great Helmsman.

The symbolism of the performance was not lost on those involved. Bill Whelan commented, "*Riverdance* is a political thing as much as a cultural thing."[1]

Riverdance in the Great Hall of the People is a suitable metaphor for the global economy. It originated in the Western world. Its roots in Ireland, one of the global economy's most dynamic success stories, are significant. It blends elements from Ireland's culture with features from other cultures and backgrounds, which are, in turn, performed by people from throughout the world. It was originally choreographed by an American and was performed on the largest stage in one of the world's fastest-growing economies: China. *Riverdance* is not insular, and no one could say that it is bland.

The World as a Stage

So how does *Riverdance* connect to the work of executives? Simply and directly. Any executive in a global corporation—and which decent-size corporation is *not* global?—is involved in similar global projects. These projects are complex, involve participants from throughout the world, demand cultural sensitivity, require global financing, and are often targeted at emerging economies.

"All the world's a stage, and all the men and women merely players...."[2] This was an elegant metaphor for Shakespeare, but for us, it is not metaphorical: It is reality. The world is one huge arena for economic activity, no longer compartmentalized by barriers or other unnecessary stage furniture. We all form part of a giant troupe of interdependent actors and actresses. We don't all recite the same lines or even perform similar repertory pieces, but none of us is entirely independent.

The interconnected, interactive, global economy is a reality. It is often confusing and disorientating: It challenges both the way we see business and the way we do business.

The global economy presents itself in many different forms, like an actor donning different masks and costumes. For example, there are the gigantic global flows of money. There is also the growing mountain of credit-card purchases, a process enhanced by the Internet. We can see it, too, in the trade deficit between the United States and China. The world's biggest economy has run up a huge trade deficit with China about which it worries incessantly; it might also worry about being technically bankrupt. China, too, has a growing trade deficit, as it seems to voraciously suck raw and semifinished materials, machines, and robots into its economy. But these are worries that belong to the old world of increasingly outdated economic paradigms and indicators.

The global economy is largely invisible. (That's why I called my previous book *The Invisible Continent*.) It should not be confused with some dark matter that hovers and lurks menacingly, ready to grab and devour the unwary. The global economy's effects are clearly evident throughout the world. We are all players on the global stage, and we all feel its effects.

A Speedy Global Tour

In fact, to set the scene, it might be a good idea to take a whirlwind tour around the world. During our trip, we will see examples of the global economy in action. So, as we began this chapter in China, let us also begin our "Cook's Tour" of the globe there.

The city of Dalian is situated near the southeastern tip of the Liaodong peninsular that hangs down from the coast of northeast China, the region formerly known as Manchuria. It is a part of China, but it faces into the Yellow Sea toward Korea and Japan.

The climate guarantees year-round ice-free status to its ports, so Dalian and its neighbors were always destined to enjoy the fruits of trade, communist or not. Dalian's immediate hinterland, on the Liaodong peninsular, is dominated by a beautiful coastline and a landscape of hills, valleys, and forests rich in natural resources, such as coking coal and iron ore. Yet Dalian has always known that it must look outward for its prosperity.

The port was established by the Russians in the late nineteenth century. The Japanese later introduced heavy industry. Dalian adopted a role as an *entrepot* for northeast China. But in the past decade, the city has changed from being a sleepy port into one of China's most important and dynamic industrial centers, with a population surpassing five million. It has combined its old industrial base in Liaoning Province, centered on steel making and chemical and machine-part manufacture, with new service- and technology-related ventures. There is a reservoir of skilled personnel, supplied by a number of universities and technical institutes. Its demand for labor appears insatiable.

The city continues to grow in physical size and population. It attracts immigrants from throughout northeastern China, drawn by wage levels that, while low by Western standards, are far higher than those available in rural China. Its citizens live in a city with its own commuter train system, as well as good housing, many parks, and leisure facilities, and, above all, clean air and water.

The city's inhabitants have more sophisticated needs than those of their grandparents. In the heyday of Maoist orthodoxy, the workers were badly paid, badly housed, and badly fed. They were given no opportunity to complain. Their leisure hours might be spent attending showings of revolutionary films or, in warmer weather, reading from Chairman Mao's *Little Red Book*.

Today's employees are provided with far better and more interesting facilities. Dalian's shops are stocked with an international range of consumer goods: everything from designer fashion to the latest DVD players. Far more people can buy these, thanks to the city's growing prosperity. Cinemas show the latest commercial blockbusters, but many residents prefer to watch DVDs, available in the city's many electrical and TV emporia.

Dalian has benefited from the seismic change that has swept aside official Chinese thinking on the economy since 1992, when Deng Xiaoping proposed the "one country, two systems" development blueprint. Long gone are the days of central planning. Instead, regional governors and bosses are encouraged to track their own course for the future. This sometimes involves bending the rules, but as long as the exceptions allowed by local bosses remain localized—and they are successful—breaches of discipline are ignored. This has been especially true after the even more drastic reforms launched by then-Premier Zhu Rongji in 1998. Mayors and other local bosses also know that if they fail to deliver annual growth rates in excess of 7 percent for two successive years, their employment will be terminated. Imagine if Michael Bloomberg in New York, Shintaro Ishihara in Tokyo, or Ken Livingstone in London faced such strictures.

In the person of Mayor Bo Xilai, Dalian possessed an extraordinary local ruler. Bo stood out from the crowd—literally—for in a land where smallness of stature is the rule, he stood well over 6 feet tall. He hailed from the western borderlands of China in Shanxi province. He came from a family with respected political pedigree: His father had taken part in the grueling Long March of the early 1930s, when Mao led his small group of followers on a two-year forced evacuation by foot from southern to northern China. Bo Xilai studied at Beijing University, newly reopened after the madness of the "Cultural Revolution" had seen students and faculty members sent to work in the fields. He was also young, in his late 40s, a comparatively brash young upstart in a land whose political leadership was dominated by 70-somethings. He joined the Communist Party in 1980 and worked in its various branches. His diligence and skill were rewarded when he was appointed mayor of Dalian in 1992. As the city opened to the outside world, Bo and his team attracted inward investment from throughout the world, especially from Japan. Today, there are estimated to be 3,000 Japanese firms operating within Dalian's city limits.

Bo redefined the job description of the typical Chinese city mayor. No longer content with managing sewerage and housing, he became his city's chief architect and marketing officer, establishing close links with the cream of Japanese industry and business. But his role did not end after the businesses were established. He recast himself as something akin to the manager of a five-star hotel, keenly and solicitously interested in the welfare of his guests. Foreign businesses were regularly contacted to find out how they were doing and whether they were encountering any difficulties that might be ironed out.

Bo was rewarded for his success in Dalian by being kicked upstairs. He was appointed governor of the whole province of Liaoning. At the time of his departure in February 2001, vast crowds of city residents (particularly women) gathered to see him off. They seemed genuinely sad. In a land long used to choreographed mass hysteria, this might have been dismissed, but the sorrow appeared spontaneous. Bo's rise continues: In early 2004, he was named the Minister of Commerce for the whole People's Republic at the age of 53.

Helped by the charismatic Bo, Dalian, along with over a dozen other regions in China, has become a *de facto* regional state, setting its own economic agenda. While still a part of China and, in theory, subject to the rule of Beijing, it is largely autonomous. The reality is that its ties with Beijing are weaker than those with business centers throughout the world.

Success breeds success, and companies that do well in Dalian act as catalysts attracting other businesses, not necessarily from the same sector. As in similar regions of China, there has been an explosion in the provision of services, whether financial or technical. Dalian is almost a self-sufficient economic entity, with many services being available to business and residents on their doorstep. Dalian has also been at the forefront of the provision of cross-border business process outsourcing (BPO) services in China, in particular in areas such as direct data entry, often for Japanese businesses. These newer developments have been spearheaded by Bo's protégé, Mayor Xia Deren. The historical memories of the Japanese in this part of China might not always have been positive, but these are left in the past, where they belong. Japanese language courses are popular and are regularly oversubscribed. As a consequence, an estimated 50,000 Dalian residents speak fluent Japanese.

It is curious that Dalian, a modern business and economic center, should also enjoy a vibrant tourism industry. Its beaches and water-sports facilities have been protected. A special tourist zone, the Golden Pebble Beach, has been erected, with marinas, two golf courses, and hotels catering for all budgets. Many of Dalian's visitors fly in from elsewhere in China. They form part of the vast and still growing consumer class in China. They have money to spend, not just on automobiles and consumer electronics, but on other aspects of the "good life," such as leisure and private education for their children. Dalian attracts visitors from outside China, too. Many Korean and Japanese tourists now prefer Dalian to Singapore.

Dalian's success relies on its willingness to engage in the new cyber-based and borderless economy. It has also benefited from being allowed to pursue its own path. It reacts directly with the rest of the world, not at the level of part of a nation-state, but instanta-neously and directly, as a region. For many decades, Dalian, along with the People's Republic of China, turned its back on the world. The rest of the world was controlled by China's enemies. Now Dalian and other Chinese region-states have enthusiastically embraced the world economy. There are 13 other cities within the province of Liaoning alone whose population exceeds one million. They are all seeking to take their place on the global stage or, at a minimum, to become part of the Yellow Sea Economic Zone. They resemble a flock of flying geese headed by Dalian.

China is probably the country that is benefiting the most from the global economy. China now has the second-highest foreign exchange reserves ($432 billion) in the world (topped by Japan at $817 billion) and domestic savings of $2.5 trillion. More than any other country, it is setting the pace in the global economy. Its 2003 GDP was estimat-ed at $1.3 trillion, and the communist state has been ranked number seven in the world (number two in terms of purchasing power).[3] Its economy grows at a rate seldom lower than 7 percent annually. Most recently, it has been in excess of 9 percent, a figure for the whole country that includes the richest and the poorest areas.

If we remember the theatrical metaphor, we can see China as being like a rented theater. It is an arena that is being used as a rehearsal studio, a testing ground for global economic realities. But a little disconcertingly, different parts of the stage are being used for varying types of performance. These differ in skill and expertise and, consequently, in audience approval.

As we shall see throughout this book, we must try to divest ourselves of old mindsets. One of the most oppressive is the notion of the nation-state. So when we think of China today, we should not think of the nation-state running from the Yellow Sea in the east to the depths of central Asia in the west, but rather an amalgam of prosperous, burgeoning regions, such as Dalian, set alongside others that might be light-years behind in economic development and prosperity. All these regions vary in size. They are theoretically under the same sovereign state, the People's Republic of China, but part of China's prosperity lies in its ability to forget about this in practice and to allow its region-states to plough their own furrows. In reality, all these regions are engaged in almost manic competition with each other for investment and resources, not as in the old days from the center, but for investment from the outside world.

Meanwhile in Ireland

We started this chapter describing *Riverdance*. Let us now look at the country that inspired it: Ireland.

For many people, Ireland summons up visions of green, mist-covered fields and valleys. But outside the tourism industry, pleasant scenery does not produce wealth. Anyway, these visions belong only in the glossy pages of holiday brochures.

When Ireland became independent as a nation in 1922, it was overwhelmingly rural. Its rulers and citizens eyed covetously the northeastern quadrant of the island of Ireland, which had been kept by Great Britain. It was richer; it was the one area of Ireland that had seen extensive industrialization. So, the rest of the island seemed destined to remain perpetually green—and poor—with its major export people. This strengthened a lack of self-confidence. There was a sense of the country being a victim of forces beyond its control.

From the 1960s onward, attempts were made to attract manufacturing industry from abroad. The Industrial Development Authority (IDA), a government agency, constructed industrial infrastructure and facilities, while the government offered generous tax breaks such as a 10-year moratorium on corporation tax payments for foreign direct investments (FDI). These moves were only partly successful. Irish competitiveness was low. Infra-structure (despite the best efforts of the IDA) in many sectors was abysmal. A former director of the IDA told of how they had brought a prospective investor to view a site for a facility by helicopter so that he would not experience the dreadful state of the roads.

In the 1970s and early 1980s, physical geography still played a big role in the international economy, and Ireland's location on the far western periphery of Europe meant that it was just too far away from potential markets. Most of those located there were attracted by Ireland's position as a European Community member. The reliance of the country on external commercial operations made its industrial sector vulnerable to trends in the global business cycle.

Emigration from Ireland increased again in the 1980s, but unlike many of the earlier emigrants, these were often highly educated. Again unlike earlier emigrants, they often returned to Ireland after gaining experience and contacts outside the country. A new self-confidence began to take hold, and with it a new attitude toward the rest of the world. It was no longer a place of exile, but one of opportunity and a source of prosperity.

The fact that the country had missed out on industrialization was increasingly seen as a blessing. It meant that there was no rusting industrial plants and no unemployed workforce born and bred to heavy industry. It also meant that the country's economy could take advantage of new trends beyond its borders in the *global* economy. Ireland could begin from scratch. In the late 1980s, developments in cybertechnology made it clear that jobs and prosperity could come at the end of a telephone line. The potential of Ireland to play a major role in the information technology sector was realized. Greater computer literacy in all sectors of the population was encouraged, and telecommunications infrastructure was enhanced. In 1992, the vision of Ireland as the "e-hub of Europe" emerged. Europe was headed in the direction of a single market, so why could Ireland not find a very profitable niche as the base for telecommunications entry into that market? Ireland already had a large base of young, educated workers who could fulfill investors' labor demands.

The visionary and almost prophetic nature of the e-hub concept is apparent when it is remembered that it was developed in 1992; that is, before the Internet became embedded in the commercial world. In the following chapter, I explain how the global economy began in 1985, and how I date developments according to my own calendar as being either BG (before Gates) or AG (after Gates). So the development of the e-hub occurred relatively early in this chronology, in the year 8 AG!

In Dublin, an extensive section of redundant docklands had been redeveloped since 1987 as a financial services center. This attracted many financial service providers to establish back-room operations. Ireland also became an attractive location for American companies' call centers in Europe. This was accompanied by a significant growth in indigenous software companies.

As we will see, Ireland is lucky; it is a nation-state that is the same size as a *region-state*. It is, therefore, capable of tapping into the dynamism of such a region state. We will see that one of the keys to the success of a region-state is being able to brand itself successfully (such as an "e-hub") and to offer something different that sets it apart from the competition. Ireland has been able to do this very effectively in the customer response management and "back office" sectors. It has also been able to capitalize on its image as a fun place to work, with a vibrant social life and abundant cultural and recreational facilities. Phenomena such as *Riverdance* and the international success of Irish rock groups such as *U2* and *The Corrs* have also played a significant part in the nation's reinvention.

For decades, successive Irish governments expended resources on attempting to resuscitate the native Gaelic language. Although English remained the vernacular of the vast majority, it was felt that the country's right to nationhood was stillborn and defective without a language of its own. But in the new global economy, where English is *the* linguistic platform of communications, the possession of English as a first language is a major advantage for Irish citizens.

Ireland's call centers are able to employ many of Ireland's foreign language graduates, but there are not enough fluent speakers of German, Italian, or Swedish, for example, within Ireland. The country's openness means that native speakers of foreign languages are attracted to it and are welcomed. Greater prosperity has also attracted immigrants from all over the European Union, within which barriers to relocation have been all but cancelled. They have added their skills to Ireland's economy and helped to make Irish society more varied, colorful, and sensitive to the wider world. Given Ireland's readiness for and commitment to the global economy, it came as little surprise that the country was ranked first in both 2002 and 2003 in the A.T. Kearney/Foreign Policy Globalization Index.[4]

Ireland has many strengths. It has a relatively small but highly educated population. It is situated on the periphery of Europe, yet it is the closest part of Europe to North America. In the economic past, dominated by manufacturing industry and physical constraints on movement, its location was a liability. But in the age of the global economy, physical location is much less important. Without doubt, the greatest advantage it possesses has been its vision of how it can fit into the new and ever-changing economic realities of the twenty-first century. This has enabled Ireland to create more than 300,000 new jobs in the areas of cross-border BPO, CRM, and R&D in just over a decade. Along the way, its time-honored social malaise of unemployment has been eliminated.

A comparison between Ireland and another island nation, New Zealand (actually two separate islands), will be helpful. Both have economies that were traditionally based on farming and processing of agricultural products. Ireland, though, has transformed itself from a country with a largely agricultural basis into a country with a strong ICT base. New Zealand is still very much playing the old game. It believes that deregulation is enough. It isn't anymore. As a result, New Zealand has not been able to come up with new types of industries. Sitting on a base of agriculture and agriculture-related industries, and applying Ronald Reagan–style deregulation, especially under the banner of "Rogernomics," is not good enough. You have to do what the Irish, the Finns, and the Chinese are doing.

Now let us leave the Emerald Isle and fly northward to Scandinavia and to its northeastern extremity, Finland.

Finland: In from the Cold

Finland has long been on the periphery of Europe, but the opposite periphery to Ireland. Where the latter looks out westward upon vast areas of ocean, the people of Finland have been able to look out upon a slightly drier landscape, but one equally hostile: mile after mile of impenetrable forest and frozen tundra broken only by icy lakes and endless, fast-flowing rivers. In fact, Finland was as far from the beaten track of commerce and trade as it was possible to be.

Finland sits on the northeastern shoulder of the Baltic, a sea by name, though almost one big lake. In the distant past, the Baltic was an avenue for primary products such as furs, timber, and amber, but Finland was really too far north to benefit from this. Its harbors have been kept open year-round only by icebreakers. Freezing temperatures bring one blessing. In the winter, some lakes and rivers freeze so hard that it is possible to drive trucks across them, thereby adding seasonally and nearly costless transport to the infrastructure.

Finnish industry has traditionally been based on processing natural resources, especially the abundant woodlands. There is also some high-quality mechanical engineering. But Finnish industry has never been static. Throughout the twentieth century, considerable amounts were spent on R&D, and production was accompanied by constant innovation.

In the last half of the century, the country was sandwiched between the spheres of influence of the rival superpowers: the United States and NATO to the north and west, the Soviet Union and the Warsaw Pact to the east and south. Although its society and government were free and pluralist, everyone in the country (and outside world) recognized that this had to be paid for by a commitment to "neutrality." *Finlandization* entered the political vocabulary as a term of contempt. No one wanted to be like Finland.

It also developed a Scandinavian-style welfare state, paid for by heavy borrowing and by some of the highest levels of direct and indirect taxation in the world. This also paid for some very high-quality education.

In the midst of this, companies such as Nokia and Sonera (now called TeliaSonera after a merger with the Swedish operator Telia in 2002) developed global trail-blazers in telecommunications. Important developments in software engineering, such as data security specialist, SSH, and the Linux computer operating system (invented by the Finn Linus Torvalds) also emerged.

As a result, Finland has achieved levels of productivity and competitiveness that are the envy of more established economic players. The Geneva-based World Economic Forum declared Finland the most competitive country in the world in 2003, for the second year running.[5] It came in ahead of the United States and Singapore. It also scored top marks for network connectivity and compatibility, and was deemed the most responsive to IT and e-business opportunities.

How has an isolated high-tax country turned the economic tide? First, the country has always recognized that its prosperity lies in looking outward toward the rest of the world. This has been something of a curse in the manufacturing-dominated past. With few mineral resources, the country was vulnerable to oscillations in energy prices. Finland was also one of the few regions outside the old Soviet bloc to shed a tear, albeit perhaps a crocodile one, for the demise of the Soviet Union. The USSR was one of Finland's most important trading partners. Cross-border visits contributed to the Finnish tourism sector. The breakup of the communist giant meant that Finnish balance of payment figures suffered a considerable drop. Finland faced an international environment shorn of old certainties and a domestic economy that showed all the signs of being in terminal decline. The Finns are a resourceful nation, and with resolution they realized that salvation could come only through openness to the rest of the world.

In addition to being outward looking, the level of Finnish education is very high. As in other parts of Scandinavia, proficiency in English is extensive, but with the Finns such linguistic skill is a necessity. The Finns are proud of their vernacular Finnish, but they are wise enough to know that only Finns (and Estonians) can learn it. It is a very complex language, unrelated to Indo-European languages such as Swedish and Russian. Few foreigners are brave enough to acquire even a basic competence. The Finns have long been compelled to communicate with the rest of the world by means of the linguistic platform of English. Knowledge of English is necessary for advancing in education; after all, not many English and American high school and college textbooks are translated into Finnish. English is the language of top-level management meetings in companies such as Nokia (Finland's largest company). English is viewed not as a threat, but as an opportunity. English instruction starts early in Finnish schools, and, increasingly, many subjects are taught *through* English. This is one of the reasons Finnish universities have exceptionally large contingents of foreign students.

Outward looking and English speaking, Finnish leaders and managers acquire an international and global outlook almost by default. Top management in Finland's corporate sector is also broad-minded and seeks to acquire and use the best talents wherever they come from. For example, two of Nokia's top directors are Norwegian and American. The Finnish stock exchange is operated by a Swedish company, OM.

The final ingredient in the Finnish success story is an appetite for technology. The Internet was adopted with gusto in the mid-1990s. Every local government department and tourism office acquired a Web presence at an early stage. Most Web pages are in Finnish, but they nearly all have English translations on another part of the site. Browser terminals have been provided in all schools, public libraries, and many other public places. In 2002, Finland had one of the highest Internet connection rates in the world: 230 connections per 1,000 people. More people were online in percentage terms than in any other country—1.5 million people out of a 5 million population used the Web on at least five days in the week.

Finland has a propensity for being at the top of league tables (see Exhibit 1.1). It holds the number one spot for cell phone usage. At the end of 2002, more than 87 percent of Finns had a mobile phone. This far exceeded land lines, but this was not surprising in the home of Nokia, which currently holds a third of global market share. Although the company is proud of its Finnish roots and Finnish headquarters, it also knows that its domestic market accounts for less than 1 percent of its global sales.

Nokia did not attain its global position by accident. Nokia traces its origins back to a lumber firm set up in southwest Finland in the mid-nineteenth century. In the 1970s, it provided communications systems for the state railways and Finnish armed forces. In the next decade, it switched to consumer electronics and suffered a severe beating from Japanese competition. Indeed, the company almost went bankrupt in the early 1990s. But through innovation and the pursuit of aggressive R&D strategies, it has come back from the brink. It does not rest on its laurels. In 1994, Nokia's CEO, Jorma Ollila, made a truly historical decision: Nokia's future was to be in mobile telecommunications. From that year, the company has unsentimentally pursued success in this market. It has divested itself of involvement in the many other areas in which it was involved.

Growth Competitiveness Ranking 2003		IMD World Competitiveness Scoreboard 2004	
1	Finland	1	United States
2	United States	2	Singapore
3	Sweden	3	Canada
4	Denmark	4	Australia
5	Taiwan	5	Iceland
6	Singapore	6	Hong Kong
7	Switzerland	7	Denmark
8	Iceland	8	Finland
9	Norway	9	Luxembourg
10	Australia	10	Ireland
11	Japan	11	Sweden
12	Canada		
13	Netherlands	22	United Kingdom
14	Germany	23	Japan
15	New Zealand	24	China

Source: World Economic Forum.   Source: IMD.

Exhibit 1.1   Competitiveness rankings.

Finland has realized the benefits of a knowledge-based economy. Much of this grew out of an existing commitment to innovation. When problems arise, they have to be solved. Solutions can then be marketed abroad.

Finns have always been realists. They know that they cannot hide in their forested country at the top of Europe: They have to be participants. They have shown that full-blooded participation in the global economy can change a nation's place in the world and prove that the rest of the world is not a place to be feared. This openness to the global economy has encouraged investors, such as American pension funds, to buy Finnish corporate stocks. Today, more than 60 percent of Finnish equity is held by foreigners. As Finnish companies aggressively master the global stage, students and tourists flock to the land of Suomi.

Finland is not alone in Scandinavia in embracing the global economy, especially through the conduit of technology. Neighboring Sweden is the home of Ericsson, also a leader in the provision of mobile technology and the development of many technical platforms.

What Is the Global Economy?

What are the characteristics of this new global economy relished in places as diverse as Dalian, Dublin, and Helsinki? Terminology is always an inexact science. Every term is a linguistic sieve. So, before attempting to define it, let's just say at the outset what the global economy is not.

What can be said is that the global economy should be differentiated from the notion of the "new economy" that sprang up in the late 1990s. This trumpeted a brave new economic order based on the fantastic technological advances unleashed through the Internet. It was a model that mistakenly saw a parallel and unstoppable rise in productivity. The wheels fell off this conceptual wagon in April 2000 with the sudden decline in technology stocks.

Apart from its manifest intellectual weaknesses, this "new economy" has very little in common with what we will talk about. The global economy is based on a world in which borderlessness is no longer a dream or an option, but a reality. This has been helped by the cyber-revolution, but it is not the same phenomenon as the cyber-revolution itself. Multiples of stock values, as well as derivatives and financially engineered products, also matter far more in the global economy.

The global economy has its own dynamic and its own logic. It is no longer theory; it is reality. It is going to grow stronger rather than weaker. It will feed on its own strengths. It is irresistible, and it is destined to have an impact on everybody—businessmen, politicians, and bureaucrats, but, most important, ordinary citizens. There is no use complaining about it or wishing it to go away. People will have to learn to live with it.

The emphasis here is on learning because success and even survival depend on acquiring novel outlooks and relationships with the rest of the world. This book hopefully goes someway toward pointing a route toward these new outlooks and relationships.

Some people and countries might be determined to fight against the reality of the global economy, using the old mind maps and the old paradigms. However, the cost in economic and especially human terms will be enormous. Progress is as inevitable as death and taxes.

Traditional nation-states and national governments face a great challenge. Some seem to want to approach this new world with one foot stuck stubbornly in the shore of the past for support while they gingerly test the water with the toes on the other.

Some are better placed to take advantage of the global economy's opportunities. History favored the United States by providing it with a truly federal form of government. As a result, states such as North and South Carolina, known as the Carolinas, can pursue an innovative economic agenda without risk of being stymied by central government. The battles between state and center have been fought over and resolved. The constituent states are each well placed to take advantage of the global economy. This does not mean that all 50 states do so. Some still seem to be wedded to a past based on Canute-like protection of "strategic" economic sectors.

Other federal states in the world do not allow their constituent members anything like real autonomy, and the central government maintains a tight rein on regional developments. Examples include India and Brazil, two of the BRICs (Brazil, Russia, India, and China), according to Goldman Sach's new jargon of promising new economies. In terms of the global economy, these nations are still asleep as a whole nation. Nevertheless, some of their regions have begun to take their places on the global stage. China adopts a somewhat schizophrenic policy; in theory, it follows a rigid, centralized political formula. In practice, unprecedented economic autonomy has been allowed to regions and cities, particularly since Zhu Rongji's reform of 1998.

But at the opposite extreme, there are states such as Japan, Russia, and Indonesia, which maintain centrality of decision making in theory *and* practice. No region succeeds because no region is permitted to succeed independently of the rest of the state. Their central governments are jealous of allowing any directional role to escape the center. They are swimming against a tide that could yet inundate them. Of the BRICs, only China has the governance structure to help its regions to work interactively with the global economy. Others have a long way to go before their central government really wakes up to the calls of the rest of the world.

The task of describing what this new world *is* may be difficult. If all the news stories and clippings about globalization are assembled, the integrated picture that emerges is distorted. Not all the components fit neatly together; it is a wild, abstract mosaic rather than a jigsaw.

But let us forget the scare stories and the merchants of bad news, and instead try and see what we can say positively and with certainty about the characteristics of the global economy: It has innate characteristics, which I list in no order of importance.

Borderless

First, as I have long argued, national borders are far less constrictive than they once were. Some of this has been thanks to technology, while some has been the result of international and bilateral agreements, especially in the area of trade. The world is an increasingly borderless place. Tariffs are evaporating as countries realize they need each other to survive economically.

It is not yet completely border free, as nation-states still have reasons to maintain controls on the movement of people and goods in the interest of security and public safety. But in terms of four key factors of business life, the world has already attained the position of being effectively without borders. These business factors I have labeled the four C's: communications, capital, corporations, and consumers.[6]

Effective **communications** always depend on the nonexistence of borders. It was one thing when communication was predominantly physical. If a person wanted to go from A to B or send something there, be it a letter or a product, the inert force of gravity often slowed the process down. Slowness of movement was further added to by border checkpoints, the need for visas, and passport control, not to mention custom and excise inspection. People viewed these as obstacles and deterrents. But technology spurred an improvement. Telephone lines allowed a person to speak with someone directly on the other side of the world, without having to go through a host of intermediate exchanges. Once such lines of telecommunication, existed they could be used for data transfer. Improvements also occurred in the production of cables using fiber-optic technology. A barrier to communications remained while the conduits of this communication still had to pass along wires, which, in turn, had to be laid across mountains or oceans. The latest technological advances do away with wires and their costly installation and maintenance. When data is carried by radio frequencies, it is absurd to believe that lines drawn on maps can have any impact on its movements.

Telecommunication benefited from a process of deregulation in the 1980s, and many former state monopolies were privatized, thereby increasing competition and lowering costs for consumers.

Domestic markets that had formerly been imprisoned in the clutches of national communications monopolies were opened up. Many communications companies co-operated and entered into alliances; others merged so that the telecommunications world was changed from a patchwork of state monopolies into a far more dynamic and colorful kaleidoscope that did not respect national borders. Many telecom operators, including TeliaSonera, Vodafone, and Telefonica, have become truly global.

Yet it was the development of the Internet from the mid-1990s onward that has probably had the greatest impact on making the world of communications truly borderless. This is a technology that is widely available, accessible from personal computers anywhere. Traffic passes through it oblivious of borders.

The second *C*, **capital**, is also a beneficiary of a borderless world. This, too, has been aided by deregulation of financial markets. It has also been assisted by the position of the U.S. dollar as a monetary platform. Not only is it the major trading and settlement currency, but it is also the currency of choice for many savers throughout the world. In most developed countries, the aging population save money for their retirement. The trouble is that no OECD member country offers adequate returns for an investment at home. This is one of the biggest reasons why a massive cross-border migration of capital, both short and long term, has occurred.

Some **corporations** have successfully responded to the borderless economy by shedding the trappings of the nation-state that hindered their self-awareness. It was far too common in the past for a successful corporation to identify closely with a "home base," a company headquarters, or a corporate "home town, where it all began." Some of this might have been sentimental, but it was outdated if the corporation saw the world as its marketplace. Improvements in telecommunications mean that companies do not feel tied down to a corporate headquarters in a certain city. If circumstances demand it, they might even dispense with legal ties to their home bases by reregistering in another, more favorable location.

The last two decades have seen a remarkable decomposition of corporate functions, ranging from R&D and manufacturing to sales/marketing and financing. It is now common within an individual company for these functions to be located across national borders—for example, R&D in Switzerland, engineering in India, manufacturing in China, financing in London, while the marketing function and HQ remain in the United States. More recently, indirect work has been outsourced: Witness the growth in call centers in India and else-where, and the outsourcing of logistics to specialists such as FedEx, DHL, and UPS.

It is in terms of the last C, **consumers**, that the borderless ele-ment of the global economy has made itself felt most keenly. Consumers have the ability to do what they have been urged to do many times: shop around. The Internet gives consumers the ability to compare products and prices and make a much more informed choice more easily. Platforms for paying by credit card then allow the purchase to be made, processed, and delivered. There might still be some who are emotionally tied to the ideal of the nation-state, who support demagogues seeking greater protection of domestic busi-nesses and jobs, but when they are presented with a choice of two similar products, one (product A) available locally at a price consid-erably higher than product B, which originates elsewhere and still enjoys a price advantage when delivery charges are added on, only the most die-hard partisan of the nation-state will opt for the pricey product A. The reality is that it is almost impossible to buy a shirt that is genuinely "Made in America." Its fabric may come from Egypt, threads from Japan, and buttons from the Philippines. If only the sewing process takes place in the United States, how American does that make the finished shirt?

Invisible

Observers might be forgiven for not fully realizing the potency and prevalence of the global economy. It is largely invisible. It might be better said that it is not totally visible to the naked eye. This should not be taken as implying that it is secretive or reclusive. It is because the actions that it performs often take place not on the streets or the debating chambers of national parliaments, but on computer termi-nals. One of the mechanisms whose development has enabled speedy cash transfer is a piece of plastic: the credit card. It is the preferred means of carrying and spending money for hundreds of millions of consumers. Yet the money that credit-card holders spend is never seen. Sometimes, payment occurs so quickly that not even the most sophisticated camera with an incredibly high shutter speed could record it.

Some of the most important developments are earth-shaking in their potential, but their implications are not fully understood outside of a small circle of players. As a result, they are not headline news; they are lucky to feature in the news at all. As for the print media, they may be buried rather inconspicuously in the business pages.

Consider a few aspects of this invisible world. Transactions and settlements of money now take place mostly on and through computers. Some products are also purchased in the plaza known as B2B and B2C trade exchanges, or as C2C auctions. Most ATMs around the world spit out local currency if you use your home country cash/credit card with Plus or Cirrus membership. There is no way for the government to know how much cash you have withdrawn abroad or how much you have spent with a credit card to purchase goods and services across national borders.

Cyber-Connected

The global economy would not be possible, or even comprehensible, without cybertechnology allowing large amounts of data to be transferred incredibly quickly. It would not be possible without the corresponding drop in technology prices. The Internet is only the most public part of this. Today, the Internet protocol (IP) is capable of handling transmission of not only data, but also images, voice, music, and videos. Voice over IP (VoIP) is rapidly making inroads into the world of traditional telecom providers, but music and movies are also downloaded across national borders, as long as there is a line with IP routers. Everything and everyone connects.

Outsourcing, for example, rests on the capability to model new processes and instantly deliver critical software components, all within minutes of a conversation. The success of Indian software houses, such as Infosys, WiPro, HCL, Tata Information Services, and others, underscores the fact that 24x7 development is no longer a wish, but a reality.

Measured in Multiples

Money makes the world go around. And so the role of money in a global economy must be important. Money is no longer seen only as a unit of value in the short term. The late 1990s and the first years of the new century have witnessed a number of corporate takeovers and restructurings that would have been viewed as surreal two decades earlier: In these, a company that had only recently emerged and maybe was not actually profitable successfully acquired a much larger, longer-established, and seemingly solid part of the corporate land-scape. None of this was possible without those who assess corporate value looking at a far bigger picture, not one based on the here and now alone and the currently quoted price on whatever share index they chose, but on what the situation was likely to be in 10 or 20 years, and on how this was reflected in price/earnings ratios.

Multiples are signs given to the management by the shareholders to shoot at the business opportunities on the horizon. If the management does nothing other than business as usual, the multiple will come down, reflecting the disappointment of the ammunition givers. Multiples are fictitious, in that they often do not reflect corporate value, but they express an expectation. This can become reality if a company is bought or a new investment is made to fully utilize the multiples.

So the global economy is borderless, invisible, cyberconnected, and measured in multiples. Many of these elements are self-nurturing: They feed off one another. They all involve taking a leap, if only an intellectual leap at first, into uncharted waters.

This global economy is in its infancy. Unfortunately, this description contains an analogy with human development, from the state of the infant, the child, and the uninformed. It might be better to say that the global economy is in the early stages of development, but there is nothing childlike or uninformed about it. It has not emerged like an extraterrestrial from on board a meteorite. It has entered the world through the actions and intellect of human beings. It has not been foisted onto the world by some small, nefarious network intent on world domination. It has developed collectively. And, as we will see, it promises to be beneficial to the world at large.

The excessive capital in developed countries is looking for opportunities to breed. If you understand the logic of the global economy, you can attract companies, customers, and capital to your region or company from the rest of the world. You do not have to be born rich or be born in a wealthy country to prosper. All four C's can and will come to you if you have the right recipe. Alternatively, if your logic and systems are out of sync with the global economy, the four C's will evaporate, and you will not have an opportunity to perform on the global stage.

To reap the benefits of the global economy, join me to better understand how the plot unfolds. Let us begin with the opening night.

Notes

[1] *Riverdance in China*, documentary broadcast by Raidio Telefis Eirinn channel 1, 9 April 2004.

[2] William Shakespeare, *As You Like It*, 2.7. 139–140.

[3] "China's GDP Expects to Exceed 11 Trillion Yuan," *People's Daily*, 27 November 2003, www.nationmaster.com.

[4] www.atkearney.com.

[5] www.weforum.org.

[6] The concept of the four C's was first explored in my book, *The End of the Nation State* (New York: Simon & Schuster, 1994).

2

OPENING NIGHT

The World AG

Written history nearly always depends on a dating system, a chronology of some sort. This is based upon some central event. For Christians, this event was the date of the birth of the Christian savior, Jesus Christ. History was divided by this watershed into events that occurred before this and were dated BC ("before Christ"), and those that took place after it and were dated by AD, the Latin *anno domini* ("in the year of the Lord"). Muslims adopted a system based on the date of the Hegira, or the Prophet Mohamed's flight from Mecca to Medina. In the Christian calendar, this took place in 622 AD. Muslims use the dating system AH. Certain more recent revolutionaries have tried to impose the singularity of the political changes they have effected by changing the calendar. In Revolutionary France, not only were the years changed but the calendar was "rationalized" and the names of the months altered to reflect changes in the seasons. So, March became *Ventiose*, the windy month, and November became *Brumaire*, the foggy month. When Pol Pot and his genocidal comrades in the Khmer Rouge seized power in Cambodia in 1975, they

declared that the calendar had been changed and that the unfortunate people of the country were living in Year Zero.

The opening night for the new economic reality that is the global economy occurred in 1985. It was in this year that the world began
to change.

For me, 1985 is the *annus domini*, and the dating system I like to
use in a light-hearted way is AG and BG—after and before Gates.[1]

Why 1985? Admittedly, there was no one Earth-changing event;
there was no equivalent to a Big Bang (that occurred in London's
Stock Exchange in 1986). Instead, seeds were planted that may not
have sprouted into abundant growth straight away but that did not lie
dormant and lifeless. At the time these seeds were sown, many commentators did not realize the revolutionary importance of what lay in
store; some more careful observers noted that they were new seeds,
of a variety of plant not previously grown, belonging to a totally novel
and unknown genus and species. None could be sure how the plants
would develop, what they would look like, or whether they would ger-
minate at all.

Leading the Dinosaur

At the macropolitical level, there was an event that most people were
aware of. The aging, creaking dinosaur of the Soviet Union gained a
new Communist Party General Secretary: Mikhail Sergeyevich
Gorbachev. At 53, he was young (well, at least 20 years younger than
his American counterpart, President Ronald Reagan) and was able to
walk freely on his own. He didn't limp along in his greatcoat, but he
strode purposefully. He spoke clearly and eloquently—his speeches
were not interrupted by paroxysms of wheezing and coughing. What
he said was also interesting. He had plans for reform.

Gorbachev's commitment to new thinking came as no surprise to
Sovietologists. He had dared to say such things within the restricted
grammar and vocabulary of the Soviet leadership prior to his eleva-
tion. But when his "election" was announced, skeptical observers in
the West felt that it must have been the result of some behind-the-
scenes deal, a Faustian compact in which he had sworn his commitment to the status quo for the chance of filling the throne.

Then Gorbachev began to use terms and principles like *glasnost*
(literally, "openness") to explain the need for greater transparency in
the Soviet system. *Glasnost* was a term that nobody cared, at first, to
define too well. It could mean a desire to see the world not through

rose-tinted spectacles, but to acknowledge that there were some plants in the garden that were far from pleasant. Although everyone knew that already, these problems could now be discussed openly. There was no longer anything to be gained by pretending that the Soviet world was perfect. The problem was that, although this was a novel and, in fact, revolutionary step, talking about a problem didn't make it go away. It produced lots of diagnoses, but no cure.

A joke was told about how Gorbachev fitted into the litany of Russian leaders. Lenin, Stalin, Khrushchev, Brezhnev, and Gorbachev are travelling on a badly maintained train. The train runs out of coal and grinds to a halt. Lenin orders the train driver to be shot. Lenin dies and Stalin takes control of the train, which he fuels with coal, wood, and anything he can steal at gunpoint. The train starts up and rumbles on for a while, but then shudders once again to a halt. Stalin has all of the train staff shot, and then he dies. Khrushchev then takes over control of the train has the former train drivers rehabilitated (posthumously), and the train starts up again unsteadily, but then inevitably it breaks down. Khrushchev is thrown off the train by Brezhnev, who says to everyone, "The train may have stopped, but don't tell anyone. Pull down the blinds and let's pretend we are moving." Eventually, of course, Brezhnev goes the way of all Party First Secretaries, and Gorbachev takes over the train, and what does he do? He sticks his head out of the window of the still motionless train and keeps shouting, "The train has stopped. The train has stopped."

That was Gorbachev's problem: All he did was highlight the problem, and no matter how well meaning you are, this is not a serious solution to anything. He had no grand vision of where he wanted to go. Maybe he chose not to have one. Maybe he realized that the Soviet Union was doomed, that it was unfixable, that it was just too big an assembly of lies and contradictions to have any future potential.

Gorbachev sought to fix problems in a piece-meal way. He was a committed communist when he started out, albeit a communist committed to reform. But as he went on, finding out that solutions even to the myriad of small problems were impossible or that one solution only occurred at the price of throwing up larger obstacles, the impossibility of the task must have become clear.

The more he tinkered with the Soviet Empire, the quicker it fell apart. The satellite states of Eastern Europe regained their freedom in the space of a few hectic weeks in the early winter of 1989, their former leaders dumped sometimes temporarily on the political garbage heap. In the Soviet Union itself, Gorbachev ended up being sandwiched between conservatives and radical reformers. The conservatives said that the disintegration of the machine demonstrated the folly of attempting to alter it and that it was best to leave it alone to stagger and splutter into the future. The radicals had a vision—or, rather, a set of often-contradictory visions of the future of Russia, not of the Soviet Union. This assembly of unwilling participants, along with Gorbachev himself, was doomed following the failure of the conservatives' putsch in August 1991. The gray apparatchiks who launched the coup to replace Gorbachev may have been thwarted in their goal of turning the clock back, but in their immediate aim of ousting the first secretary, they were successful beyond measure.

Gorbachev may be reviled in today's Russia, the world would be a very different place without the reforms he introduced. These spelled the end of the "Evil Empire" and of the Cold War. The Soviet empire would no doubt have collapsed at some stage, but whether it would have been sooner rather than later, and whether it would have been with a loud bang or a faint whisper, nobody can say with certainty.

What Gorbachev missed was the effect of globalization. The desire of young Russians to open up and reform the country (which I wrote about in my 1989 book *The Borderless World*) was precisely due to the information they had been receiving, albeit confidentially. In the same book, I predicted the demise of the Soviet Union as a country. The forces at work on Gorbachev's Soviet Union were such that one could not open and reconstruct the economy simply by fixing what was wrong in comparison with Western economies. The reforms Russia had to go through were at least two-dimensional. At one level, there was the shift from the socialist planned economy to the capitalist market economy. The other dimension was remodelling to incorporate the global economy. This is where the Russians and their American advisors failed.

The demise of the Soviet empire and of world communism has meant that we now can largely speak of a world without borders and barriers. But without Gorbachev, it might not now be possible to speak of a truly global economy.

The View from the Hotel: Detroit

The second epoch-shaping event occurred in September 1985 when the finance ministers of the Group of Five—the United States, the United Kingdom, France, West Germany, and Japan—met for a meeting in New York's Plaza Hotel. There was nothing unusual in the meeting. Such get-togethers had been occurring for the previous 10 years. In the early 1980s, though, worries had grown in the United States about the nation's industrial base, especially its traditional manufacturing sector. Areas that had once been the heart of American industry, such as Detroit, were coming under increasing pressure from imports (especially from Japan).

Part of the problem went back to the oil crisis years of the mid-to-late 1970s when the American public had ended its love affair with home-produced gas-guzzlers. As a result, cars that were smaller (and also cheaper) became more popular. The same thing happened with consumer electronics.

It is always unfortunate when economic questions get mixed up with political sloganeering. Simplistic and crude xenophobia raised its ugly head in areas that were fast becoming rust belts, such as Detroit and Milwaukee, and references to Pearl Harbor started appearing on radio talk shows and phone-ins. These were not made by respectable commentators or politicians, although Lee Iacocca, then CEO of Chrysler, used the phrase "yellow peril." But although they were ugly, they could not be ignored by politicians who court votes from everybody, no matter how unattractive they may be. Outright tariffs or trade barriers were viewed negatively, but there was a perceived need to try to make Japanese exports less competitive, especially in the American market.

National currencies had long been recognized as a means of helping to leverage a country's exports and imports, and thereby improve balance of payment figures and competitiveness. Part of the problem was that the American dollar was perceived to be overvalued. This meant that Japanese exports were cheaper, more competitive, and more desirable in the United States.

The agreement reached by the finance ministers of the G5, the so-called Plaza Accord in 1985, is complex, as such documents usually are. But the most important element was that the central banks of the countries represented would seek to allow greater flexibility in rates of currency exchange. They agreed that the dollar would have to fall in value. It should not fall freely, but the yen and the Deutsche Mark should be made stronger. Let the dollar fall—without jeopardizing the whole financial system.

The Plaza Accord had two objectives: to reduce the overall U.S. debt, which consisted of a triple deficit on the current account, the trading account, and the government budgetary account. The dollar was to be allowed to fall quite quickly, but in a controlled way. On the day the accord was signed, the exchange rate was 235 yen to the dollar; in 1994, it was 84, an almost three-fold strengthening of the yen.

In domestic American terms, some bankers, headed by Federal Reserve Chairman Paul Volcker, were partisans of the robust dollar. Indeed, for some strange reason, Volcker was labeled "the vanguard of the dollar" during his reign, despite the fact that the dollar carried on falling throughout. The conclusion of the Plaza Accord gave these bankers greater political leverage.

My view is that the strength of a national currency should never be confused with fetishes of the nation-state such as "national strength." A country can have a very strong currency, no doubt a reflection of confidence in its macroeconomic management. But it can then experience the painful effect of its exports being more expensive in the marketplace. This can be very uncomfortable indeed if its exports are based on commodities.

Some expected, while others hoped for, a reinvigorated American export scene to result from the Plaza Accord. Yet their hopes and expectations were largely misplaced. True, Japan's stronger yen might have caused difficulties for Japanese exports (the Japanese business association, the Keidanren has always thought so), but it also meant that its imports were cheaper. Such imports included iron ore and other metals used in automobile manufacture, as well as a host of other commodities and unfinished goods. Japanese auto manufacturers were able to produce cars that retained their competitiveness, especially in the American market. Japan's exports retained competitiveness throughout the turbulent 1990s. This is still reflected in the country's surplus on its current account.

What the economists and ministers missed is the fact that competitive global corporations can always find a way to compete, by either raising prices, investing in R&D, relocating to cheaper countries (the U.S., in this case), or using better branding and marketing. Strong Japanese companies remained strong or became even stronger, and the monthly trade surplus with the U.S. has remained at the $5 billion level ever since.

Why did so many economists and experts miss this? This is examined in Chapter 4, "Playmakers," but basically, economists retained nineteenth-century thinking in which most products traded across national borders were largely price-elastic commodities. Now, for manufactured goods, there are many ways to overcome currency fluctuations or directional changes. Most German and

Japanese producers have survived severe currency appreciation by producing better products and selling them at higher prices while continuing endlessly to improve productivity. In a borderless world, if these measures are not enough, companies can migrate to lower-cost countries for production or other overhead work while keeping the most critical functions at home.

Busting the Budget

Meanwhile, back in the beginning, a little farther south of New York, in the corridors of the U.S. Senate, the final touches were being put on a bold piece of legislation sponsored by Republican Senators Phil Gramm of Texas and Warren Rudman of New Hampshire. The Gramm-Rudman Act was the final result.

The act offered a solution to another economic headache of the mid-1980s: the budget deficit. Ronald Reagan had been elected president in 1980 with a promise to roll back the deficit and end the spiral of America living beyond its means. Big deficits were a result of big government, and most of those who voted for Reagan viewed government in a negative light, the cause rather than the solution of a host of problems.

There was an element of blurring between the worlds of macro- and microeconomics. The stereotype of being a spendthrift nation and never paying today what can be paid for tomorrow or next week was one that most Americans wanted to forego. Some were no doubt influenced by David Ricardo's comment, "What is wise in an individual is wise also in a nation."[2]

The dangers of continual and accumulating budget deficits are manifest to everyone. Deficits have to be paid for, and the only sensible way this can happen is through borrowing. With an increasing, rolled-over budget deficit comes an increasing amount of money that has to be paid merely to service the interest on the debt. This amount seldom remains static for long. It does not actually buy anything; there is no benefit in terms of schools, hospitals, roads, or public transfers. There is no argument about the principal, the amount that was originally borrowed and lies at the heart of the loan. That stays the same, but the interest payable on it can rise and fall, depending on interest rates. Both principal and interest must be paid back, but the more and the longer a budget deficit is allowed to fester, the greater the burden is passed on to the next generation, or maybe to generations not yet born, who certainly were not responsible for running it up in the first place. Big deficits and massive foreign debts can also have a destabilizing effect on an otherwise healthy economy, causing interest rates to rise and maybe even leading to inflation.

But an allied danger is that deficit spending creates an aura of unreality. It breeds irresponsibility. A window shopper who probably finds the area of personal finance a dreadful bore and an inconvenience can be easily enticed by a promotion offering a product on "Buy now, pay later" terms. The Day of Reckoning can be pushed into the future. This is a bad habit. Governments should encourage personal responsibility by their citizens in all walks of life. But how can a government do this when it is consistently practicing irresponsible economic behavior?

President Reagan's chief of staff, Donald Regan, worked with Senator Gramm to craft a package of legislation that would mandate a balanced budget. The bill was then sponsored by Senator Rudman, joined by Senator Ernest Hollings of South Carolina. The legislation passed the Senate in the fall of 1985 and was signed into law by the president on December 12 of that year.

The deficit was so huge that an attempt to curtail it could only be made in stages. So the law made provisions for a scheduled reduction. In the fiscal year 1986, it was to be slashed by $11.2 billion. Equal reductions were to be effected in the following four years until, by 1991, the hoped-for Holy Grail of a balanced budget would be reached. If the targets in any one fiscal year were not achieved, the president, as chief of the executive, was empowered to make the cuts in government spending necessary to bring the deficit reduction into line with the law's prescribed schedule.

Almost immediately, it became clear that, although a balanced budget was a very good and worthwhile concept, it conflicted with the needs of American politics. There is nearly always an electoral race going on somewhere in the United States. The staggered nature of political contests means that, in addition to presidential elections, there are senate and gubernatorial races, as well as those for Congress—not to mention those at county level. In the week following the Senate passage of the Gramm-Rudman Act, the very same legislative body enacted a package of aid transfers to agriculture amounting to $52 billion. This was at a time when the federal courts' service was so short of cash that it was often unable to pay jurors' travel expenses. The year 1986 was an election year for one-third of the members of the Senate. Those with well-organized farming votes were alive to this electoral contest facing them, and being able to go before their electorates as a proven friend of the farmer was advantageous.

The budget deficit, though trimmed, did not go away. But it became less of a bogeyman. By 1991, the year that was supposed to see the end of budget deficits as previously known, the main provisions of the Gramm-Rudman Act were allowed to lapse because of President George H. W. Bush's desire to extricate himself and government from financial and governmental gridlock.

Gates to the Future

But let us return to 1985 and to its early months. On the other side of the American continent from Washington, a 30-year-old bespectacled college dropout named William Gates, who had established a computer company called Microsoft in Seattle a decade earlier, launched a new computer operating system called Windows. Its first version appeared in 1985.

By the mid-1980s, most people in the Western world had been exposed to computers. The machines still held mystique, even terror, for many. They were vast inhuman mammoths capable of storing huge amounts of information. They could also manipulate people. Some could even play chess and challenge grandmasters.

Other people had gotten their hands on their own computers, especially designed for home use. They were anything but powerful or awesome. They allowed users to play simple arcade games, but little more. They were often the preserve of the hobbyist, who often got the thrill of putting them together.

Then still faster computers, with greater memory-storage facilities, came to market. The possible applications were more sophisticated. But there was one gaping hole in their usefulness. A computer is an assemblage of circuits encased in a metal box, usually with a screen and one or two input devices, such as a keyboard. Unless it can share information with other computers, it is useless.

Numerous computer-programming languages were available. Some were fairly accessible, allowing home users to write useful, if simple, applications. Others were more complex, the realm of the specialist programmer. But programs written in one computer language seldom worked with applications in another.

That is where operating systems came into their own. They allowed different types of applications to be run on the same machine, side by side with each other. But operating systems had one other, far bigger advantage. Operating systems did away with the need to use computer code. They allowed nontechnical people to use computers and to gain value from them. In some ways, operating systems were like the ignition key in an automobile. With a good operating system, it was possible to do useful things with computers, not just play Ping-Pong.

Among those who had developed operating systems was Bill Gates. In particular, in the early 1980s, he had developed the MS-DOS operating system, which worked on IBM machines. He had the vision to believe it was possible to create not just another operating system, but *the* operating system that would be used on computers and desktops throughout the world. It would also redefine the relationship between user and computer, even the way in which the user entered information. The interface would no longer center on the input of code by a device such as a keyboard, but instead it would allow the operator to use a device such as a mouse to choose material presented graphically on the screen. This was to become a world-changing platform.

Other operating systems would exist. Windows might not be the best operating system in the world, but Bill Gates had the vision that his company's system would dominate the market. Where an application was needed, Microsoft could provide one that worked seamlessly in the Windows environment. This might be a word processor, a spreadsheet, a database, or any computer technology for work or leisure. As the speeds of computer circuits improved, so did the sophistication of applications that Microsoft could provide. There was a blurring between home and office computer utilization. The same application could find a use in both environments, on similar hardware, though the uses to which it might be applied would be different.

The Windows operating system has never stood still. In the 1990s, a neat marketing shift occurred. Instead of referring to each new version with a serial cardinal number—Windows 1, 2, 3, and so on—Microsoft identified the version by reference to a year. First there was Windows 95 and then Windows 98. Microsoft developed a Chinese version, which was just as well because 1998 in China would see truly revolutionary changes, under Zhu Rongji, in how the economy worked.

Each new development in personal computers either has been anticipated or has been provided for by Microsoft Windows. When Internet usage took off in the mid-1990s, Microsoft developed Internet Explorer, which soon ousted its rival Netscape from any hope it might have of providing a platform in Internet browsing.

Simulation applications aiming at copying all types of leisure activities, from playing cards to playing golf, also hit the shelves. In the early 1990s, there was a shift in storage devices for personal computers, from small magnetic discs toward hard discs and CD-ROMs, capable of storing hundreds of times more information. Microsoft (and others) seized upon this development to provide reference material and multimedia application content.

Bill Gates has achieved dominance with his software platform. Some might grumble about the bugs in the software, as well as expensive technical assistance, but the fact is that Microsoft has created one of the key platforms of our age. This is the communication tool we use throughout the world today, overcoming national borders and traditional protocols that dominant carriers and/or host governments imposed on their people. Today, all governments and companies either must use the Windows protocol themselves, or must be capable of interfacing with those who do.

14 AG: China

So, 1985 was a starting point for the global stage of 2005 in a number of ways: ideological (Gorbachev), economical (Plaza Accord), fiscal (Gramm-Rudman), and technological (Microsoft).

The years since 1985 have seen some hectic developments. It would be tiring to list them all, let alone talk about any of them in detail. Yet the events of one year, 1998 (14 AG), represented a further blossoming of many of the seeds sown in 1985. They have, in turn, added their development potential to the development of the global economy.

Nobody can talk about the global economy and leave China out of the discussion. China seeks to compress 200 years of post–Industrial Revolution development into a couple of decades. It disproves the notion of "first mover advantage" in the AG era. China is also trying to work with the global economy by dissecting its vast empire into digestible units, what I label "region-states."

Selecting crucial moments in China's recent hectic development is difficult. You could point to Deng Xiaoping's pronouncements in the early 1990s. Deng's observation that all Chinese couldn't get rich together was an important political landmark, accepting inequality as the price of progress. The Chinese Communist Party was dedicated to bringing progress and prosperity to all in China. Traditionally, it had sought to do this by following the path of Marxism-Leninism, as refined by Mao Zedong. But "prosperity" (viewed as nonpoverty) was the goal, and the theories were but paths to that end, not ends in themselves. As Deng observed as long ago as 1962 (and repeatedly thereafter), it doesn't matter whether the cat is black or white, as long as it catches mice. Deng was the first to recognize the power of the global economy as a means of making the country stronger and wealthier. He realized that strength and wealth could not be simply extracted from within the confines of China's national borders. He then opened up a number of regions by way of experiment and witnessed the remarkable power of global corporations in Shengzang and Shanghai. In a famous speech of 1992, he added dozens more regions to the open zones.

The year of 1998 is perhaps even more significant to China because of the reforms introduced at a party conference in March of that year, the party's eleventh. Their architect was the newly appointed Prime Minister Zhu Rongji. None of these reforms came out of the blue. Zhu had served as deputy prime minister and central banker for a number of years, and had already introduced many alterations in the economic system. His moves had been hampered by die-hard but rapidly ageing conservatives in the party, including his predecessor, Prime Minister Li Peng. Zhu's reforms were prompted by a need to remove three cancers that were adversely affecting China's society and economy.

One problem was endemic corruption in government, which flourished in all sectors and regions and which had been incited into greater fury by the opening up of the Chinese economy. Graft had been the target of numerous "mass mobilizations" in the past, but these tended to be rather crude and largely ineffective. Weeding out corruption could not take place without developing the rule of law and firm legal standards. This had been hampered in the past by the perception of positive law as "bourgeois."

Second, there was the need to reduce China's crippling bureaucracy, an inefficient weight around the neck of China. Zhu Rongji set the goal, which he subsequently achieved, of cutting Chinese central government bureaucracy by half. In a country that still paid lip service to the tenets of Marxism-Leninism, such a massive downsizing of the government sector was dramatic. The task was made even more Herculean by the centralized structure of decision-making. It was natural that a government that knew the value of keeping a tight-fitting lid on its country should concentrate as much power in the center as possible. But in a country as vast as China, where internal communications are often made impossible by natural barriers and vast distances, such an ideal was unworkable. Even though China had started to open up to outside investment in the 1980s, potential investors were stifled by this overcentralized approach. Developments affecting activities in local areas could not take place without the seal of approval of a central ministry in Beijing.

The third element of Zhu Rongji's reforms was to clear out the dead weight of government firms and *parastatals*, or state-owned enterprises (SOEs). Over half of them were losing money, most were inefficient, and many were technically bankrupt. They were a constant hemorrhage on the Chinese government's funds. Traditionally, the Chinese central government had acted as a milk cow for state industry. It provided protection, by giving companies a monopoly or by restricting the access of foreigners to lucrative local markets. But as the likelihood of the state ever seeing any return on these projects declined, the government was throwing good money after bad.

Zhu instituted a package of reforms known in English translation by the rather uncomfortable title of "The Three Respects." The reforms saw parastatals, such as television manufacturer Haier and computer producer Legend (since rebranded as Lenovo), cut loose from the state and removed from the safety net of state injections of capital. They were now on their own. If they needed money, they could seek it from Chinese investors, especially through the stock markets of Shanghai, Shenzhen, or even Hong Kong. But before they could do this, they would have to restructure and behave like worthy recipients of investment. Those that did not—or could not—were free to fail. They could take over other firms or be taken over themselves.

This was nothing short of a revolution. Former government thinking had said that these were "national" corporations. They had a legitimate communist reason to produce and provide for the people of the People's Republic. In the 1980s, party ideologues had attempted to rationalize the introduction of free-market precepts in terms of an analogy with a birdcage. In this birdcage economy, the bird of free enterprise was free to sing as sweetly as it liked, but it remained within the constraints imposed by the party-state. Without the cage, the bird might fly away. But Zhu was advocating the destruction of the birdcage. It was an idea that was based on the knowledge that not only would the bird not fly away, but it would attract flocks from overseas.

Zhu's attitude toward parastatals and SOEs was harsh but, in retrospect, heroic. Much of the market was simultaneously opened up to foreign companies, who were free to compete with Chinese companies. Those who had the will and the ability could try to survive using whatever methods they felt beneficial. They could take over other companies and consolidate their activities. Another option was to form joint ventures with foreign companies.

A further element of Zhu's strategy was to decentralize the management of many former "national" corporations away from central ministries into the hands of municipalities and the provinces. This was tantamount to the economic breakup of the country. China moved from being a single nation-state into a nation of region-states. It is not inaccurate to call it the United States of Chunghua, the Chinese name for the center of the universe.

The heads of regions and cities now worried about the future of their local companies, with wealth creating potential. Some were able to turn them into success stories. Others sold them to foreign corporations. Mayors and governors speedily began to act like entrepreneurs, or, as we have seen in Dalian, as CEOs of region-states.

Zhu's remarkable reforms were prompted by the realization that he could not save all the national companies that were crowding out the Chinese economy and draining it of resources and vitality. He recognized that the solutions to China's problems were not internal. The only source of assistance was external: the rest of the world.

China today contains the most brutal, inhumane, and unsentimental capitalism imaginable. Its own people are exploited. Those from the interior, from areas of traditional poverty, are brought in to work for wages that are higher than those to be earned at home, but they are not always paid on time—or sometimes ever. Health and safety issues are generally ignored, and there is hardly any welfare safety net. Working conditions are never part of the equation. The attitude of management is often heartless and never sentimental. What matters is getting the job done, hopefully before target and below budget.

China exhibits capitalism in the rawest form. A factory manager in Guangzhou finds that the eyesight of some workers deteriorates as a result of the work they do. He fires them with one week's pay. They are no longer his responsibility. Were a Japanese manager to act like this, he would risk imprisonment. Were a U.K. firm to do this, it might be both sued and prosecuted.

In China, the capitalist can do anything he or she wants. If wages rise, the entrepreneur relocates to a lower wage environment. This might be further inland in the central and western backlands, where there is a vast reservoir of underemployed rural labor. He sacks the workers who are too expensive, who work less, or who may tire more easily. This is the purest, most unadulterated form of capitalism on the planet today. It is a world taken from the pages of Charles Dickens or Theodore Dreiser.

It is a primitive form of industrialization, not to be found in today's Japan or the United Kingdom or the United States. Ironically, it evokes Friedrich Engels's descriptions and denunciations of the barbaric conditions of the English working class in the 1840s, as well as his denunciation of the greed of the English manufacturers as a class:

> For [them], everything in the world exists for the sake of money, itself not excluded. It knows no bliss save that of rapid gain; no pain save that of losing gold. In the presence of this avarice and lust of gain, it is not possible for a single human sentiment or opinion to remain untainted.[3]

Engels, of course, was a member of the Communist pantheon. Banners in the People's Republic carried his bearded image beside Marx, Lenin, and Mao.

Why did this change occur in China? Some of Zhu's reforms were compelled by circumstance. The financial meltdown in Asia in 1997, while not affecting China directly, had repercussions. There was also the prospect of China's membership of the World Trade Organization. Part of the changes can be put down to the critical migration of the most important resources of management: the four C's: communications, capital, corporation, and consumers. All these critical resources have criss-crossed national borders. This is now entering China.

For generations, China was a predominantly rural and poor nation. This was exacerbated by the explosive rise in population in the nineteenth century. Many outside observers considered that it had great potential—in the future. They said it was a sleeping giant. While it slept, the Western world industrialized, and alongside these developments went all the necessary steps for nation building. China has now woken up and aspires to the same position in the world as these developed economies.

China will probably be able to achieve this more quickly and more cheaply than traditional developed countries. It can learn their lessons and benefit from their technological developments. As I write this, in fall 2004, the Chinese economy is ranked number seven in the world (see Exhibit 2.1). If present rates of growth continue for the next three or four years (a prospect that is entirely feasible, despite the warnings of observers), it will pass Germany to become the world's fifth-largest economy. Were the much sought after (in the United States) revaluation of the Yuan renminbi (RMB) to occur, this would further propel China up the GDP league table.

Top 10 Countries in the World by GDP

GDP Ranking in 1990			GDP Ranking in 2003		
Rank	Country	GDP (Trillion$)	Rank	Country	GDP (Trillion$)
1	U.S.	5.8	1	U.S.	11.0
2	Japan	3.0	2	Japan	4.3
3	Germany	1.5	3	Germany	2.4
4	France	1.2	4	U.K.	1.8
5	Italy	1.1	5	France	1.8
6	U.K.	1.0	6	Italy	1.5
7	Canada	0.6	7	China	1.4
8	Spain	0.5	8	Canada	0.9
9	Brazil	0.5	9	Spain	0.8
10	China	0.4	10	Mexico	0.6

- Assuming that China keeps growing at 8% p.a, it will:
  - Catch up with the U.K. in 2007.
  - Catch up with Germany in 2008.
- Assuming strengthening of RMB by a factor of two after its float in 2005–08, its GDP will:
  - Double in dollar terms.
  - Catch up with Japan in 2008.
  - Become the number 2 economy in the world by 2010.

Source: World Economic Outlook, April 2004 (IMF).

Exhibit 2.1   Top 10 countries in the world by GDP.

Putting an "e" in Christmas

Once again, the final key is technology. The work of computer pioneer Sir Timothy Berners-Lee shaped the world as we know it and appreciate it today. In 1989 (5 AG), Berners-Lee developed the Hypertext Markup Language on which the world's Web pages are based, and the code that millions use to communicate with them and with others.

The history of the Internet has been written elsewhere, but its impact has been as sudden as it has been dramatic. After all, in the early 1990s, who beyond a group of computer-science cognoscenti knew what the Worldwide Web or a Web browser was? In the mid-1990s, Web awareness in the developed world grew apace, thanks to faster computers and routers, better modems, and the availability of browsing software, but this awareness was accompanied by uncertainty. Even Bill Gates was cautious, not initially believing that it could have any lasting impact on the expanding computer using public. It was not until 1994 that he announced that the long-awaited Windows 95 operating system would come with Internet connectivity. Everyone agreed that the Internet was very powerful, but for what? Could it change the world?

In the history of the Internet, the period surrounding Christmas 1998 (14 AG again) stands out. This was when the public in the developed world began to purchase items over the Internet in a phenomenal fashion. The online shop Victoria's Secret became the talk of the season. Until then, scholars and commentators had doubts about the Internet's capability for e-commerce. The Internet had a great potential, already realized, for providing information, but it was felt that it would not be used for purchasing goods, with the exception of online bookstores, such as Amazon.

Christmas Day 1998 stands out in my memory as Portal Memorial Day. It was then that the amazing realization sank in that e-commerce could really work. This Christmas season was one of euphoria. Christmas usually is a time of hectic purchasing, followed by the January sales and a slump. But in the early weeks of 1999, there was no falling off in the cascade of Internet purchasing. After Christmas Day 1998, e-commerce became a legitimate citizen of the economic world. Of course, as we all know, there have been many oscillations in technology stocks since then, but strong portal companies have continued to grow. Look at companies such as Amazon, eBay, and Victoria's Secret, to name but three that are doing far better than they could have imagined. The CEO of eBay, Meg Whitman, commented in an interview with the *Far Eastern Economic Review* on how the main items sold in 1998 were cuddly toys called Beanie Babies. Now, the site sells millions of dollars worth of automobiles. "I don't think I'd ever have predicted we'd go from Beanies to Beamers," she observed.[4]

This cybercontinent is greater than any country on Earth or even the extended European Union. For the first time in human history, the world changes its habits in a matter of days rather than years. By the end of 2004, 800 million people had a URL or were connected to the Internet. This is the same number of people who lived in countries with a per-capita GDP of more than $10,000 10 years ago. These people are all connected, one way or another, and ready to use Google to search for anything either in their own language or in 40 different languages. Consumers are in a constant state of readiness. Eight hundred million people are ready to read, listen to, or watch anything available in cyberspace. Given this, it is little wonder that Tower Records, the long-established recorded music retailer, filed for Chapter Eleven protection one year after Steve Jobs and Apple introduced the iPod. The sudden death of a company or an industry such as recorded music or film and analog cameras is now a frequent reality.

Technology was the final building brick to create today's global stage that represents a decisive break with the past. Maybe it was coincidence that saw three of the most seminal contributions occurring in one year: 1985. The year before, 1984, apart from being the title of George Orwell's novel was also the year in which Michael Dell established Dell Systems in Austin, Texas. Dell went on to revolutionize supply-chain management. The year 1984 also saw the launch of Cisco Systems in California. In the same year, George Soros's Quantum Fund emerged on the world's financial scene, making hedging "multiples" and derivatives routine in the financial world. Time frames have shrunk in the global economy, as we will see. More can happen now in the space of a few months than occurred previously in decades.

Yet, even today there is still a remarkable degree of lethargy as many decision-makers hold instinctively to structures that are old and enfeebled. In the next two chapters, we will see just how outdated traditional attitudes toward economics and political organizations have become in the era of the global economy.

Notes

[1] Convenient though it is as a means of understanding the global stage, the dating system used in most countries has achieved the status of something of a platform, so I do not suggest that people start using the "AG" system.

[2] David Ricardo. *Principles of Political Economy and Taxation* (Loughton, Essex: Prometheus Books, 1996), 172.

[3] Frederick Engels. *The Condition of the Working Class in England* (Oxford University Press, 1993), 281. Edited by David McLellan.

[4] "CEO, call, Meg Whitman, eBay," *Far Eastern Economic Review*, 29 April 2004, www.feer.com.

3

THE END OF ECONOMICS

Reinventing Economics

Let us repeat that the global economy is a reality—it's not a theory. But so many of those who should know better, especially those whom people expect to know better, seem to be still asleep. The majority of the world's economists remain cocooned in a pleasant dream.

The old economy grew up to explain the relationships between demand and supply, and supply and employment. It tried to explain how supply/production and inventory increase as the interest rate or money supply changes. Because the economists are convinced that the equations among these factors are well established, they can recommend that politicians and bureaucrats use one or more factors to influence the other, to generate employment, to increase gross national production, or to simulate housing starts. When none of these levers seems to be responding sharply, they have invented still another tool to borrow money from the future: minting promissory notes or bonds. Most governments with the privilege to do so have done so and have used the money in public works to artificially inflate the economy, almost like plastic surgery. This, of course, is a bad joke

and is certainly not what such towering figures as John Maynard
Keynes or Friedrich Hayek originally meant. But governments interpret that they are still within the bounds of the economists' theories.

Since the early 1900s, when these original thinkers were active
in framing the economics with the then-known economic parameters, the world has changed dramatically. The economy is no longer
closed in a country, nor is the world an assembly of the autonomous
and independent nation-states, a model most of them have assumed
as underlying structure of economy. Instead, the world consists of
interdependent units of nations and regions. Some regions have a
population of millions, but others, such as the European Union,
have hundreds of millions. Hayek is still correct, as Adam Smith and
Milton Friedman are, in that eventually the market mechanism or
the invisible hands of God will sort things out. The legacy they have
left behind is so strong that the economists today, including most of
the recent Nobel Prize laureates, are working on a variation of their
old masters' themes. The economists are not looking straight at the
economy itself, but are trying to interpret the economy through the
lenses of the old masters, by modifying the antiquated equations
and developing mathematical models that explain only a part of the
global economy.

Another problem is that economic theories are believed to
explain causality. For example, if you decrease the interest rate, you
would expect to stimulate the economy because businesses can borrow money and make necessary capital investments. Likewise, an
increased money supply by the central bank would drive down interest rates, making credit cheap. Businesses could then make aggressive capital investments because they could also expect higher prices
and increased consumption from the market. This type of causality
has been the reason behind the confidence (or ignorance) of politicians who make a big promise of "recovery of economy" or "increase
in jobs." Most of them casually hire economists to crank out the policy statement, which normally boils down to large government or
small government, and increased welfare or tax cuts.

The problem is that no one is thinking about the global economy
and its cause and effect on a national economy. For example, a higher interest rate is good to attract money from the rest of the world, as
Greenspan under Clinton's presidency demonstrated. The U.S. economy from 1992 to 2000 was euphoric, despite high interest rates,
because the rest of the world pumped money into the country to
enjoy high interest rates. In fact, we can also argue that a high interest rate is good, period. In the aging society of the advanced world,

most consumers have more money than they can possibly spend, so the money is put into financial instruments "just in case" they have a problem in the future. Their balance sheet is healthier than their government's. A higher interest rate means that they can increase their financial asset base faster, and their borrowing capacity increases although their nominal income may not. This is why consumption— and, hence, the economy—often moves against the preachings of the old masters who lived only in the society with the majority as workers, not as wealthy consumers with 401(k) plans. If the money comes from the rest of the world, businesses can raise money in the capital market and do not have to borrow money from the banks. So, again the interest rate is no longer a decisive factor in a business's decision for capital investment.

In the borderless world, an excessive money supply by the central bank can slip out of the country if there are no attractive opportunities within the nation. In this way, a government is constantly arbitraged, or disciplined, by its own citizens and by the investors in the rest of the world.

There is no model to describe the global economy as such because we are dealing with so many parameters and variables, and so many "units of economy." These can be strongly interlinked, as with currency exchange rates, or loosely interlinked, as with real estate investment trusts (REITs) and tax rates. Cross-border investment decisions are made to take advantage of the differences in these and many other factors.

Furthermore, advances in IT have made inventories significantly less necessary. Companies such as Toyota, Dell, and Inditex have demonstrated that they can make their products "just-in-time" and in response to orders. So, the grand theories of adjusting interest rate downward to expect the business to stockpile inventories is no longer that effective. They know that cash is the best form of inventory as it is tangible and exchangeable for other goods at a moment's notice.

Another complication is that the cybereconomy is growing fast and the cross-border exchange of goods, services, and even financial instruments is taking place in areas unbeknownst to the economists, let alone to the government.

Finally, though this may not the final item by enlightened students of the global economy, there is an increase—or even explosion—of funny money. Bonds and Treasury bills are funny monies from the point of view of the traditional economists because they are not exactly money, but they act as money with liabilities for taxpayers to pay later. The trouble is that the buyers of these public liabilities are no longer the residents of an issuing country. For example, over the past 20 years, Japan has financed about a third of the entire U.S. Treasury deficits. At the end of March 2004, IMF published statistics revealing that Japan had a foreign reserve of $817 billion, while China had $432 billion, the European Union had $230 billion, and Taiwan had $227 billion. Most Asian countries keep their reserves in dollar-denominated instruments, such as 10-year U.S. bonds. In fact, two thirds of the reserves by the central banks of the developed countries are in dollars, whereas the U.S. economy is only about 30 percent of the global GDP. In addition, the private sector, such as banks, private pensions, and insurance companies, maintains a high portion of dollar-denominated products in its portfolio. In Japan alone, the size of such portfolios exceeded $14 trillion in 2004.

So overall, the effectiveness of any government's fiscal policy is at the mercy of not only what businesses and consumers do at home, but also what other governments and the individual companies and consumers in the rest of the world do. Public debts, such as bonds and bills, are like a forced-circulation device and are meant to absorb money in the market, to be spent presumably to create jobs and enhance consumption. At least in Japan, the government has made the public believe that the tax money is spent to provide basic public services, and bonds are issued to stimulate economy and create jobs. Bonds are sponges to absorb excess money sitting (idle) in the private sector in passive instruments with a high degree of security and medium return on a longer time horizon. Therefore, American investors who are looking for high return and more short-term results do not favor U.S. bonds. In addition to overminting the green backs, Uncle Sam has developed a habit of printing promissory notes, primarily for the foreigners. This is one of the reasons the funny money, USGS, has become even funnier: Its effect on the entire globe has become huge, even to the point that many non-American corporations and consumers want the dollar to remain strong. In many ways, they trust the U.S. government's fiscal policies more than they trust those of their own governments.

Over the last 15 years, this funny money has been joined by many other new types of funny monies, produced using techniques such as derivatives and multiples. Assortments of these techniques are actually offered in the form of hedge funds and structured bonds. Most of these instruments are based on mathematical assumptions that ordinary people find difficult to comprehend (yet are sold to them). Many developing countries have fallen victim to arbitrageurs who use many of these funny monies with bold interventions, such as short-selling with high multiples.

At this stage, we simply have to acknowledge that in today's inter-linked global economy, the money sitting in one side of the globe could be deployed, with huge multiples, halfway around the world either to accelerate the prosperity of a region or to destroy a nation's economy. There is no formal or effective mechanism globally to govern the superliquidity produced as a result of an individual government's political situation, even though the collective effect is globally serious and sometimes destructive. Likewise, no economic model can begin to address this issue and the previously described issues.

I do not believe that we are at the stage of being able to establish a mathematical economic model. Too many variables and other forces are at work, many of which are not even discernible or documented with credible statistics. However, this should not deter us from exploring the new global economy. In the end, there may never be a suitable mathematical methodology to describe the twenty-first-century economy. But there may be an approach possible through a different model, such as theory of complexity, to begin to address the issue in totality. This may be decades away, but we can begin to gather the evidence of global and cyber economics as fundamentally different from—and many times opposite of—twentieth-century economics.

Economic Theories That Once Fitted the Times

Part of the paradox that surrounds economics is that it is often divorced from the world in which it has been developed. Economic theories, like laws of physics, hold good whenever or wherever they are applied in the universe with clear boundary conditions. But if we look very briefly at a handful of economic thinkers, we will see that their ideas are products of their historical environments. They also contain manifest logical flaws.

For Adam Smith, a pin factory was the state-of-the-art of technical innovation. He lived in the eighteenth century, and because the service sector in his day was miniscule compared to ours, he disregarded it. He also considered that value was closely linked to the cost of labor used in an article's production. Smith distrusted combinations of either producers or workers, seeing them as deliberate attempts to distort the market. His prognostications of future business activity were also wide of the mark because he considered that greater competition would ultimately reduce profits. But Smith conceived of markets in a localized sense. He knew about international trade, but the reality of most people's lives saw them born, bred, and buried in one location. He wrote, "A man is of all sorts of luggage the most difficult to be transported." His world was beset by a host of barriers to movement: economic, political, and physical.

David Ricardo (1772–1823) knew a lot about wealth. He made a fortune as a stockbroker in the early nineteenth century before he took early retirement. As a rich man, he knew about and consumed many of the benefits of international trade, especially wine. National wealth was still based on precious metals such as gold and silver, and the introduction of a paper currency in the early nineteenth century was viewed by many as state-sponsored robbery. Trade still relied on bills of exchange. Ricardo's law of comparative advantage emerged at a time when his native England was an economic powerhouse in the world. Yet it was an England that was just starting to industrialize. Much of his writing centers on questions such as the economic rent of land and the wages of agricultural workers. Manufacturing was an important but ancillary and somewhat volatile economic activity. He wrote:

> A great manufacturing country is peculiarly exposed to temporary reverses and contingencies, produced by the removal of capital from one employment to another. The demands for the production of agriculture are uniform; they are not under the influence of fashion, prejudice, and caprice. To sustain life, food is necessary, and the demand for food must continue in all ages and in all countries.[1]

Ricardo thought in terms of national economies, wedded permanently to nation-states. He was not a nationalist, but to think in any other geopolitical terms would have been absurd for him. Ricardo was also one of the first to apply a rigid cause-and-effect methodology to economics. Factor A caused effect B in factor C, which, in turn, had a generally predictable impact on factors D and E, and so on. He was one of the earliest and most eloquent advocates for untrammeled international trade and was a vociferous critic of the English Corn Laws, which precluded the importation of cheaper grain from North America and Eastern Europe.

Similarly, John Maynard Keynes's "general" theory of economics was written in response to the Great Depression that swept the world in the early 1930s. It was a time of economic hardship that seemed to defy all existing economic nostra for its alleviation. Unemployment remained stubbornly high, while on the wings of economic debate stood extremists such as Adolf Hitler, who were only too willing to lull the embittered millions into supporting him. Keynes's theory had many flaws, but it has been overtaken by world developments. Keynes thought in terms of a closed economic model, not one that was intimately linked with the outside world. Keynes was a descendant of the political economic tradition that placed great emphasis on the role of labor and employment. In today's world, humans are being replaced by robots and automation in a growing range of activities. If we need proof, we only have to look at the way economic improvements are not accompanied by parallel increases in employment. In fact, in recent years, when the number of jobs has increased, the stock market has tended to go down. Investors know that increased employment is a sign of poor productivity gains and, as a result, a potential cut in the bottom line.

Keynes argued that much of the failure of "classical" economics was because it had been time specific, a factor he considered dangerous. Yet he did not see the danger of his own theories having the same incipient risks.

Keynesian economics grew out of a serious economic crisis. Its lessons have a certain allure in similar moments of economic disruption, such as when there is either high unemployment or high inflation. High unemployment was accompanied by low consumption levels and massive overproduction. Smith's "invisible hand" was arthritic, according to Keynes. The market also lacked equilibrium in the long term. The answer was for the government to inject demand into the economy and to supplement deficits in consumption. It is a central tenet of Keynesian economics that demand breeds supply, with supply come jobs, and with jobs come higher levels of consumption.

Keynes earned considerable sums in the financial markets, and, like Ricardo, he knew much about the nature of wealth. Neither Ricardo nor Keynes was an ivory tower theorist. Keynes responded intellectually to the world he could observe. It was a world of nation-states, so the governments of these nation-states could provide solutions to problems within closed economic systems.

Keynes might be forgiven for allowing his horizons to be limited by the prevailing landscapes. When a problem occurs in any organization or system, however large or small, there is a tendency to spend time searching for a scapegoat when it should be spent searching for a solution. The economic order that had been prevalent until the 1930s had failed to provide solutions. If anything, the solutions seemed to have contributed to ultimate economic dislocation. The age of imperialism had been replaced by an era of nationalism. In economic terms, this pointed toward protectionism. In such an environment, the nation-state stood out too prominently. Keynes was not an open advocate of protection. The scapegoats he sought were often those whom he described as "slaves of some defunct economist" who saw the past as a paradise to which it might be possible to return by turning back the economic clock. (Keynes's sense of intellectual superiority prevented him from believing that his theories might ever one day be defunct.) Government had also grown extensively. Whereas the governments in the days of Adam Smith and David Ricardo were responsible only for overseeing wars (and usually doing a bad job), governments in the early half of the twentieth century were responsible for a lot more areas of life, including education, health, and housing.

Keynesian economics relied heavily on a linear approach, based on identifiable and measurable inputs and outputs. As I've said, it was a closed economic model in which jobs, demand, supply, interest rates, and money supply were all related. It was an article of Keynesian faith that the government could control economic activity by adjusting one or two of these factors. This is similar to the Newtonian model of physics known as conservation of mass (or energy) in a closed system.

The flow of money in such a closed, regulated system can be predicted with lesser or greater certainty, but in an economy that is interlinked and through which money can flow with ease, such certainty is elusive.

The situation quickly becomes complicated if two countries start trading a multitude of different products and services, or if they start communicating with ultrafast computers. A total of 189 countries are doing this. Money flows through credit-card transactions or across trading floors. Borders are less like barriers, and even though restrictions still exist, people cross them more readily. In Japan, 20 million people leave the country annually and outspend the Japanese trade surplus. The money is moved by interbank transfers. So credit-card buying is both cross-border and through cyberspace. In fact, a Chinese ATM provides renminbi notes in response to a Japanese cash card, as long as it is endorsed by Cirrus or Plus. This is true in most of the countries I have visited in the last year or two.

If the citizens of all 189 countries started doing this, what economic model works? What use are nineteenth- and early-twentieth-century models based on the nation-state economy when I am in Dalian taking out local currency with my Japanese card?

There are other players in the money game of today: private and institutional investors, not to mention arbitrageurs. All these participants interpret moves by central bankers in different ways, so a simple linear model based on inputs and outputs is simplistic in the extreme. Linear models work best with exact variables. The present-day money markets with their complexity seem to veer more toward chaos and random patterns. It is still possible to say what may happen or may not happen, but not with certainty.

Through an excessive reliance on such modalities, those who make economic decisions informed by Keynesian expectations of macroeconomic realities in the changing global economy may find that the results that are achieved bear no resemblance to what they had intended. An analogy might be with a chef using tried and tested recipes and methods from a well-respected cookbook. But the dishes he produces are inedible. An example of the application of Keynesian economic nostra to "real world" economic problems and the results can be seen in the United States. At present, it enjoys a low interest regime. This should stimulate economic activity, but in practice, much of the surplus money in the economy seeps out in pursuit of higher yields from other, maybe riskier markets.

New Fundamentals Require New Thinking

The economic realities in which economists such as Smith, Ricardo, and Keynes lived are distant worlds away from the one we inhabit at the beginning of the twenty-first century. No one could have possibly imagined the impact that technology would have on information or the business world. After all, perhaps the greatest examples of "new" technology known to Ricardo was the Rothschilds' use of carrier pigeons to bring the news of Wellington's victory at Waterloo back to London in 1815.

Technology has also transformed work. It has changed perceptions of the world we inhabit. Thirty years ago, Americans viewed Europe or Japan as places on the other side of the world. Letters took more than a week to move between them. Communications were possible but expensive. Today, documents can be sent to the "other side of the world" within the space of the time taken to click Send on a screen. Greater use of Voice over IP (VoIP) telephony allows friends and family members to chat casually and frequently. Some of these changes are thanks to technology; others, especially within telecommunications, have been made possible by deregulation.

But most important of all is the way technology has transformed geopolitics, turning old-style nation-states into anachronisms. The global economy has also generated or raised the profiles of new business elements that were unthinkable before, such as multiples and derivatives. The role played by multiples or price per earning ratios in today's business world is a deliberate challenge to traditional ways of looking at companies. These are also a defiance of time. They seem to rely on nonstatistical elements, often nonrational or even irrational. One of these is euphoria. During the heady days of the technology-inspired new economy in the late 1990s, most people felt positive about the U.S. economy. It was on the right road and it was growing apace, so, not surprisingly, multiples grew exponentially.

And yet, economics as a discipline still seems to be stuck in the old world. Post-Keynesians, such as Paul Samuelson, basically offer variations on the same central themes. Economic education still revolves around the frameworks encapsulating the old paradigms. Some may be useful, but their assistance is, at best, confined to asking new questions instead of providing answers. Their relationship is akin to a jigsaw puzzle that has maybe two-thirds of its pieces missing.

In the global economy, the Keynesian model is defective; it does not work. Why not? Why does common sense not work? It's because time stops for no man. Economic environments are no more permanent than the weather.

Turning the Taps On and Off

Money supply is fundamental to the macroeconomic model. It is the water in the Keynesian bathtub. Yet, if we look at the global economy, we see a constant flow. We don't even see absorption anymore. The world is awash with money presently, but if it were absorbed, it would cause inflation. Traditional economic theory cannot explain this.

Many reasons exist for this abundant cash liquidity. As mentioned earlier, governments bear some of the responsibility for minting too much money. In the early 1990s, there was a morbid fear among the governments of many developed countries that they would run out of money or that money would begin to run short.

There was also a desire to assist the banking sector. But injecting money into the system on a large scale is merely a symptom of how frightened politicians are. They fear that people might actually panic and raid the banks, fearing a crash. The populations of the OECD countries are aging. They are putting ever-greater quantities of money aside for their retirement years. But once those are reached, they no longer need money because most of their wants are provided for.

Pension funds, managed by either private companies or government agencies, cannot find suitable sources for investment within their traditional nation-state economic borders. Money no longer is transferred into inventory. In fact, the very nature of inventory has changed. The best type of inventory is money. Large inventories are potential profits, but not yet profits. They may soak up considerable amounts in menu costs. The desirability of extensive inventory is debatable, especially in those environments utilizing just-in-time procedures.

Technology and deregulation have liberated money from national economies. Money flows to areas of highest return, no matter where that is. Money (and money traders) is unsentimental and is not troubled by old notions such as patriotism. We might say that the world has responded to its positive liquidity by creating liquidity buckets where financial resources reside when they are not absorbed into traditional conduits, whether savings or consumption. As a result, many OECD countries have more money in their economies than they can efficiently use.

To prove the effects of this overliquidity, we can use a function developed by Alfred Marshall around the end of the nineteenth century. The ratio, known to economists as Marshall's K, depends on the relationship between money supply and the gross national product. Many economists believe this to be constant. Because it is unwavering, it is said that a country suffering strong deflationary pressure should raise the money supply. This will cause prices to shoot up and will set off an inflationary situation. In very simple terms, the solution to deflation is inflation, a form of economic vaccination. This treatment was what the economist Paul Krugman prescribed as an antidote for Japan's deflation, but it is also the prescription most other economists offer.

In reality, no matter how much money was pumped into the Japanese economy, the expected inflation did not take place. In fact, money was not absorbed by the real economy. Industry did not utilize the capital to invest in machinery or to stock inventory. Nor did the aging population hurry to buy goods for fear of inflation. Consumers knew, better than economists, that they did not have to hurry to convert money into goods.

Deflation and the GDP Deflator

Macroeconomists are also wedded to the notion of the GDP deflator defined as how much a product or service costs in terms of its former price. For example, the gigantic investment by all sectors in computers is now only one hundredth of the cost in the past, so the deflator kicks in. Japan is therefore defined as deflationary because computers are cheaper for the same level of functionality (that is, per gigabyte of memory). But I think that such a definition of deflation is highly questionable. In the example of computer hardware, there is an ongoing move toward producing cheaper and faster chips and microprocessors. According to the guardians of macroeconomic definitions, this produces deflation. But that is not how consumers feel. The consumer price index may not move at all, yet governments such as Japan's announce a certain rate of deflation. When the economy is flat and the government states that there was 3.6 percent deflation, a disingenuous government can claim that the real economy grew by 3 percent. This is misleading.

GDP deflators are yet another element that macroeconomists will have to examine afresh. The definitions of the deflator made sense in the commodity-dominated trading environment of the nineteenth and early twentieth centuries. This was the economic background against which the high priests of macroeconomics made their definitions of elements such as the GDP deflator. At that time, they were acceptable because they made sense. Yet in the days of superfast and supersmall microprocessors and flat-panel visual displays (getting larger and cheaper) and phone bills getting cheaper per unit of usage, what is the best way to define the GDP deflator? This is, or should be, the job of economists. Every time governments publish statistics for national accounts, I have to reexamine the definitions being used for the labels contained in them. I have a sense that these figures just are not realistic. I don't see such levels of growth as are proclaimed. But if the Japanese government published national accounts of a 7 percent growth in the economy, journalists writing for news magazines would proceed to write about "Japan's Solid Recovery." Readers like a feel-good story, even if it doesn't square with economic reality.

Interest Rates and Nest Eggs

Another aspect of monetary policy that the advent of the global economy has altered is the position of interest rates. For so long, they were a core doctrine, especially for the Keynesians. The interest rate was a phenomenon that dominated old-style national economies with national currencies. For Keynesians, interest rates and money supply were the only two forces that a central bank had at its disposal for influencing the macroeconomy.

Since the days of Lord Keynes, the U.S. dollar has become a new monetary platform, acceptable and preferable as a currency for trade and savings. Consider the influence of the dollar on the economy of Australia. Interestingly, in Australia, most people end up saving in U.S. dollars. The Australian currency has shifted or oscillated greatly in value: It appears unstable. Savers have responded by shifting their savings to whatever currency they want, something that is possible only in a deregulated economy. People's psychology does not track their currency's up-and-down fluctuations. Australian industry does—it has to because most companies are involved in commodity trading—but the Australian saving public does not. Savings and pensions are hedged against the Australian dollar. Most savings are in U.S. dollars, so even if the Australian dollar lost value dramatically, Australians would not be alarmed and they would not see their financial nest eggs threatened.

The Australian economy has been improving over the last six years for totally unknown reasons. In a commodity-based economy, economic orthodoxy teaches that the weaker its currency becomes, the more export competitiveness rises; the economy should improve, and vice versa. But this has not happened, even when the Australian dollar has alarmingly strengthened. The dollar has effectively neutered its Australian namesake. During 2003 and 2004, the Australian dollar gained 40 percent against the U.S. dollar—the largest among OECD currencies. This is because most Australians have now switched their savings back to their own currency to enjoy higher interest rates.

The Australians are not alone. The savings of Argentinians and Russians are also mostly in U.S. dollars (particularly after their economic crises of 1997–1998). Similarly, consumption in these countries does not pick up even when their currencies do so.

By globalizing the portfolio of assets for individuals in a similar way, a national government can avoid mounting pressure from mismanaging its own economy. Those saving predominantly in their beloved "national" currency are not so neutral to currency fluctuations. British savers, whose savings are in pounds sterling, have to worry about that currency's fluctuations against the euro, in addition to movements against the dollar. If the United Kingdom joined the euro zone, life might not be so uncertain for British savers. It might even become quite boring.

Can Physics Help?

Another way of looking at the relationship between the old and global economies is to return to the science of physics. Isaac Newton laid its foundations in the seventeenth century. Many important additions arose over the next two centuries, none greater than Albert Einstein's Theory of Relativity. While Einstein is viewed rightly as a great thinker, his radical theory did not dispense with Newtonian physics; it refined and added greatly to it. Let's see Newtonian and even Einsteinian physics as an equivalent, though far from perfect, metaphor of the old economy.

This didn't provide all the answers to what was going on in the universe. In particular, these theories could not explain the actions of the basic units of the universe, the atoms. In the early years of the twentieth century, Danish physicist Niels Bohr worked out a new quantum theory of the atom. In the next decade, a German physicist, Werner Heisenberg, established that there was another realm of physical reality below the level of the atom in the world of the sub-atomic particle. The laws of the Newtonian universe did not work here. Heisenberg postulated that a given bit of matter could be measured either as a particle (in terms of charting its position) or as a wave (by measuring its velocity), but not as both simultaneously because the act of measuring one characteristic rendered the other measurement uncertain. His theories were elaborated into quantum mechanics. At the realm of the subatomic, things do not happen as they are supposed to. Maybe we can see the world of quantum physics as similar to but far from identical to that of the global economy.

Another scientific analogy might be made with the world of chaos and complexity, of activities that cannot be ascertained with certainty, maybe because simply too many nonstandard variables are acting on the outcome. By way of a simple example, consider the fall of a leaf. In classical Newtonian physics, it is possible to say how quickly the leaf will fall and, all things being equal, where it will fall. But what if there is a gust of wind? Maybe the effect can be measured on the leaf's fall, but the gust itself and its interaction with the leaf are important. How fast is the wind? What direction does it flow from? What is the shape and texture of the leaf, and how does this influence its fall and its contact with the wind? Already a simple leaf falling toward the ground has become a very complex act that can be foreseen and modeled with great difficulty. This can be done at a simple level, but the issue has always been that many experiments have to account for "noise" that will distort the experiment's results. But how far are the final results distortions at all?

A Complex World

I see a number of parallels between the global economy and the world of complexity. For one thing, it is clear that the former has many variables influencing each other. It is a system that is inherently dynamic but not always predictable. The expected results do not occur as they should. A small change in one variable can have a huge and inexplicable elsewhere. One area that attracted the attention of those interested in complexity was the study of phase transitions— what happened when a body changed from being a solid to a liquid, or a liquid to a gas. Maybe the global economy reflects such a change, from the old world of manufacturing to the new world that owes so much to technology and that was not previously possible. Perhaps the greatest similarity is in attitudes toward order and equilibrium. Much of traditional economics (including Keynes's writings) accepted that economic systems moved toward equilibrium. This reflected the influence of physics. Complexity theory holds that "classical" equilibrium is an attractor toward which some, but by no means all, events conform. For these there are other attractors, which are imperfectly understood but which infuse events with their own order.

The global economy is something that has developed only in very recent terms, whereas the forces behind quantum mechanics and the axioms of complexity theory have been around for as long as there has been a universe. Nobody realized this before the advent of Heisenberg and Bohr or Mitchell Feigenbaum.

Quantum mechanics has not replaced traditional Newtonian/ Einsteinian physics. Much of the latter's discoveries are still valid, but not at the level of the subatomic. Similarly, quantum mechanics doesn't operate above this level. It is as if there are two separate realities, both informing each in certain instances. Both are equally valid within their separate spheres, but both are separate. The global economy has a number of similarities with quantum physics. Nobody is completely sure how it works, least of all the physicists. Experts agree on little apart from the certainty of its existence. Even some of the experts admit that they don't know all the answers or really understand the phenomenon.

The same observations can be made regarding the impact of complexity theory on accepted science. The former seeks to add to existing knowledge and never to be satisfied with answers that rely on accepted ignorance. As a result, the response of the scientific community has often been skeptical and a little defensive.

Theorists from the Santa Fe Institute have applied complexity theory to economics. Not surprisingly, they have rejected much of traditional economics in light of complexity, believing that it makes fundamentally erroneous assumptions about the effects of technology and the behavior of economic networks.

We should not minimize the role of psychology. Many of the players develop their own psychology, so we can talk of government psychology, politician psychology, and trader psychology. They are all connected. The development of Russia today is different from that five years ago. Developments in Brazil are different than what they were ten years ago.

All the different actors are alive and sensitive to changes in the world. Interaction takes place not only across borders, but also between industries and across cyberspace. Interaction seems to have a built-in desire and ability to challenge and defy physical distances and obstacles. This interaction is nonlinear, and there is no equilibrium. In the world of physics, it cannot be described in terms of an equilibrium equation. For one or any input, not only are the probabilities very different, but the bipolar opposite of what is expected may result.

The best way to cope with this new reality is to cast one's mind back over the last ten years and observe how the same phenomenon could lead to different returns, especially in countries such as Russia, Brazil, Mexico, and even China. Consider Brazil as an example. People used to say that it was a high-risk environment. Now it is believed to be an acceptably risky environment, and money rushes in. This could be the right amount of money, so there are healthy returns. If too much money rushes in, it could become extremely volatile and unstable—and risky once again. That's the nature of physics and dynamics.

This is a function of time. It is also a function of your sophistication—how quickly you can bail out and also how skillful you are in playing the game while at the table. I started out characterizing the nature of this new economic sphere as a jungle. Many dark shadows there appear reasonable upon closer inspection.

The reality is that although the effects of the global economy can be observed, as can some of its inner workings, such as the behavior of money, its mechanics remain something of a mystery. It is slippery and hard to get a grip on. Quantum mechanics has seen the arrival of a plethora of subatomic particles—gluons, gravitons, and so on—that help to explain its workings. The global economy also throws up new business particles. One of the most significant is the multiple and the derivative. Probably others are waiting to arise. Arbitrage across time zones and national borders is commonplace.

For generations, notions of corporate value rested upon staid statistics that were comprehensible and also predictable. A company had a size and weight that depended on its capital and stock at a certain moment in time. There were profits and losses, both of which contributed, though never totally, to a stock's value. But in the late twentieth century, a fairly well-established accounting ratio, the price per earning ratio, came into greater contact with the concepts of discounted cash flow and net present value analysis. This sought to look into the future and to appraise the changing value of money over time.

The Curve Ball

Most branches of science regard empirical inquiry as necessary. One of the criticisms leveled at quantum physics was that so much of it was theoretical and unobservable. Complexity theory also had to deal with demands for acceptable proofs. This has never been true of economics as a discipline because there has always been a lot of data to work with. As an example, consider one particular data thread that has traditionally been important in economics: the flow of money.

Alfred Marshall once casually equated the flow of money in the economy to oil in a machine. In Keynesian economics, money was the blood of the *corpus economicus*. But in the late twentieth century, money started to act unpredictably.

Central to Keynesian economics is an obsession with money supply. The key question is, "What is money?." Does it include credit, airline mileage, and bartered commodities? A nation's economy may be compared to a huge bath with separate faucets marked as fiscal and monetary policy determining the amount of money that flows in. At the other end are two plugs for draining money out of the bath. The central bank stands alongside the bath with a thermometer testing the temperature, to ensure that it gets neither too hot nor too cold. The amount of water in the bath is all important. Too much water leads to inflation; too little leads to unemployment. But what constitutes the water?

So, there has been a trade-off between jobs and the value of money. The price of maintaining the value of the money in people's pocket was traditionally a high level of joblessness. Even today economists talk about a *natural level of unemployment*, one that it is more or less impossible to go below without accelerating inflation. The term is a Keynesian legacy.

This model is neat but not elegant. And let's remember: one nation, one bathtub. Within it, the water is supposed to cause little patterns identified as consumption, investment, and government spending. Taken together, they are called the gross domestic product or aggregate demand.

The theoretical trade-off between jobs and inflation was solidified by the economist Jack Philips. In a possibly unintended tribute to Alfred Marshall, he exemplified the relationship in terms of a curve to which his colleagues added his name. The Philips Curve seemed to make a lot of sense in the 1950s and 1960s, but the connection between high unemployment and low inflation soon started to part company.

For much of the 1990s and the present decade, the United States seems to give the lie to the Philips Curve. Low rates of inflation have been accompanied by low levels of unemployment. Inflation has rarely climbed above 3 percent, and unemployment has stayed below 6 percent. There has been no oversupply of labor, no producers unable to sell their produce. No inflation, no deflation gaps. So where is Professor Keynes?

Oscillating Wildly

The reality is that the global economy renders Keynesian economics obsolete and its theories somewhat jaded, if not altogether defunct.

These include much of the thinking about exchange rates. We mentioned earlier that borderless capital is one of the symptoms of the global economy. One way in which this has to happen in a world where borders are less impenetrable than before is in the area of currency exchange rates.

Since the early nineteenth century, economic thinking on exchange rates has been dominated by David Ricardo's paradigm of Purchase Power Parity (PPP). Boiled down to essentials, this teaches that rates of exchange are determined by the relative purchasing power of the currencies concerned. So if 100 units of currency A were needed to buy a list of commodities in market A, while the same group of commodities could be bought with only 150 units of currency B in its home market, the exchange rate between currencies A and B was 1 to 1.5.

This theory was so elegant that it did a violent disservice to the real world. It failed to take into consideration a whole host of cost features that could account for differences in price between two markets—and even within the same market on different days, depending on supply. There was also the question of elasticity for produce in a market. This had nothing to do with the currency used.

It is important to remember when discussing PPP that it was always based on tradable items that could be transported across national borders before they were bought and sold. These might be finished goods or commodities such as wool or wine. But these are not the totality of products and services that are bought and sold and that filter into national accounting mechanisms. Many physical items cannot be traded over borders or over any distance. These naturally include nonmovables such as houses and parking lots, as well as domestic services. Tradable items can vary in their contribution to a nation's economy. In Japan and the United States, tradable items make up only about 10 percent of the GDP, whereas in many Nordic countries, the figure is nearer to 50 percent. This is a function of each country's economy and lifestyle.

But in Ricardo's day, exchange rates could oscillate widely, but no one except those involved with foreign trade would know much about it. After all, there was no flickering ForEx screen to inform interested parties.

Apart from the odd wild fluctuation, currency exchange rates remained static and unchanged for years. They were often cemented in bilateral agreements. These sought to establish exchange rates based on a nation-state's holding of gold.

Ricardo's Purchase Power Parity, though long respected, must be treated as a fundamental of the old exchange rate paradigm. As I will demonstrate, there have been a number of paradigm shifts in currency exchange thinking, so exchange rates according to Ricardo can be seen as Paradigm I.

People are still stuck in this old mindscape. Some commentators say that the strengthening of the yen (or any other currency) represents an improvement of that country's fundamentals, and vice versa. This is incorrect. At the moment, the yen is strengthening because the Japanese don't want to hold it. They know that the Bank of Japan is in favor of buying dollars to prevent the yen from getting too strong. There is a guarantor of dollar purchases. While the financial currency dealers and arbitrageurs buy dollars, it is a safe currency. Most of these traders are ignorant of economic theory. If the Japanese economic fundamentals improved, would they buy yen? Certainly not. These dealers always have what they call a "position," a financial and psychological comfort zone. This can be informed by what others will do in response to news. They anticipate a certain response. The traders' psychology has as much influence on currency exchange rates as any other economic judgment. This is obviously far from the practice of the Efficient Market Hypothesis.

Until very recently, the Japanese financial authorities detested the expensive yen. They may have been under pressure from Japanese industrialists. They bought dollars, thereby making the dollar stronger. In 2003, Japan bought $200 billion using taxpayers' money. In March 2004, the Bank of Japan signaled an end to this interference. It would intervene far less, even when volatility might seem to warrant it. The bank sought to defend this turnaround by referring to the strengthening position of the Japanese economy, which showed signs of emerging from its long sleep. Japanese exports were also growing, so there was no longer a need to maintain a weak yen. More important, perhaps (though not stressed by the Bank of Japan), was the fact that Sino-Japanese trade had entered the realms of a trade surplus. There was also the looming specter of inflation in America, combined with the expected response of the Federal Reserve: a rise in interest rates.

This retreat from intervention does not represent a long-delayed conversion to reality or a determination to escape from old mindsets. The Korean financial authorities, who traditionally pursued a similarly interventionist policy to keep their currency, the won, at a low level, have flagged their determination not to sit on the fence. According to Choi Joon Kyung, director-general of the Korean Finance Ministry's International Finance Bureau, "Our foreign exchange policy remains resolute. We'll use every won to protect the foreign exchange market from...moves that go against economic fundamentals."[2]

The collective psychology of maybe a handful of currency traders is causing volatility. No matter what happens, if the yen becomes too strong, they know that the Japanese government will come in like the good father and rescue the yen and the country's economic competitiveness by buying dollars. Most countries want their currencies to be strong. Yet many trading nations, such as Japan, Korea, and Germany, cry foul when their currency gets too strong to maintain their trading competitiveness. So there is always a final buyer in this system: their central banks.

In the very dangerous, risky, and volatile jungle of currency trading, this is a "sure bet." It is as if there is one stupid merchant always willing to buy the dollars to support the dollar level. This is why dollars continue to be traded vigorously. It has nothing to do with the fundamentals in Japan or in the United States. It cannot be explained in terms of Ricardian Purchasing Power Parity.

Paradigm II

And so we move on to Paradigm II. Ricardo's theory has already been dealt a knockout punch by the notions of financial equilibrium and its applications to currency exchange rates.

Let us demonstrate this through a scenario. An imaginary investor arrives on Earth from Mars. He has a certain amount of money with him (let's not ask where he got it). Should he convert it into Japanese yen or U.S. dollars? The question would have to be asked: What would be the expected return in a certain period of time in the future, taking into account inflation levels in both countries, the interest rates, the country risks, and so on? What is the equivalent number to make the profitability of the investment equal? This is totally different than Ricardo's Purchasing Power Parity. Is it beneficial to keep the money in pounds, in yen, in dollars, or in some other currency?

This is financial equilibrium theory (also known as Paradigm II). It was very much in vogue in the mid-1980s. People actually believed that this desire to achieve equilibrium was a stronger factor governing the exchange rate than Ricardian Purchasing Power Parity.

The Power of Politics

From 1985 to 1992 (and beyond, for a while), a third paradigm entered the picture: a political paradigm. America argued that the dollar was too strong for the country to be competitive. That was a political paradigm because neither the bankers nor the economists were saying it. This was the position of the politicians, who, in turn, were being lobbied by American industry. The country's business leaders were armed with self-confidence in their own competitiveness, yet they were finding it difficult to export their products. They blamed this on an unfriendly exchange rate.

As we have seen, one of the upshots of this paradigm was the Plaza Accord of 1985. It is true that the agreement reached then covered more than the exchange rate between the yen and the dollar. But the attempt to improve American competitiveness at the expense of Japanese competitiveness failed.

This political paradigm was not even economically or factually supported. Everyone believed that America could get by with this political paradigm because it was such a strong country. Because of it, the American public and the government started to accept weaker and weaker dollars. This is irrational. The dollar fell in value and reached its bottom in 1994, when Japan was in its deepest trough of its depression. (The bubble burst in 1989, so 1990–1995 saw Japan as an economic basket case.) The fundamentals were very bad, but the yen hit a high mark of 84 yen to the dollar in 1994: its high-water mark (compared with a rate of 235 yen in 1985). This has nothing to do with economic fundamentals. It was based on the expectation that the yen would get stronger.

In the wake of this high-water mark, it was felt that the yen had become too strong. In this way, the whole of the United States could, in theory, be bought up by collateralizing Japan. It was realized that the fall in the dollar represented something of an overshoot, so its value began to come back to 135 and 180, gradually approaching a narrower band between 110 and 125 yen to the dollar.

In the late 1990s, yet another paradigm appeared. Let us call Paradigm IV the *trader's paradigm*. A handful of traders throughout the world might have a collective sense, or a shared gut feeling, that there exists a perfect position at which they are safe and their debts are cleared. A trader then feels discomfort, maybe panic, the further he feels himself distant from this perfect cleared position. For a Japanese trader (or a trader in the yen of any nationality), this might be 108 or 107 yen to the dollar. Programmed trading may add to this sense of a perfect position. Once the level is reached, yen are either bought or sold automatically without human intervention. Traders aren't worried about Purchase Power Parity. They don't care much whether the fundamentals are good or bad. They are ambivalent of what politicians are saying. But they are not ambivalent to the politicos in their totality. They pick up on the particular politician who is saying what they want to hear.

These traders are an extremely scared group of people. They stand to lose a lot of money overnight or even in a split second if they misread a signal. Like scared people, they are generally always looking over their shoulder or through the corners of the eyes at what other people are doing, waiting for the signal to act, never wanting to be the first to jump themselves. They always sense what others are likely to do and what other positions are like. For the exchange rate, the position of fellow traders dictates what the optimal exchange rate is at any one time.

In Japan, there has traditionally been an interference level, and when it is reached, the Ministry of the Treasury steps in to buy. Currency trading would be very dangerous if there were no equivalent to a Japanese treasury office that stood as a guaranteed buyer. As a group, the traders would be far more cautious. Sometimes what amounts to a game of hide-and-seek develops between the traders and the treasury ministry. The traders try to find a position that is both comfortable and safe. They also try to second-guess the ministry's intentions and the level at which it will intervene. The traders can afford to be more aggressive because there is and will always be a buyer of final resort. The more aggressive they become, the more volatile the market becomes. Consequently, there are more opportunities to make money—and also to lose it. The more money the traders make, the more aggressive they become because they can afford to take higher risks.

Built into their aggregate psyche is the knowledge that when the yen starts to become too high, people—including the Keidanren and the trades unions—will start to demand intervention. This is a traditional Ricardian-conditioned response.

So, over the last century, we have seen the currency exchange rate paradigm constantly shifting. It has shifted three times, from Ricardo's Purchasing Power Parity to the traders' paradigm based on their collective psychology.

The Difficulty of Changing Habits

In spite of what we say about the reality and potency of the global economy and its paradigms, most countries on planet Earth seem addicted to pursuing old and tired economic policies. Let us look at just two, the first of which is a definite case for economic counseling; the second, the United States, has exhibited very definite but confusing signs of waking up to the new reality.

There is a proverb that you cannot have your cake and eat it. The Japanese government wants foreign direct investment. It has a very vocal and visible campaign urging investment in Japan, headed by Prime Minister Junichiro Koizumi. But once foreign investors come in, they are taxed and the money taken from them is used to subsidize inefficient industries and sectors.

Let us look at the importation of American and Australian beef. Its world price is very low, compared to that of Japanese beef, and Japanese consumers love it. However, it can be sold only above a certain price. Part of the price charged for the imported beef goes into fiscal pools, used to subsidize Japanese beef producers. The loser is the Japanese consumer, who is not able to enjoy the cost benefits of consuming American or Australian beef. The protection is sometimes helped by "acts of nature" such as an outbreak of disease in American herds. Such an outbreak led to a complete ban on imports of American beef into Japan at the end of 2003. A popular Japanese dish is *gyudon*, or beef served with rice and a spicy soy sauce. But it has to be American beef—not even Australian beef has the accepted taste or color according to the top gyudon chain, Yoshino-ya. In response to the ban, a chain of restaurants specializing in the dish were forced to shut their doors for some time. An interesting adjunct to this is that there have been nine cases of BSE reported in Japanese cattle and only two in the U.S., yet the Japanese government has banned American beef imports.

There is the equivalent of a damping mechanism for helping old Japanese industries survive. They survive, but artificially. They exist on the fiscal equivalent of a life-support machine. In the process, they are so spoiled by the subsidies coming from this damping mechanism that they make no attempts to improve their productivity or competitiveness. More money has to be pumped in to help them survive. And this applies not only to beef, but to rice, wheat, corn, dairy products, sugar cane, and so on. The full list covers most agricultural products.

Some of the most costly government intervention comes in the sphere of agriculture. We have already mentioned the protection afforded to beef producers. The Japanese government regularly spends billions of dollars in subsidies to rice farmers. It is estimated that no less than $400 billion has been transferred in this way over the last decade. But the more subsidies are spent, the less competitive the farmers become. The situation hasn't changed, despite the massive investment by Japanese taxpayers. The only beneficiaries, in fact, have been construction companies because most of the money was spent "modernizing" the rice paddies.

These payments stem from a wish to protect Japan's "food security." Such notions are truly archaic, a rural delusion. They see the nation-state as a fortress under present or potential siege by the rest of the world. As a result of this malignant belief, Japanese consumers have to pay dearly for their rice, although rice produced in Australia could be supplied at one tenth of the price to the Japanese.

Such subsidies to rice farmers are only part of the general benevolence of the Japanese government when it comes to making transfers to protected groups. Subsidies are accompanied by selective tariffs against imports from countries such as China that can produce the same food at a much lower cost. These moves may be attempts to protect the economic basis of rural life. They are also a response to the power of Japanese farmers whose organizations are very vocal, and the influential but often woefully inefficient agricultural cooperatives who have been very powerful lobbyists on behalf of their members.

Japanese farms are structurally inefficient. They are too small, far smaller than their American counterparts and well below the EU average. Transfers and tariffs are said to protect the Japanese farming sector, but this has meant higher food prices and restricted choice for Japanese consumers. It has led to inefficiency and waste in the sector itself, but most significantly, it has not prevented a numerical decrease in its membership. Not only are there fewer farmers, but they are also older. The average age of Japanese rice growers now is 59 and rising.

These measures may be dressed up as helping the farming sector, but in reality, they have done nothing of the sort. The only sectors that have been truly aided are the construction industry, the central bureaucracy, and those in the spectrum of affiliated agencies dealing with agriculture, food, and forestry.

One of the most extreme examples is the subsidy paid to mulberry growers for more than a century; the growers have only recently ceased to receive government largesse. The Japanese silk industry is all but dead.

In Japan's case, the desire to help weak and uncompetitive businesses may be heightened by political considerations. Such an industry may be a big employer in an area providing strong and staunch support (and money) for candidates from the ruling Liberal Democratic Party (LDP), or a particular faction within it. There may also be completely irrational considerations. An industry may be considered traditional to an area, wedded to it by history and heritage. There is then a perceived but misguided duty to protect it and its workers.

The Japanese government still directs monetary policy from its nineteenth-century comfort zone. It tries to help export-orientated industry by ensuring a weaker, more business-beneficent yen. At times, it seems that the Japanese government is still dealing with the early paradigm and that it hasn't gone much further than Ricardo. It seemed to believe in this paradigm with an almost unshakeable faith, intervening in a vain attempt to keep the yen weak. It pumped in more than $200 billion in 2003 alone in support of the weaker yen. And yet the government could not stop the yen from strengthening. The Bank of Japan and the Japanese treasury seemed stuck in a groove of consistent intervention in the currency market. Each time they intervened, it became less effective. Whenever they bought dollars, they actually weakened the American currency and strengthened the Japanese. Each intervention caused an even greater cumulative loss to the Japanese taxpayer, who must ultimately pick up the tab. By the end of 2003, Japan had exhausted much of its budget reserves in this idiotic ritual.

This is such a blessing for America, with its huge deficit. One person in the market is buying dollars. Having bought these dollars, the Japanese government has nowhere else to channel them except by buying American Treasury bonds or government securities (GS). There is one constant buyer for this unpopular government financial instrument. This is a double whammy for the American government: The Japanese keep buying dollars, but they don't hold on to them and put them in a vault or under the mattress. Instead, they buy American government securities with them. In 2003, the Japanese alone bought about one third of the total number of American GS issued in that year.

The Japanese government was trapped. It was making its decisions based on outmoded macroeconomic axioms. It has been acting with the economic mentality of an export-led manufacturing nation-state. But the major economic activity in Japan is now the service sector. Even a majority of the manufacturing sector is taken up by back-office activities. It has even sought to defend its long overdue policy switch by referring to improving export figures. The stronger yen would have been a blessing to consumers as it would have allowed them to buy the best and cheapest from anywhere in the world. However, the Japanese government retains a protectionist mentality and a faith in the nation-state model that precludes giving consumers the opportunity to enjoy a strong yen.

Uncle Sam Goes Global

Japan is far from being alone in its commitment to the old economic paradigms. Except for a few very notable exceptions, the American government is still wedded to them.

Consider America's earlier attitude toward China. In the mid-1990s, it argued that the Chinese should strengthen the renminbi (RMB). Among those aware of the new currency exchanges paradigms was Federal Reserve chairman Alan Greenspan. During the euphoric eight years of the Clinton presidency, he stealthily raised the Fed's interest rate and, in the process, sucked money from the rest of the world. This was done under the premise of curbing inflation. This sleight of hand was successful. Many thought that he was pursuing the Keynesian approach of increasing the interest rate to suppress the overheating economy. In terms of the bathtub metaphor, he was pulling out one of the plugs to let some of the bubbling water flow out. He appeared to be an economic old-timer, a macroeconomic Archie Bunker.

The *eminence grise* behind Greenspan was Robert Rubin, formerly of Goldman Sachs. Rubin and company knew what they were doing—but they were never going to say publicly that their real intention was to drain money from the rest of the world. For the Federal Reserve *not* to correct the errors of the past was beneficial. There was no benefit in telling the world that this move was motivated by the new global economy and its paradigms. It is like in judo when you use somebody else's force to throw an opponent. Or it may be like a magician who suddenly learns a new and fascinating trick. He is able to charge high fees because he can draw large crowds to watch him perform. But he doesn't tell anyone the secrets of the new trick—certainly not other magicians—unless he is a fool. He allows them to mislead themselves into thinking that he is performing it in a certain way. When anyone is successful and they really know what the source of their success is, they shouldn't tell too many people, not even their closest friends. This may be a very Machiavellian attitude but, as Phineas T. Barnum quipped, "Never give a sucker an even break."

The high interest rates that followed the Fed's decision ushered in a boom period for America. This is one of the reasons the Clinton presidency was—or seemed, in retrospect—such a good time. There were years of euphoria. About one third of the money boosting Wall Street and the NASDAQ market was coming from abroad. The American public didn't seem to know this, and they certainly shouldn't have worried about it.

Many sources of money, such as those acquired by workers who reach retirement age, can remain as a stock or financial asset. They can and, no doubt, will be invested and, in turn, will accumulate in value. During the 1990s, in the heady days of the Clinton presidency, some stocks produced returns as high as 400 percent over eight years. It was the financial asset, the stock, that accumulated, without it being used. It could still generate cash by being collateralized. In such a way, it could produce a flow or income for the average worker or retiree.

So, as long as stock prices went up and kept going up, Clinton remained a "good president," no matter what he got up to in his private life. In an opinion poll (in connection with the Monica Lewinsky affair), Americans were asked whether they thought Clinton was lying: A majority responded yes; when they were then asked whether they thought he was doing a good job as president, a majority also replied affirmatively. They were saying that they did not care about his private peccadilloes with members of his staff, as long as he kept Wall Street humming and the financial futures of their 401(k) plans secure.

Whether President Clinton realized it or not, he was performing a type of magic dependent on the new paradigm of the global economy. The traditional Keynesian approach has always been that high interest rates are bad for the economy. It is my belief that in a developed economy such as the United States, high interest rates are a very positive feature because they draw money from the rest of the world, where it is in surplus. Where there is an excess of stock or financial assets over income, it is not to be expected that the flow or income from these assets will grow at 10 percent per year. However, if they are invested wisely, financial assets can easily grow by more than 10 percent per year. In terms of the flow or drawing effect of this stock, in terms of collateralization, for example, this also can grow exponentially. This is the stock's flow impact. So, high interest rates are good for mature economies.

In fact, one can even argue that a high interest rate, sustained over a period, is a symbol of a strong economy because other countries that cannot match it will end up "contributing" their currencies to the countries with high interest rates. See Exhibit 3.1. On the other hand, a high interest rate in a country that is ignored by the rest of the world would simply depress its economy. In such a country, Keynesian economic theory still holds true.

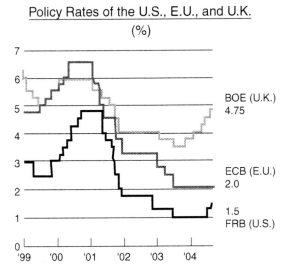

Policy Rates of the U.S., E.U., and U.K. (%)

Note: U.S. = Federal funds rate, E.U. = ECB interest rate, U.K. = Bank of England rate.

Source: FRB, ECB, BOE.

Exhibit 3.1 Policy rates of the United States, the European Union, and the United Kingdom.

When America had a high-interest environment in the 1990s, it enjoyed euphoria because it attracted funds from less stable areas such as Latin America and eastern Asia. Its high interest rates offered a haven. America had a better economy with high interest rates. Financial assets such as pensions and 401(k) funds were inflated. Bill Clinton should be given the credit for his staffing wisdom because it was a policy formulated by the three wise men (Greenspan, Rubin, and Summers). The "feared" inflation never occurred during this period, not because of the high interest rate, but because America is an open market and cheaper products and services came in from other countries to arbitrage otherwise high price–seeking domestic providers.

As I write in 2004, it is apparent that George W. Bush and his advisers do not understand the new paradigm. As a result, Bush is going back to the old, traditional "supply-side" policies of lowering taxes and, thereby, stimulating the economy. Of course, there is an element of economic populism in this. Low taxes are popular; they win elections. Unlike the policy of the 1990s, this is based not on inflating or augmenting financial stock, but on adding to the flow or income.

A low-tax environment is essentially saying that the government is charging less for the flow or income from financial assets or labor. The concrete results of this are that individuals have, say, $500 more in their pockets at the end of the year. This is income money that it is hoped they will spend. But although this may induce a temporary feel-good sensation, some rudimentary financial arithmetic shows how facile it is. In an environment of high interest rates, a sum of money in a pension fund—say, $200,000—can quadruple in value. But the maximum a government pursuing "flow policies" can provide is $500, or maybe even $1,000, per capita per year in tax concessions. Even this has major repercussions on the economy, leading to a higher budget deficit. Its positive impact on individuals, though, is considerably less than the amount coming from higher interest rates. The extra $500 or $1,000 is also insignificant because it is not going to enter the market. The larger amounts earned as appreciation increase consumption far more because the holders of funds feel a greater propensity to consume. In fact, this is true in most developed countries. Policies to increase stock (such as higher stock prices or interest rates) are far more effective in stimulating consumption than policies to increase flow by reducing either tax or interest rates. See Exhibit 3.2.

Greenspan, still chairman of the Federal Reserve Board, naturally does not like the Bush doctrine. All he can do is try to float the economy by trying to boost construction, a typical Keynesian tactic.

Those who do not understand the new economic paradigms are liable to become a victim of someone else who does. It is important, perhaps essential, to highlight the merit of knowing the economic paradigm. In the developed world, the economic policy formulators should focus on asset appreciation, which has a much better impact on the economy, than focusing on increasing flow of income. President Bush's preoccupation with cutting taxes is making the United States very vulnerable to a large-scale hemorrhage of American money into markets offering higher returns than those available at home (such as the European Union).

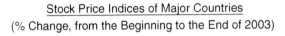

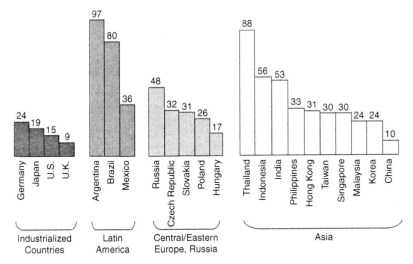

Source: Yahoo! Finance.

Exhibit 3.2 Stock price indices.

Among the few governments that do understand this is the Chinese, especially people such as former premier Zhu Rongji (1998–2003). Zhu very wisely invited foreign capital to China. He did this knowing that it would bankrupt many old-fashioned industries that were the backbone of the Chinese economy, and even of the Chinese state. China is now the largest recipient of foreign direct investment. In the following chapters, we look at others in the world attuned to the global economy.

The New Economic Paradigm

To summarize how the economic world has changed, and its ramifications for you and your organization, let's recap. The global economy has created its own paradigm. Some of its characteristics are novel; they are all interesting.

For possibly the first time in human history, prosperity and riches are not dependant on existing wealth. To put it bluntly, you don't have to be rich to get rich or richer. In the past, especially during the time of Smith, Ricardo, and even Keynes, the prosperity of Great Britain depended on industry, large resources of coal, and a network of colonies producing raw materials. The

prosperity of the United States was also based on industry and innovation, as well as a seemingly inexhaustible supply of land, natural
resources, and workers. Both countries converted much of their
advantages into tangible wealth that was used to sponsor industrial
and infrastructural development elsewhere in the world.

In the global economy, there is no need for mineral resources or
colonies. An area can be very poor in "traditional" resources. Consider
Ireland and Finland. Both countries were part of others' empires,
historically unable to support their populations. Both experienced
devastating famines that wiped out significant sections of their population, either directly through hunger or indirectly through disease.

Yet both countries are now at the forefront of the global economy. They looked to the rest of the world for prosperity, and because
they are areas that were attractive to investment, it came and shows
every indication of staying. China, too, is a poor country. It is very
rich in mineral resources. It is the richest in the world in terms of
population, but it has never succeeded in providing sufficient
income levels for all its people. Those region-states that are prospering do not have natural resources—remember Dalian. The parts
of China that possess these, such as the far west and northeast, are
still poor. China has allowed wealth to come in from the rest of the
world to certain areas.

The world has an excess of capital. Mutual and pension funds
can be added to traditional forms of investing. As prosperity spreads
in the world, so does the number of investment funds. Locations
include not just the traditional G7 economies, but areas such as
Singapore, Latin America, Russia, Australia, and India. These nations
are all cash rich, and they are searching constantly for investment
opportunities. It goes without saying that fund managers are not care-
less or negligent in making decisions about fund allocations. One of
the largest investors in China is the Singapore Central Provident
Fund, and CalPERS, the largest U.S. pension fund, is also present in
every prosperous region. A region has to show itself worthy of consideration. Every region knows that it is in a buyer's market in which
it must compete for investment. Money is not necessary for prosperity, but investment is.

Size no longer matters. Another element of competitiveness
that has been altered by the global economy is attitudes to size. It
followed from the traditional obsession with nation-states that,
before a company could be successful internationally, it had to cut
its teeth at home. It needed a substantial domestic market. So,

international success was not available to companies from states with small populations. It was a Big Boys' Club.

To see how this is no longer the case, we need only to go back to Finland and Nokia. The Finnish domestic market numbers a mere five million, less than the population of a large U.S. city. But its success has depended on looking not inward, but outward. Less than 1 percent of Nokia's sales in 2003 came from Finland. Such global success is no longer a rarity. Danish companies are also successful global niche players: Think of William Demant in hearing aids, Danisco in food additives, and Vestas and NEG-Micon in windmills.

Real success never comes from your backyard. As we shall see when discussing the nation-state's obsolescence, large domestic markets are one more of the traditional factor endowments that are no longer applicable.

The reality is that some individuals establish companies that are the equivalent of capital magnets. They attract funds and investment from around the world. One of these individuals is Michael Dell. But the investment flows would have been impossible without the deregulation of the financial industries in Europe and North America.

The global economy must be treated as a totality. It is not the sum total of all the 189 national economies put together. It is an entity on its own right, *sui generis*. We have no model to describe it. We have just begun to observe its emergence, like from sort of primeval soup.

The global economy has yet to produce its theorist, its answer to a Keynes. There has been no development of a quantum economics. Yet, too, clinical of a diagnosis will prove elusive, and the moment it has been dissected, it will change into something else. Maybe it is permanently changing and in a state of flux, with perpetual metamorphosis as a defining characteristic. But we are able to discern the internal circulation of the global economy. We know how the money that is its lifeblood flows: We know how it travels and where it goes. What we need now is a means of understanding, a theory to make sense of the global economy, stage directions for the global stage.

Notes

[1] David Ricardo, *Principles of Political Economy and Taxation* (Amherst, NY: Promethus Books, 1996), p. 183.

[2] "Dollar-Wary," *Far Eastern Economic Review*, 15 July 2004, www.feer.com.

PART II: STAGE DIRECTIONS

4

PLAYMAKERS

Finding Your Bearings on the Global Stage

Our landscape has changed radically. The world is beset by a world war between the shibboleths of the old economic thinking, with its allied baggage, and the global economy. We have already examined some of these obsolete notions and fading nebulae of the old economic order. Now we will examine the way in which we look at the world and how we divide it into discrete geographical and political entities is being undermined by the global economy. Although our thinking is dominated by the atlases of the past, with their maps of continents containing a collection of different-colored political units, the global economy is strange and alien. When we start to jettison the straightjackets of this old thinking, the global economy not only makes greater sense, but it is seen as one grand continent of opportunity whose exact contours still remain vague in places but that will amply reward brave exploration.

For me, the geographical and economic unit of the global economy is the region. Let us imagine a region as a theater. It may be a slightly smaller, more intimate theater than the Bol'shoy in Moscow or La Scala in Milan. The stages of these theaters are designed for big spectacles, whose value is often caught up in shortsighted impressions. The productions are, to paraphrase Shakespeare's *Macbeth*, full of strength and fury but signify nothing. A smaller stage can be far more useful. A good producer knows that the actors won't get lost on it; there will be a more direct and intimate contact between performer and spectator. With a smaller production, a producer can make changes from performance to performance when and if something goes wrong or doesn't go according to plan. There are more opportunities for concentrating on the science of acting rather than on choreography.

Putting regions at center stage demands some radical rethinking of the way we view the world. The global stage is borderless. This means that a lot of our nice cozy concepts about geography are going to have to be discarded. The most obsolete of these notions is the nation-state.

We have seen that the study of economics has been bound up with the nation-state. Economics and the idea of the nation-state grew up together. The nation-state was the arena for political and economic activity, and for over a century after its birth, the discipline of economics was labeled *political economy*. The nation-state and economics have seemed inseparable, but they are not related biologically or scientifically. Indeed, one has had a very bad influence on the other.

The nation-state has become firmly embedded in the intellectual, cultural, and political landscape. But it is a smooth-talking squatter rather than a rightful resident. This has been due to a process of ingratiation. The nation-state concept presented itself as an organic development, a natural development of human organization. The nation-state protects, it provides, it is the source of solutions to its own problems. How can we live without it?

Because it seems so immutable, many people think that it is very old. This is a mistake. In the parade of human history, the nation-state is a recently arrived interloper.

It was first defined by Jean Bodin, a French lawyer in the middle of the sixteenth century. Bodin looked at the myriad of small political entities that were often at loggerheads with each other. The reasons for disputes were many and varied, and often very trivial. In Bodin's time, differences over religious worship injected real bitterness into these contests.

Some of the political entities of Bodin's time were little more than city-states with some attached countryside—places such as Genova in Italy. Similarly, Venice had originally been a region-state, very badly endowed by nature. By the end of the medieval epoch, it had established its own empire, though by Bodin's day this was starting to fall to pieces. Bodin knew there was a political institution that was broad in its geographical scope: the Holy Roman Empire. Even at the time, this inspired the joke that it was neither holy, nor Roman, nor an Empire. Whatever strength it had came from its mass, the unity of its parts. This was combined with an ideology, something capable of attracting and keeping loyalty, not dissimilar to a contemporary brand. The concept of a universal emperor was something that commanded both recognition and respect. If a lesser ruler could find some type of unifying ideology, his own distinct political brand, based on common origins or language or tradition, maybe he could have the same type of recognition, respect, and power as the emperor. This was attractive to some rulers, who thought it would bring not only loads of prestige, but also greater wealth.

There were a number of technical problems with Bodin's idea. Most of them have been solved over time. The first was the lack of a big bureaucracy. Without this, a nation-state was a paper tiger, a cozy concept—no more. A real nation-state had to be staffed, policed, and defended, but courts and armies had to be paid for. The most effective means of getting money was taxation. This, in turn, needed tax officials, as well as custom and excise personnel. There was a need for policemen to assert the state's uniqueness, as well as soldiers to guard its borders. So, early on, it was apparent that the nation-state was an expensive ideal. As devotees of big government have discovered to their cost since then, the bigger the government, the more expensive. No matter how much they are paid, some of the money that should be going to the center is rerouted into collectors' pockets.

European exploration and colonization grew after the sixteenth century. So if nation-states were successful, they could become very wealthy. There was still a need to assert their power economically. This was done by the mercantilist system. People went from the mother country to exploit the treasure chest of the New World. They then sent these riches back home for processing and resale. But those settling down in the far-off territories were never permitted to produce anything tradable themselves or to trade with any other country or colony. They were entirely dependent on the mother country for all their finished goods and equipment. The development of indigenous industry and trade was prohibited. This signaled the arrival of one of the nation-state's most long-lasting and pernicious economic "assistants": protectionism. If you rule a nation-state, you must protect its interests, including the nation's economy; it was mistakenly believed that the best way to this was to establish a system of regulations and tariffs limiting or excluding the products and services of other nation-states from those of the mother country. This doctrine may not be as popular as it once was, but it is certainly far from redundant in today's world. Calls for protection also inspired the notion common in the writings of some early economists that the state was the ultimate arbiter of its own problems. The state had to solve these as best it could. There was an external world beyond its borders, but its role in the solution of economic problems was, at best, secondary and indirect. The rest of the world was quite literally foreign. The concept of the closed economy was born long before John Maynard Keynes.

Mercantilism in practice was a big blunder. It led to the American Revolution in 1776. Mercantilism sought to protect the economies of the mother countries. Instead, as with any prolonged form of protection, it led to inefficiency, high taxation, and ultimately the bankruptcy of the nation state.

In the nineteenth century, the concept of the nation-state discovered a new lease on life by attracting greater ornamentation and symbols. This form still haunts our world today. Each state had its own flag, its symbols—such as the American eagle and the Russian bear—and its national anthem. These were meant to inspire loyalty and near religious devotion, a sense of oneness. They can be viewed as a further part of the nation state's brand creation. But the parallel with modern branding breaks down with the fact that those involved sought to lock people into loyalty. There was no room for choice or "shopping around."

Another vitally important part of the nation-state brand was "national territory." Particularism and regionalism were seen as bad, pernicious, and invidious to the state ideal. Shadows of these thoughts are still with us.

In the economic sphere, the nation-state had its own unique currency and, to protect it, a national central bank. The German economist Friedrich List wrote a blueprint for the nation-state's economic activities. National economies were to deliberately look inward; they were to be shielded from the shrill winds of competition by high tariffs. One of the countries where List's theories were received and applied was the United States. They were also applied throughout Latin America well into the twentieth century, with ultimately fateful results. In the twentieth century, each nation-state had to have its own "national" airline, its "flag carrier." Most of these could not make money because their markets were too small. It is hardly surprising that many of these flag carriers have now gone bankrupt or have merged with other carriers.

Another "must-have" for the nation state was an army—the bigger and better equipped, the better. At this time, the nation-state attracted a very dangerous element to its entourage: nationalism. The two got on very well. The state was an embodiment of a "national spirit" that was found (and only to be found) in people of a particular ethnic group and speakers of the national language.

From the late nineteenth century, the idea of a nation-state was exported from its European homeland. It became prominent in Latin America, where a number of small, sometimes miniscule political entities had grown up. All claimed to be distinct. But their ruling castes all spoke Spanish (Portuguese in Brazil). That did not stop them from drawing maps to emphasize *their* territory, and fighting costly and disastrous wars when these were breached. Their economies were dominated by exports of a limited number of primary goods. In the twentieth century, each one tried to strengthen its economy by building up uneconomic and uncompetitive domestic industries to supply substitutes for imports. Exporting was discouraged as the state unrealistically turned its back on the outside world. But the more they industrialized, the more dependent they became on outside capital. They discovered the importance of the rest of the world through a very bumpy, costly, and, in some cases, bloodstained journey.

In Asia, the nation-state brand was viewed as the height of political sophistication. Rulers saw it as a way of consolidating their power. It smelled of modernity and progress. Only by conforming to the nation-state concept could rulers be viewed seriously by Europeans and Americans. When Japan opened up to the West in the late nineteenth century, the country's rulers borrowed the centralized form of government used then in France and Germany. It has never been seriously changed.

Consider Korea, where the nation-state ideal remains very influential. Many people in South Korea dream of the emergence of a Great Korea, stretching from Cheju Island in the south to the Yalu River in the north. This will come about when North Korea opens up (or falls) to the South. This will happen when its economy responds to its internal contradictions and collapses, with either a bang or a whimper. The Koreans believe that the rising of the curtain on the Korean peninsular will usher in great business and commercial opportunities from which Korea will emerge as a true rival to both China and Japan. It will have a combined population of nearly 70 million people and might also have nuclear weapons at its disposal. But while Korean nationalists may look forward to "reunification," what they really hope is that the communist North will become an economic colony ready for a process of modernization to be carried out, naturally enough, by South Korean companies such as Samsung and Hyundai. Appetites are already being whetted by talk of undertaking joint ventures and establishing facilities in new industrial parks. It is as if there is an undiscovered pot of gold, whose discovery is simply a matter of time. By looking north, South Koreans are able to avoid competing with countries to the west and east. South Korea can opt out of the future because it believes it has its own rosy destiny.

This sentimental vision blinds many in Korea. While they look only to their north, Korea's real strengths lie in its position in the Yellow Sea region, facing the markets of China, Japan, and the United States across the Pacific Ocean. These are the zones that should attract more Korean attention (see Exhibit 4.1). The Yellow Sea may be vibrant, but it is not a nation-state. It cannot stimulate the same irrational emotions, no matter how powerful the economic forces at work are.

At the moment, trade between China and Korea is growing steadily. But because of their myopic insistence on looking north all the time, Koreans do not realize that a "hollowing out" is occurring, in which Korean businesses are increasingly relocating outward from Korea toward China. Products exported from China by Korean companies are all reassembled in the port of Pusan and then are exported officially out of "Korea."

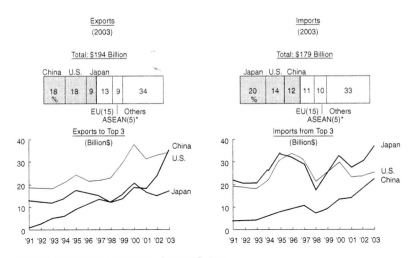

*ASEAN5=Indonesia, Malaysia, Philippines, Singapore, Thailand.

Source: KITA.org.

Exhibit 4.1   Korea's trading partners.

How Nation-States Retard Economic Development

Modern abuse of the nation-state concept can be seen in the Soviet Union, which inherited the Czarist conquests of Central Asia. Stalin paid lip service to the notion of national self-determination, and ethnically based socialist republics were carved out. These seldom bore much relation to the nationalities they were supposed to represent.

When the Soviet Union collapsed in 1991, these republics had independence and sovereignty foisted upon them. They were completely unprepared for it. Having formerly been intimate members of the highly entwined Soviet economy, they were cast adrift in a completely foreign ocean. Their new rulers (usually the former communist bosses) acquired all the previously mentioned trappings of the nation-state: flags, symbols, national anthems, and currencies (often worthless) and national banks. Integration of their respective markets has been delayed by personality differences among the rulers, as well as by border disputes. Ethnic differences are magnified to absurd proportions. Vast natural resources are left untapped or are inefficiently exploited by one nation-state acting independently. In fact, nobody knows how many nation-states have been born out of the former

USSR. The same is true of the former Yugoslavia. If an overarching dictator emerges in the future, these "regions" could once again be united as "one nation."

But it is in Africa that the nation-state concept has had the most disastrous consequences for people and economies. In 1885, the European powers met in Berlin to carve up the continent among them. The entities they created are still with us. They were not making states at all in Berlin; they were establishing colonies or protectorates. When a growing tide of African resentment forced the rulers of Western Europe to concede independence and political self-government to their African holdings, it was agreed that the border demarcations drawn up in Berlin should serve as the borders of the new crop of nation-states. This was to avoid border conflicts and the incipient risk of conflicts. Nation-states were born that made no sense. They had territories comprising few natural resources, a food production sector dominated by subsistence cultivation and chronically vulnerable to natural calamities. Not surprisingly, many of these states have remained at the bottom of the world's GDP league.

Apart from the economic myopia of these policies, ethnic and religious borders were ignored. Many of the new states contained festering internal conflicts. In the case of Nigeria and the Congo, these have spilled over into bloody civil wars with predictable impacts on resources. Other areas that had the potential for growth, such as the Niger Delta region, were divided between two separate nation-states (Nigeria and Cameroon), neither of which was interested in cooperation—both wanted only total control.

The Nation-State Fetish

All of this matters because nation-states continue to hold sway over our thinking. Look again at economics. The nation-state produces statistics known as national accounting aggregates. These include tables of the gross domestic product or aggregate demand, and are supposed to show the economic health of a particular nation. When the GDP is divided by the state's population, another magic number is found: GDP per capita. This figure can act like a combination to a safe. When it is above a figure of U.S.$10,000, the country's rulers believe that they have arrived as a state, that they are no longer dirt poor, and that they are important players in the world's economic game. This allows them to become members of the Organization for Economic Cooperation and Development (OECD).

Gross domestic product, a nation's total value added per year, is a very bold measurement. It relies on information supplied by a population, mainly as a result of tax receipts or shipment records. Of course, few people like paying tax. For some, it becomes a matter of duty and honor to pay as little as possible. A separate arena of economic activity emerges—a "black economy" that may be as big or bigger than the legitimate one.

As its name implies, a GDP is domestic, looking at activities that take place within a state's borders. The figure of gross national product (GNP) is more relevant because it includes economic activities by the state's citizenry beyond its borders. As we have seen, the global economy does not respect national borders. Both the GDP and the GNP include only finished products and services. Many goods and services can be initiated in one country, but they are completed in another. If we look at cross-border business process outsourcing, we see that much of the back-office work involved in the provision of a service is carried out in a low-cost environment. Only the finished service is consumed in the "host" country, yet the contribution made by people in another country is not properly registered.

GDP and GNP figures offer only averages for a whole nation-state. The major engines of economic activity in the global economy are not nations, but regions. The contribution and vitality of a particular region will not be discernible in a nation's accounting aggregate figures. The growth level of China averages around 9 percent per annum. But this is a figure for the whole country. It embraces vibrant region-states such as Dalian and Guangzhou, whose growth rates were between 13 and 15 percent per annum for 2003, and regions farther west such as Ningxia and Gansu, which are still enmeshed in poverty. There are China watchers who like to pour cold water on China's continued economic growth trends, stating that it is impossible for the country as a whole to maintain growth rates of 9 or even 7 percent. But such responses fail to take account the reality that it is not China as a whole that is growing, but certain regions within it. The concept of the totality of the Chinese People's Republic exists at the political level only.

So, whether China continues to grow at a high pace depends on whether it can grow the number of megalopolises or region-states, along with the growth rate of such regions. China produced 146 new cities with more than one million people in the 10 years between 1990 and 2000 (see Exhibit 4.2). There is no reason to believe that it cannot repeat this. There are, after all, still 800 million people living in the Chinese countryside as farmers.

Sadly, these inadequate numbers are used in assessing a state's economic health. If they show growth compared to the previous year's figure, this is evidence of a strong and healthy economy.

As another example of using outdated theorems to explain the global stage, consider the conventional supply/pricing curve. If you plot the capacity of suppliers on the X-axis, in the order of lowest to highest producers, and the cost of production on the Y-axis, you can explain the pricing curve and how it is going to drive out the weakest suppliers as price competition becomes tougher when demand shrinks. Usually, this supply curve is constructed only using domestic suppliers. Increasingly, you now have to construct the curve for the entirety of the EU or North America. The curve is increasingly meaningless if it is construed simply in insular terms. For example, we are now witnessing China's demand pulling Japan's marginal producers' supply and getting mordant plants to wake up. So, here again, the national model needs to be modified to reflect the semipermeability of borders.

Chinese Cities over a Million People

Population in Millions	Number of Cities	
	1990	2000
1-3	17	156
3-5	3	4
>5	0	6
Total	20	166

Source: Chinese Statistics on Population, 2001.

Exhibit 4.2   Chinese cities with more than one million people.

Strong States

Similarly, a strong currency is given more importance than it now deserves. The logic is that a strong currency suggests a stable economic base. Such a nation would find it relatively easy to borrow. Funds might be accessed from international financial institutions, or government securities and bonds would find ready buyers. It might even have a good credit rating. Its currency would be desirable.

But a nation with such a "strong" currency soon finds that its currency is overvalued. If its economy relies heavily on the export of commodities, its exports are too expensive. At times, the Japanese yen is strong against the dollar, but although the Japanese economy is not in the best of shape, its exports are still very tradable. The reason is that these exports are largely branded, manufactured goods, not commodities. A strong yen, though the bane of the Japanese *Keidanren*, means that import of materials and components is cheaper.

In the world of near instant communications, the nation-state is irrelevant. One of the outward symbols of its existence is the national border, staffed by uniformed officials checking papers and manning barricades. But what use are such border controls in the world of the Internet, for example? Does a stream of data passing along a fiber-optic cable stop at each national border it crosses so that it can be inspected for contraband?

The nation-state promised much but delivered little. In today's world, far from making things better, it threatens to make them worse. It has the potential to hold back human development through artificial compartmentalization of skills and markets. Quite simply, the world has moved on.

Our world is now interdependent to a greater degree than ever before. But global interdependence is *nothing* new. The idea of a hermetically sealed nation-state fully self-sufficient in all its needs is absurd. There has always been trade. Throughout human history, technology has made trade possible over greater distances. Now technology and improved logistics allow trade to occur at greater speed.

By breaking up the world's population into supposedly self-sufficient entities, nation-states have stymied the realization of interdependence. Political entities, whether large or small, still believe that, at the end of the day, they can survive on their own, though things might be a little tough. Confrontation rather than cooperation has followed in its wake. It sets a high price on a specious and nonexistent uniformity. This can be achieved only at the cost of great human suffering. Economies and societies thrive on diversity. If we look at a city such as Dubai in the United Arab Emirates, we see a prosperous metropolis. It is situated in a part of Arabia on the shores of the Persian Gulf, but many of those who work there and contribute to its prosperity are not Arabs. They may be managers from Western Europe or taxi drivers from India or Pakistan. Its nightclubs are adorned by beautiful Eastern European girls. In fact, it is so dependent on managers and workers from India that its airport offers direct flights to 15 Indian cities. The same diversity is at the heart of Singapore's continued success.

In Asia and Africa, the benefit of new European technology has
sometimes been resented. In some countries in Africa, it became government policy to reject all aspects of Western "civilization" while
holding on to the trappings of power, which were largely inherited
from the West. This was sometimes done on the grounds of self-
styled nationalism or Africanism (it has had many titles). It was often
accompanied by government takeovers of the factors of the economy—once more, in the name of the nation-state. Development and
poverty alleviation have often been set back decades.

The Rise of the Region

We must look for the new centers of growth in our world, and we
can find them easily enough in the regions. Some of these regions
are component parts of old nation-states; others spill over existing
borders.

In the opening chapter, I mentioned how the global economy has
infused new life into regions around the world, whether it is the
Shandong peninsular or Finland. Some old-style nation-states are
lucky and are small enough to act like region-states. These include
Ireland, Finland, Denmark, Sweden, Norway, and Singapore, though
they have more going for them than size alone.

The ongoing development of the global economy will lead to an
inevitable undermining of the nation-state in favor of the region. This
is anathema to those who believe in a big, centralized state as *the only
way* to run politics, society, the economy, and culture. For many such
"statists," the concept of the national centralized government was, in
its day, progressive and forward looking. The regional could too easily be the seat of the local, the parochial, and the inward looking.
Limited areas bred limited horizons. Those who thought in terms of
small units could never think big. But this has changed, thanks largely but not solely to technological breakthroughs. In the twenty-first
century, the opposite is true. It is the nation-state itself that is anti-
progressive and introspective, and it is often the regions of the state
(though, admittedly, not every region) that are outwardly mobile and
that work and think within a truly global and borderless perspective.
They no longer think in terms of states as political monoliths, but of
states that are amalgams of regions. They also look to the rest of the
world for capital, technology, and markets. They do not need to possess all the elements of economic prosperity, as long as the world
works for them and with them. For this reason, the global economy

acts to discipline governments and to streamline regions. Borders are nothing but a burden for old nation-states. In this context, it is amazing to see how many border disputes continue to rumble on.

What is happening is that economics and technology are enforcing a new scale on geopolitical organization. There will remain boundaries, but these will be transparent and will represent opportunities and supporting diversity. The demise of the nation state will not usher in a bland, one-dimensional, monocultural world.

A region-state is not a political, but an economic unit. Some region-states are equal to political units. Singapore, for example, is more like a city-state than a sovereign state, with its minuscule area. The Republic of Ireland is also fortunate to be open to the global economy and, at the same time, retain the traditional trappings of statehood. But these are accidents of recent economic history and geography.

The notion that region-states can act as foci of prosperity is not a novelty. I mentioned Venice; this great city was originally a region-state that grew in the later medieval period into an empire. Italy was studded with such centers: They were the cradles of the Renaissance and other contributions to our world, including double-entry bookkeeping. Farther north in Europe was the Hanseatic League, a collective of trading cities on the shores of the Baltic and the North Sea. These centers, such as Riga, Tallin, and Danzig, were the region-states of their day. They looked outward for their prosperity rather than looking to central government with their hands outstretched.

Regions are already sizable economic players in the world. If we look at Japan, we see that the Shutoken metropolitan area (the Tokyo, Kanagawa, Chiba, and Saitama prefectures) has a gross national product of $1.5 trillion and that is in the top three in the world. The Kansai area centered on Osaka has a GNP of $770 billion, which occupies seventh place in the world, after China. Both these areas are entitled, by numbers at least, to qualify for membership of the G7. Of course, in reality, the level of local decision-making allowed to them by the centralized Japanese political system is miniscule.

Defining the Region-State

We must be careful not to define region-states too tightly, especially in terms of population. True, many region-states share characteristics, but these should be seen as points of reference rather than hard and

fast definitions. No aspiring region-state can attain success by merely
marshalling a set of ingredients, as in a recipe for a cake or a specification for a piece of equipment.

Population size is important but not crucial. This is an elastic
variable.

In many ways, size is a state of mind. A region must have a sizable
domestic market to attract internal investment, so a lower floor of half
a million or, better still, a million is desirable. If there are too many
inhabitants, it may be impossible for investors to maintain a clear
marketing focus. The often-intangible sense of solidarity, a fabric
holding and motivating its population, may also be absent. The ceil-
ing, on the other hand, seems to be around 10 million people,
although Shutoken around Tokyo has 30 million inhabitants but is still
a natural community, thanks to its excellent commuter networks.

There are no magic numbers. An area might have the "right" population level—the same as other successful region-states—but still be
mired in poverty. Similarly, an area that seems a gargantuan parody of
intimacy might be a successful region-state.

An international airport and at least one large and efficiently
functioning harbor capable of handling international freight, as well
as a good transport infrastructure, are necessary, too. A sprinkling of
forward-looking universities and research facilities capable of attracting good students and turning out highly trained workers and graduates is very important.

But the most essential element of any successful region must be
openness to the outside world. The rest of the world must be viewed
positively, as the source of prosperity. Xenophobic notions must be
expunged. The concept of native versus foreigner must be erased, so
rules limiting foreign investment or foreign ownership of land or capital must be abolished.

Pernicious antiforeign measures have to go, too. These include
laws prohibiting cabotage (such as tariffs) in the carriage of goods,
either by land or by sea. There must be no barriers to companies from
outside the region coming in and either taking over local enterprises
or setting up joint ventures. In today's business world, mergers and
acquisitions are a very cost-effective means of entering a market or
augmenting market share.

When I discuss company structures, one of the points I will make
is that it no longer matters where a company is based or "headquartered," so this reality must play a role in attitudes toward outside

investment. It may well be that more "big players" start to relocate their headquarters to region-states. This might be aided by laws allowing easy company registration. This already exists in the United States. If we see its 50 states as constituent region-states, then Delaware already enjoys preeminence for company registration. Its separate business courts system is also attractive to those wanting to do business there.

Not only must a region-state be a good place to do business, but it also must be an attractive place to work and to raise kids. This is important, as can be seen by the constant attempts in areas such as Singapore and Dalian to enhance the physical environment through the maintenance of beaches and parks. Although "eye candy" is important, it is meaningless on its own. Much of the promotion of regions carried on in the past has focused on such issues. Glossy brochures attempting to attract inward investment were produced singing the praises of an area and displaying its natural beauty and landscapes, so much so that all the separate images of pretty flowerbeds, marinas, and manicured golf courses became an undefined blur.

A powerful definition of a region-state is that it is a unit for creating a positive virtual cycle. The more people who come in, and the more varied their backgrounds and skills are, the more varied the region becomes over time. If it starts out in manufacturing, other services associated with the manufacturing sector enter the region, too. In time, financial institutions arrive, along with those offering domestic and retail financial services. A positive cycle thus occurs, and the region becomes a totality with a deeper, wider economic and business base. It is amazing how quickly industries and service providers are attracted to prosperous regions and assemble there to support some of the industries that are already spearheading industrial acceleration.

When new industries of a varied background are attracted to a positive area, a whole plethora of affiliated nonbusiness services mushrooms. Schools will inevitably come in to meet the need for education and an educated workforce. Hospitals and clinics will be built to meet the medical and healthcare needs of the region's inhabitants. There are also automobile dealers, not to mention restaurants and supermarkets. In short, once there are people on the ground, they have needs that must be serviced.

This model is repeated in many places. In China, many regions are literally unrecognizable from what they were like 5 or 10 years ago. In 5 or 10 years' time, who can say what the situation will be?

If we look at Dalian, we see a bustling metropolis. Just about everything that is to be found in any city anywhere in the world is to be found there. The different services are available neatly in a geographically sectored environment. People doing business in Dalian don't have to invite civil engineers to perform environmental assessment surveys and the like. They are there already: mechanical engineers, computer scientists, cartoonists—anyone offering a service. It is as complete a city as Paris, London, or Tokyo.

We may ask, "Has Dalian always been a big city?" No. But remember that it is a central plank of the paradigm of the global economy that an area does not have to be prosperous before it can become rich.

Indian Summers

Rapid transformations of this sort have not been confined to China. India is also a land of great contrasts. At nearly every level apart from the geographical and the political, the very notion of unity among such diversity seems artificial. India's many princely states were united under in the British Empire. When the British left in 1947, a federal constitution based on a collection of states was initiated. Most power still remained at the center, though, a phenomenon that was seen as vital for long-term political stability and the continuation of the politicians' control. India's leaders dedicated themselves to alleviating poverty, but they never gave any thought to creating wealth, so the economic models constructed by Ghandi, Nehru, and their successors had the effect of redistributing poverty. In the 1990s, thanks to far-seeing and determined leaders in a handful of states such as Andhra Pradesh and Maharashtra, new areas of prosperity developed, utilizing India's huge and literate population, as well as the reservoir of technical talent that existed in cities such as Bangalore, Hyderabad, and Pune. Once the foundations of prosperity had been laid in these centers, they attracted the usual range of service industries—usual in a Western country, but novel in India. Government regulations were relaxed to allow consumers access to products and services from throughout the world. Much prosperity was known to be available through telecommunications, but the telecom network in India was a long-standing disaster, the source of numerous horror stories. Rather than waiting for an acceptable India-wide fixed-line telecommunications system to be rolled out, satellite connections were established in southern India to bypass the national telecoms service altogether.

The transformation in cities in India such as Hyderabad has been near miraculous. There are now malls lined with shops selling everything from consumer electronics to Western clothing. It is not uncommon to see people walking along the streets speaking into mobile phones, (that is, if they can hear over the cacophonous traffic). Traffic congestion is still endemic in Indian cities, but whereas up to a few years ago the traffic streams were made up of battered, standard-make cars that were fashionable in the 1950s and early 1960s (along with the odd cart pulled by a bullock), India's streets are clogged with a far more up-to-date sample of automobiles (and still a good many cattle).

These region-states in India are now more closely integrated into global business because they are not only developing software and systems, but they also are conducting fixed-line, outsourced business functions on behalf of American and European companies. They have become part of an integrated whole of global corporations.

The experience of places such as Hyderabad is seen as a phenomenon to be emulated by other Indian regions. The most startling of these is West Bengal and Kolkata, for so long the cockpit of militant trade unionism. It is even more surprising that these moves are being spearheaded by a state government dominated by one of India's communist parties.

The same phenomenon of self-sufficiency can be observed on the other side of the Pacific, in California. San Jose today is almost as autonomous and self-supporting as San Francisco. It is not necessary to go to San Francisco to get every service. In the mid-1960s, San Jose was a veritable no man's land, a wilderness. The title of the Dion Warwick song said it all: *Do You Know the Way to San Jose?* Most people did not. Now there is a direct Tokyo–San Jose flight every day, and you may have to ask, "Do you know the way to San Francisco?"

Does Dalian or San Jose worry about intangibles such as "identity"? Does the average resident care where his or her food comes from? Consider Singapore. Notions of nationhood do not perturb it greatly. True, it has all the usual trappings of a nation: a currency, a flag, a national anthem, and so on. It does not worry that no domestic farmers produce its food. It is not troubled by "nightmares" about food security. What is important is that the food Singaporeans consume is inexpensive and also nutritious. It can get this from other food producers in the region. Singapore enjoys the luxury of being both a region-state and a nation-state. It has always been able to set its own agenda.

A typical region may defy existing political borders. In the 1990s, Catalonia in northeastern Spain became a successful economic region. A zone of success tends to spread, so neighboring areas in southwest France, such as Languedoc-Roussillon, have also benefited.

We should not think only in terms of geopolitics. Just as a very talented actor can bring crowds to his performances far more readily than any theater, no matter how prestigious, a particularly gifted individual can establish not only his own identity in both a location and a business sector, but this person also can help draw businesses from other unrelated sectors, as if by a power of magnetism. Such a human magnet is Michael Dell. Since its foundation in 1984, Dell Computers has rewritten many of the rulebooks, especially those dealing with logistics. But its impact on its original location, Austin, Texas, has been no less monumental. Not only have a number of software and IT engineering facilities grown up there, but there has been a huge surge in biotechnology startups, to mention just one sector. It is as if Austin has grown from being an IT cluster to its own region-state.

Carried Away in China

The country where the phenomenon of the region-state has taken off most successfully is China (see Exhibit 4.3). In the 1980s, the Chinese government opened up a number of special economic zones aimed at attracting foreign direct investment. One of the most successful was in the Shenzhen area facing Hong Kong. It attracted investment not just from Hong Kong, but from throughout the world. Many local leaders chafed at the amount of central interference from Beijing-based bureaucrats in day-to-day decision making. They sensed that the prosperity they were experiencing was but a taste of what could be achieved by a more active involvement with the world economy and its major actors.

The response of Beijing was predictably cautious: Let's not get carried away, they said. After all, if they allowed greater economic freedom to Guangdong province, might this not turn into calls for greater freedom overall? Might not Shenzhen's calls be echoed by

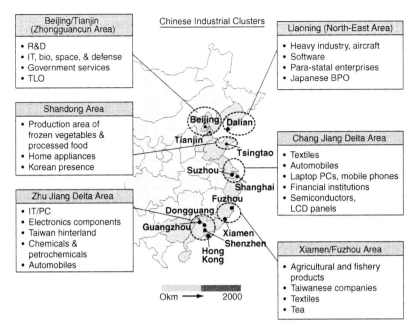

Source: BBT Research Institute.

Exhibit 4.3   United States of Chunghwa.

other cities, especially those that had been granted special economic zone status? How could the central government, which had a duty to care for all regions of the country equally, allow only a few regions to prosper, while allowing unashamed poverty in areas not too far away such as the Guizhou province?

The People's Republic of China is still a communist state (if only rhetorically), and one of its tenets of government is the euphemistic Democratic Centralism. Bitter debates raged within the secretive ranks of the Communist Party in the 1990s between reformers and conservatives, federalists and centralists.

In the late 1990s, a new vision took shape. At the theoretical level, China remains a communist, centralized state. In practice, provincial leaders are allowed to do pretty much as they like, as long as this is not accompanied by egregious displays of self-enrichment.

The per-capita income of residents in areas such as Dalian, Zhejiang, Beijing, and Shanghai is approaching $5,000 per year. It may have already surpassed this level in Guangzhou. This has been a massive jump in less than a decade. It is also huge compared to the figures hovering between $2,000 and $1,000 (and lower) elsewhere in the country. Many residents of these poorer regions are flocking eastward to share in the prosperity of China's region-states. The Chinese government has recently announced initiatives to reduce income disparities between rural and urban areas.

There are estimated to be more than 100 million migrant workers in China today. Many have not permanently settled down in the regions of prosperity. Instead, they send part of their paychecks back to their poor home areas when they get paid. This allows for a circulation of wealth between rich and poor areas. The latter can, therefore, participate vicariously in the success of the former. The money transferred may be used by those in the home region for an investment in machinery, which, in itself, can improve rural productivity and efficiency. It may also go toward education for younger members of the extended family. The migrant workers who ultimately decide to return can bring with them new and valuable skills, especially those who have worked in the service or construction sectors.

There is a worrying downside to the attraction of large population groups in search of wealth. In the Shandong peninsula, one of the prosperous regions of China, there have been clashes between natives and newcomers, especially between ethnic Han Chinese and immigrants from the far west such as the Hui, a Turkic people. Such tensions are an age-old part of any area's rise from poverty to prosperity. We need only note how an influx of Irish migrants into industrialized areas of the north of England led to anti-Irish protests.

Rapid helter-skelter economic growth is also accompanied by negative phenomena such as homelessness and pollution.

The current boom in demand by the Chinese economy is mostly based around businesses in these successful regions (see Exhibit 4.4). They are not powerhouses of the Chinese economy alone, but of the world economy, and we can see the magnitude of trade with China for each of the key regions of the world (see Exhibit 4.5). The writing is on the wall for nation-states. Just because it is in Chinese characters does not mean that it should be indecipherable to the rest of the world.

If one looks at the Chinese megaregions as region-states, then 9 of the top 15 Asian "countries" are Chinese, or Chunghwa (see Exhibits 4.3 and 4.4). However, if we literally interpret the meaning of "chunghwa," or prosperous centers of the universe, then we have to include Taiwan, Hong Kong, and perhaps Singapore because 70 percent of its population is of Chinese origin. This means that 12 of the top 15 Asian countries, excluding Japan, are Chinese. China was always a political power, but now its economic size is a power felt throughout Asia.

Nine *Chunghwa Region-States* Are Among Top 15 Countries in Asia

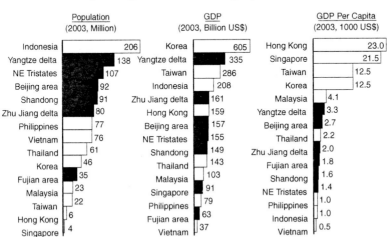

Source: China Statistical Abstract, UN.

Exhibit 4.4   Nine Chunghwa region-states compared with other Asian nations.

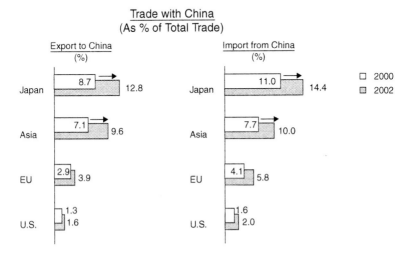

Source: International Trade Statistics 2003 (WTO).

Exhibit 4.5   Trade with China.

Not All Regions Are Created Equal

The region state (wherever it is located) is the engine of the global economy. But even though the success of greater economic decentralization is on display for all the world to see along China's eastern coast, there are still entrenched obstacles to other nation-states joining in the prosperity that can come from letting regions do more for themselves.

The constituents of a federal state, even one that is federal in name only, are better placed to become region states. They have a slight infrastructural advantage. One of the powers that is often divested or devolved to a state in a truly federal constitution is that of finance and taxation.

There is also a reservoir of politicians, administrators, and decision makers whose mindset is shaped by the regional rather than the national. In the United States, there is the state government, whose chief executive is an elected governor. The state governor can be a very effective agent in the promotion of his or her state as a place of investment. This can be done directly, ignoring the center at Washington. Ironically, but sensibly, governors frequently become presidents—think of Jimmy Carter in Georgia, Bill Clinton in Arkansas, Ronald Reagan in California, or George Bush in Texas.

The United States has been a truly federal nation for more than two centuries. Although there are continuing tensions between state and federal government, the two spheres of government are acknowledged as being complimentary and central to political culture. The United States emerged onto the historical stage as a federal state—it didn't become one over time. People talk of the American Revolution of 1776, and although this was motivated by the collective desire of the Americans for freedom, it was enacted at many levels by the unique states. Once they had gained freedom, they decided to come together. They were anxious to ensure that they had not swapped one tyranny for another nearer home.

Surprising China

It is all the more surprising (though also welcome) that the People's Republic of China should become such a trailblazer in this regard. Although the People's Republic granted a measure of freedom to certain areas under the title of "autonomous regions," residents of these areas knew that their autonomy did not surpass the semantic. The concept of the whole of the country being held together by a strong hand was one that they inherited from ancient Chinese rulers. It was updated through reading the works of Lenin and Mao.

The surge of the Chinese economy can clearly be traced back to the reforms of 1998, when Zhu Rongji became premier. Troubled by the inefficient parastatal corporations, Zhu declared that they would be left to sink or swim without help or hindrance from Beijing. This effectively transferred responsibility for these enterprises to the regions because failure would cost them dearly. So, without a declaration, Zhu effectively brought central control to an end and decentralized. The cities and provinces then set out to get help from the rest of the world. FDI surged in.

More recently, day-to-day management has been devolved to certain potentially prosperous regions. Most have, at their heart, an urban core of cities, maybe embracing five million inhabitants (often many more).

What has happened in recent years in Guangzhou or Dalian is a novel experiment. The center pays lip service to unity but allows economic autonomy. However, were this economic autonomy to be accompanied by demands for political autonomy, it is doubtful that the center in Beijing would allow this.

Microregions

Are region-states the last word in geographical terms of the global economy? Or is it possible to see, like Bohr and Heisenberg, useful activity at an economic subatomic level?

Clusters of industry have been around for a long time. They are very different to a region-state and take a number of forms, but one of the most long lasting on the human psyche is that of a forest of tall chimneystacks belching black and, no doubt, toxic fumes into the air. In Shenyang and throughout China's Liaoning province, there are lots of "smokestack" industries, operated by old, inefficient, and unprofitable state-owned enterprises, usually in heavy industries such as iron mills, steel works, and precision-machine tooling. In the heyday of Maoism, industrial icons were prominent in the aesthetics of socialist realism. Now they are fast becoming the rust belt of China. These are old-style clusters.

In other regions of China, such as Chungshan in the Guangdong province, approximately 3,000 companies are making lighting fixtures, lamps, and related items. This, too, is a cluster. They breed exclusiveness because companies from other sectors are highly unlikely to try and set up shop there. Traditional clusters are one-dimensional phenomena.

But clusters are not always a negative phenomenon in the global economy. A lot depends on the nature of the business behind the cluster. In the Pearl River Delta area of China, there are 50,000 electronic component suppliers. This cluster is a good industrial hinterland for manufacturers of goods such as plain-paper copiers, tape and disk recorders, desktop computers, televisions, and printers. This cluster is a fertile industrial hinterland that is *not* exclusive or one-dimensional. If anything, it is magnetic, attracting dissimilar industries that need the components in production there. Today, the entire Pearl River Delta is an ideal location, comparable to the Greater Shanghai area, in which all the benefits of Just-in-Time supply chain management can be contracted within a day's drive.

I mentioned earlier that one of the defining elements of a region state is the variety that is created through a positive business cycle. The economy becomes multidimensional. It is not like a region that attracts only textile industries; in turn, other textile industries pile into the region, attracted to it as if to a lodestone. This creates a monodimensional economy.

Europe has seen its industrial clusters. They still exist, but on a much smaller and more specialized scale. They are also much more sophisticated.

There are clusters of clusters in northern Italy, especially in the province of Emilia-Romagna just south of the river Po. The town of Modena has a cluster of producers of fast sports cars. It has the production headquarters of Lamborghini and Maserati, and neighboring Maranello is home to the Ferrari automobile assembly works. Parma has a cluster of famous cheese producers. Nearby Carpi similarly contains a cluster of knitwear manufacturers. Carpi has a high ratio of local enterprises: 1 business for every 12 inhabitants. Every business in Carpi, a town less than 60,000 inhabitants, is related in some way to knitwear. Each has less than 15 employees, but, collectively, it is the Mecca of knitted fabrics, where buyers and designers flock from all over the world to get the newest fashion. Bologna, the provincial capital, has a cluster of packaging industries.

Italy has maybe 1,500 towns specializing in one sector, maybe even the manufacture of one unique product. Each represents a specific cluster, which has probably become the world's foremost production center for that item in terms of innovation. What is true of Carpi for high-quality fashion is also true of Sassuolo in the manufacture of tiles. Italy as a nation economy may be going through a hard time, but these urban regions or townships, with their associated clusters, provide a dynamic element within the region state. Italy may be floundering at the national level, but the province of Emilia-Romagna is not. Places such as Carpi and Modena are microregions because they work with the rest of the world other than with Rome.

These microregions are very competitive, although once again this stands in stark contrast to Italy's noncompetitiveness. Italy's taxation system encourages small companies. It is particularly benevolent to small, almost "mom and pop"–size businesses, with fewer than 15 employees. Everyone wants to stay at this level of fewer than 15 employees. Highly specialized clusters develop, sometimes concentrating on manufacturing or processing a segment of one product, such as metal clasps for belts or bags; luxury shoes; or silk products. This is niche production, and Italian producers achieve global dominance in the supply of these high-end, price-inelastic products.

An amazing aspect of this Italian cluster-centered, microregional niche production is its ability to thrive in the global economy. For one thing, it can survive the challenge from China of low production cost. In cost terms, Italy just does not bother competing with China. The result would be a foregone conclusion. But in the world, there is enough appetite for these deluxe products, where high standards of manufacture and craftsmanship are combined with high prices, to make a desirable product. A Gucci, Versace, or Prada handbag does not sell because of its price or because it is cheaper than any other. It sells because it is a brand with high recognition and brand loyalty. To succeed in a niche market demands the development of a brand. The Italian niche producers serve a market of conspicuous consumers— so much so that famous French brands also use Italian producers for the production of apparel, bags, and shoes.

A brand on its own does not guarantee success. Some brand managers of the past, such as Pierre Cardin, made the mistake of thinking that the whole value of a brand resided in its name. Once a company had that, it could be apathetic and lazy and could afford to take loyalty for granted. There was no need to nurture the brand with further activity and innovation. As a result, the brand was allowed to desiccate and become lifeless. There was also a tendency to "sell" the brand too often and without discrimination. This allowed others to manufacture products using the brand name—a sure way to hasten a brand's death or, worse, its slow yet inexorable decline. There are Pierre Cardin undershirts, handkerchiefs, and trousers all over China. And at that level, a brand is nothing more than a label on a commodity.

Flexibility

One of the successful traits for any prospective region or microregion must be flexibility. This may demand a willingness not to be imprisoned by the paradigms of the past and, if necessary, a reinvention of itself to meet the changing global economy.

Some Italian townships and microregions are armed with an innate survival instinct. They put their success down to specializing in one aspect of manufacture. People in Carpi say that this was necessitated by the annihilation of much of the traditional European textile industry by the Japanese in the 1960s and 1970s. This did not directly affect small manufacturers, such as those in Italy. The mom and pop shops could not move out of their own hometown, let alone Italy, in search of a lower-cost production environment. Some larger French apparel companies, such as Pierre Cardin, switched manufacturing to Japan, Taiwan, and, eventually, China. These firms began a long and rather pathetic trek, migrating from country to country in search of a sustainable low-cost production base. Most perished along the way, usually somewhere in Indonesia or maybe in China. Others stayed in Europe but went to Spain or Portugal, only to meet local competition from the like of Zara (Inditex) and Mango. Most may maintain a presence in the apparel market through managing their brands and by designing. They have also invested heavily in retail operations throughout the world. Most manufacturing, however, has come back to Italy.

The Italians were too small to globalize, so they took the only alternative: specialization. In Carpi, they used to make a very broad spectrum of apparel, but they decided to concentrate instead on one area: knitwear. By specializing, they hoped to maintain a respectable price for their products. This was their wisdom for survival. The threat from Japan in textile manufacturing was a warning signal. Size and good sense allowed small Italian manufacturers to respond correctly. The townships and microregions defended and protected themselves as if they were Renaissance city-states. They have always been good at protecting themselves from external threats and marshalling native pride.

A Japanese city, Tsubame also survived as a high-tech metalwork specialist. It shifted to titanium production—for golf clubs, watches, spectacle frames, and the like—when cutlery production was challenged by lower-cost Asian producers.

The enemy against which the Italian townships have to defend themselves is no longer the forces of either the Pope or the Emperor, the Medicis, or whoever, but the forces of cheap production, such as China and Vietnam. Italy is therefore a tapestry of small townships, each one of which has been able to survive in the global economy by specializing and maintaining the ability to price high, producing items for which there is an inelastic demand. That is how they escape competing with the Chinas of this world.

But they do not seek refuge from harsh economic winds behind their city walls. They may be exclusive, but they are active participants in the global, borderless economy. As I mentioned earlier, many of the constituent parts of high-end French fashion goods are manufactured in Italy: knitwear in Carpi, silk in Como, and shoes in Bellagio, for example. More recently, they have been shifting eastwards to Turkey and Romania.

These niches may be highly specialized, but they do not exist in splendid isolation. In the case of the knitwear Mecca of Carpi, it has links with the broader fashion world in Milan, Paris, and New York, and, through them, with the wider world. By specializing, they have been able to experience globalization, but on their own terms. So, the manufacturer of fabrics in Italy is indirectly linked to the outside world. A fashion designer in New York or Tokyo is able to take advantage of the latest advances in manufacturing fine fabrics in Italy and incorporating them into his or her design portfolio. The fashion industry is but one sector that is built upon what are essentially individual capabilities that have become sanctified by time. They are narrow but deep.

Size and Scale Matter, But Not in a Traditional Way

This is an interesting antidote to the general theory that you have to be able to compete with the larger regions to survive in the global economy and, therefore, attract global capital and finance. The Italian townships seem to have done the exact opposite. They have survived and prospered on their own by using the rest of the world as their customer. They do not have to move because the rest of the world comes to them to buy their products.

This demonstrates another facet of the global economy that enterprises overlook or forget, at their peril. The products may be glamorously presented in cities such as Milan, Paris, London, New York, and Tokyo, but unless the designers and the managers of the global industry have a deep feeling and knowledge of their respective supply chains (in this case, originating in Italy), they cannot stay at the head of their business.

The townships of Emilia-Romagna also offer an alternative strategy. They do things better, through a deepening and narrowing of production and servicing. This may seem like a retreat from the battlefield of competition on a global scale, but it involves only a tactical withdrawal, in search of more favorable battle positions. The theater of competition remains the same.

This approach would not work for companies such as Ivrea for Olivetti, and Torino for Fiat, which are in megacompetition with global players. There is no haven in electronics and automobiles to escape to while still maintaining thousands of workers.

There are not many examples of such successful, Italian-style townships. Many are called, but few are chosen to the banquet of ultimate success. For some, specialization can be a very prudent strategy for some areas. There are other examples in Europe, such as Sheffield and Solingen, both of which specialize in silverware. We might also mention the glassware industry in the Czech Republic (known as Bohemian Glass), as well as Ireland's Waterford Glass, a company that owes much of its continuing success to its possession of an identifiable brand. In these cases, there was a strong historical precedent leading to the specialization. An expertise in metal and craft working had been built up over generations, maybe centuries. A microregion cannot simply wake up one day and decide that it is going to specialize in the production of high-end cufflinks (or anything else) if it has no tradition of involvement with it. The critical test is whether consumers around the world are willing to pay premium price for deluxe items. This, in return, requires that the producing regions need to be intimately linked to high-end customers.

There are other companies that, while starting small, have gained an international respect and following, far greater than the market available domestically. They include the Spanish company I just mentioned, Inditex, along with such brands as Zara, Massimo Dutti, Stradevarius, Pull and Bear, and Oysho. It has more than 3,000 shops around the world with which the company, based in La Coruña in northwest Spain, is linked logistically using Just-In-Time methods.

Regions Are Gaining Their Deserved Recognition

The advent and success of region-states is being recognized throughout the world. Sometimes, the response is rather negative, reflected in attempts by those at the political center to bolster their importance. But these gestures are bound to fail. They are like the medieval English king Canute commanding the sea's waves to flow back.

The importance of regions is increasingly noted by economic statisticians. For example, the Swiss-based Institute of Management Development has begun to include regions as well as nation-states in its lists ranking world competitiveness. The regional units tend to reflect existing regional and provincial boundaries. Among those in which competitiveness is recognized are the states of Maharashtra in India, Sao Paulo in Brazil, and the province of Zhejiang in China, and then Emilia-Romagna in Italy. In countries with huge populations, the centers of prosperity may be even smaller than a province, such as Dalian, which is merely a municipality, though an extensive one. But the inclusion of data according to regions rather than outmoded nation-states is very significant.

It can be problematic in the short term to enhance the power and influence of regions. There are a number of challenges: practical, political, and psychological. But none of these is insurmountable. On the political level, there may be an inertial resistance on the part of national or central government decision makers to devolve effective day-to-day decision-making power to the regions. Smaller countries with populations of 3 million to 10 million, such as Singapore, Denmark, Finland, and Sweden, are able to make organizational and system changes relatively quickly. They do not have the problems that larger countries face, with the center having to coordinate regions with conflicting interests. Nevertheless, friction between the center and the periphery has been evident in the recent past in nations such as Denmark and the Irish Republic.

Devolution of decision making, especially in the area of economic and trade policy, has to happen if regions are to attain their potential. Leaders at the national level are not motivated to or are incapable of taking effective measures to embrace and interface with the global economy. They carry too much excess baggage. They are also answerable to too many economic dinosaurs and shortsighted constituencies.

Once a region seems to be on the way to success, there may be envy at the center and in other less well-endowed or fortunately located areas. This envy may manifest itself in peevish attempts to sabotage a region's success, probably packaged in a benignly packaged policy of national equity or solidarity.

The center may also seek to press the brakes on local autonomy too often, as if reminding the region that it is still the boss and that there are limits within which it can play. Italian governments have tried everything over the last 40 years to fix its perceived problems to no avail. Ironically, micro-regions and high-end branding prosper without governmental intervention or subsidy. Italy is not the exception, but the rule—witness the efforts of the American, French, Japanese, and other governments to "save jobs and manufacturing industry."

If the political structures of the host are inflexible and the region-state as a separate economic entity shows signs of wanting a divorce instead of a separation (or simply more space), military force might be used to bring it back into line. (Witness Northern Ireland.) The detrimental consequences of this type of action on economic development need hardly be elaborated.

Practical Considerations

When an area becomes successful while still remaining part of a nation-state hanging on to nineteenth-century constitutional models, there is persistent tension. This centers on the question, what right has the region to hold on to the wealth it has generated, and how far must it share this with its "parent" state and its less prosperous siblings?

One of the charges that may be laid against region-states by centrists is that they are pursuing selfish, shortsighted, regionalist agendas. Centrists are, to a greater or lesser degree, nationalists. They believe in the righteousness of the nation-state model. This may be the limit of their nationalism. They see those in the regions pushing for greater freedom as mininationalists, competing for and diluting their power.

But the most intelligent leaders in a region know that a region cannot solve its problems by itself. It can do so only by working with the rest of the world. This does not mean that it turns its back on the parent state or the historical center. In some cases, these linkages add to a region's attractiveness in the eyes of outside investors. Some of the appeal of a region such as Hessen can be ascribed to it being a part of the Federal Republic of Germany. But it must be assertive. Its prosperity depends on either an explicit or an implicit renegotiation of its relationship with the center of power.

One of the central beliefs of centrists is that in a nation-state, all resources most flow outward, in a centripetal way, toward the regions from the center. We have seen how forward-looking U.S. governors have done their own successful marketing of their states, avoiding the center altogether. If a region is to prosper, it must be able to do this. It must also be able to attract investment from the rest of the world without going through a central middleman. The sophisticated center should also recognize that if a region draws in capital, corporations, and consumers from the rest of the world, its ability to tax will increase and its obligation to distribute decreases. This creates a win-win situation.

It may not seem a nostalgic idea to call for the re-establishment of regional stock exchanges and money markets. These were a feature of nineteenth-century Europe and America. They helped to finance much of the industrial development of areas such as Northern England and Pennsylvania. In the 1960s and 1970s, there was a move toward amalgamation. So the regional money markets disappeared, replaced by national bourses (with the occasional, often token satellite maintaining a fitful existence). In today's borderless world, finance does not respect borders. Arbitrage and leverage make sure that any residual national feeling in the money markets is dissolved. The national bourses are often meaningless. They may be under the ownership and management of non-nationals. (For example, the Danish and Finnish stock exchanges are owned and operated by the Swedish company, OM.) They can be as much a burden to economic growth as the other nation-state fetishes.

What a Successful Region Has to Do

There are many potentially successful region states in the world today. For many (probably most), that potentiality will remain unrealized. Some regions stubbornly refuse to wrench themselves out of their torpor, no matter how much money could be attracted or how much positive development could take place there.

Even better-placed regions cannot rest on the laurels of future success. In the global economy, there are few dead certainties. They may well enjoy all of the necessary factors for success, but a host of objective factors, from interference by the center to poor marketing strategies, will get in the way.

Choices have to be made. Not being distinctive can be the fastest route to commercial ruin. It is impossible to be a jack-of-all-trades, trying to do too many things and specializing in nothing. A region that seems to be offering all things to all potential investors will soon be exposed as a cheap, talentless auto salesman with nothing worthwhile to offer. A potential investor develops a long list of candidate locations for setting up operations elsewhere in the world. But the real decision makers look at only the short list, typically three to five names. Unless the region remains in the short list, it will not be considered at all. So the real name of the game is to get into the short list. This is the reason a spike of characteristics compared with other regions must be developed and presented. Both Ireland and Singapore have succeeded in labeling themselves as the e-hub of Europe and the de facto ASEAN capital, respectively. Such labels get a region on the short list. Then you have to deliver: Singapore declares that it can off-load a cargo container within 25 minutes of arrival 24x7.

Look at the Irish Republic. Its pursuit of the e-hub vision demonstrated a commitment to telecommunications, but with special emphasis on areas such as back-room services and customer response management. The country has been able to attract call center operations, either standalone facilities or affiliates of large organizations. In just over a decade, it has built up an unrivalled expertise: It has the physical, logistic, and legal infrastructure. It has achieved a very strong position. Those thinking of opening CRM facilities often ask themselves, when discussing location, "Why not Ireland?" rather than "Why Ireland?"

No position in the global economy is completely unassailable. Probably because of its long and bitter history of economic poverty, the Irish Republic does not take its position for granted. It knows that it still has to compete to win and that it must contend with other heirs apparent, such as Holland and, increasingly, Poland and the Czech Republic, for the European CRM crown.

Ireland is interesting because it shows the benefits of concentration on one area. It also shows that benefits from one sector do not preclude other actors. Ireland is in no danger of becoming a hybrid, old style/new style call center cluster. Other high-tech industries have been attracted, and these, in turn, have led to the formation of their own technology and R&D–based clusters. In the summer of 2004, Bell Laboratories announced plans to establish a specialized R&D center in Ireland.

Another vital ingredient for success is, as I've mentioned, flexibility. We have seen how the Italian townships survived by reinventing themselves. We can see that at a higher order in the case of Singapore. Essentially a trading and communications center until the 1950s, it then entered an era of industrialization. However, it had to fight off competition from other manufacturers, and in the 1980s, it switched from its emphasis on manufacturing to the service sector. There was no hope of winning in manufacturing against the much larger and cheaper labor pool of Indonesia, Vietnam, and Thailand within ASEAN countries. It simultaneously promoted itself as a strategic location for multinationals in Southeast Asia who were persuaded to establish regional headquarters there. It trumpeted its logistics and positioned itself as a professional and financial services provider to neighboring countries. In the late 1990s, in the face once again of competition, it has had to change its development goals in the area of biomedical technology and telecommunications technology.

Each change of direction has been difficult, but Singapore has constantly come up with new projects, achieved them, and then moved on to the next. The human costs have often been high. But Singapore has recognized that, without such flexibility, it would be dead in the waters of the South China Sea, both as a nation-state and as a region-state.

Branding Places

Beyond flexibility, regions need marketing. There is an old proverb about the uselessness of hiding a light under a bushel or hood. A successful region-state has to adopt an effective marketing strategy. This can take many forms, always informed by the realization that this is what everyone else is at, too. One of the most important assets in such a marketing campaign is an effective marketing manager. I return to this when we talk in greater detail about leadership. The job description of this marketing manager may have an existing title. In the United States, he or she might be a state governor; in Germany, the premier of a Land; or, in China, a city mayor. Whoever or whatever such leaders are, they must be untiring in their efforts to preach the distinctiveness and the investment friendliness of their region.

They must learn from other successful regions but never slavishly copy them (see Exhibit 4.6). They must be aware of local differences and what assets make their region unique and uniquely attractive. Some of these may hinder the search for inward investment. Others call. But whoever is in charge must not become indifferent to success. Even when hordes of companies set up plants and invest heavily, either directly or indirectly, regional leaders must remember that investment is like seawater: It can flow out as easily as it flows in.

Globally Active and Prosperous
Megaregions, Region-States, and Microregions

		Functional Specialist	Multiple but Sporadic	Full Range or Controlling
Breadth of Industrial Spectrum	Broad	Shandong	Pearl River Delta Greater Shanghai	Tokyo Metropolitan Area
	Sector Specific	Irish CRM Dutch BPO	Singapore Indian BPO (Bangalore/ Hyderabad)	Silicon Valley Greater Boston Medicon Valley
	Niche	Italian Towns	Chinese CRM (Dalian)	Austin

Business System Leading to End Users/Customers

Exhibit 4.6   Globally active and prosperous region-states.

The Will to Succeed

Most important, if not vital, is motivation—the will and hunger to succeed. For, unless this is taken collectively to heart and becomes part of the fabric of a region's identity, the desire to participate in the global economy will remain mere rhetoric.

Sometimes, the will to succeed stems from a deep aversion to failure and is the result of an unsettling period of dislocation. Finland is a good example, in which the society was shocked by the disaster of 1992 and 1993. The country was compelled to think about its future. With the collapse of the Soviet Union, they could no longer play the role of playing one power bloc off against another and then take advantage of both sides. There was the realization that their traditional industries based on forestry, timber products, and copper smelting could not afford them a high standard of living or, certainly, the standard of living to which they had become accustomed. They had to move into ICT- and IQ-based industries. The financial catastrophe made them think about how they could live in the future. There was only one conclusion: for the country's population to put their mind and strength and apply their sinews to moving into an ICT environment, not merely superficially, but intrinsically at all levels.

Organizing Regions

The world must start thinking in different scales. It should start to think smaller (in terms of regions), but it should simultaneously think bigger in terms of the global totality and amalgams of effective and progressive regions. Large economic groupings such as the European Union and the countries of ASEAN can play a vital role on the new global stage.

The most successful to date has been the European Union. It was founded as the European Economic Community in Rome in 1956. Its aim was to be, first of all, an economic union that would embrace a Customs union and free trade area.

Its founding document was the Treaty of Rome, amended at the Heads of Government conference at Amsterdam in 1992. There was a commitment from the start that this union would not be a mere talking shop of European politicians exchanging platitudes and indulging in a paper chase of worthless utterances. Free trade was defined as freedom in four vital "factors": freedom of movement of goods, of people, of capital, and of freedom of establishment, so that a citizen of any member state could set up a business in any other member state without discrimination.

These and other core principles were enshrined in the founding treaty. They have been refined and augmented by regulations and directives issued by the Council of Ministers. These form a body of positive law or European Community Law, separate from the laws of the member countries. Most important, a European Court of Justice was established in Luxemburg to adjudicate on European Community Law.

In 1962, this court flexed its muscles for the first time. A Dutch retailer, Van Gend en Loos, was in dispute with the Dutch Customs Administration, and the case was referred to the European Court of Justice. The retail company argued that the actions of the Dutch authorities had violated the Treaty of Rome, and the court found in its favor. In its judgment, the court stated that where there was a conflict between national or municipal law (the laws and regulations of the community's constituent nation-states) and European Community Law, the latter always took precedence. So, Community Law existed not alongside national law, but effectively above it.

The court explained its stance by pointing to the EEC (as it then was) as a unique and unprecedented organization. When its members established it, they consciously ceded a section of their national sovereignty to this new structure, in the interests of the common good of their citizens.

The Dutch (and every other) government could have ignored this judgment, but they didn't. Such judgments are not binding on the parties. Indeed, the judgments are always described as clarifications of European Community Law. After the court pronounces its findings, the case goes back to the national courts for conclusion, with the clarification and judgment made by the European Court. Early on, the European Community demonstrated that it wasn't a paper tiger.

The original Rome Treaty had a very open-ended attitude toward trade restrictions. Apart from fairly visible tariffs, it sought to eradicate less manifest means of distorting the market. These were lumped under the heading of Measures Equivalent to Quantitative Restrictions (MEQRs). In the 1970s, the European Court of Justice identified quite a number of measures by national governments that seemed innocuous on the surface but that it identified as having a deleterious impact on trade. These might include measures designed ostensibly to protect health and welfare. But any measure that made a product or service from another member state less attractive was viewed as a restriction and distortion of trade.

Traditional nation-statists were outraged by much of this. It was a full-frontal attack on national sovereignty and integrity. Worse still, many argued (disingenuously) that it was dictatorial and antidemocratic. The stereotype emerged of a bureaucratic European Commission staffed by jackbooted officials who were intent on homogenizing Europe into a bland and borderless Euroland. These were garnished by absurd "urban myths" about how the EU was planning to ban coasters in bars and enforce standardization of sausages.

But all EU legislation is made by the Council of Ministers (which includes representatives from the national governments). Directives, an important part of the EU legal armory, have to be made into national laws first by national parliaments before they can have any clout. The simple truth is that EU Community Law touches only a portion of the activities of EU citizens, although it is a very important portion.

There are still tensions between those who have a vision of a far more borderless Europe and those who are wary of integration. The nation-state still has its dedicated partisans, as witnessed by the row over voting weights and vetoes in the Council of Ministers at the end of 2003. It may be significant that one of the nation states most adamant in this dispute was Poland. For over four decades, its sense of national identity had been subsumed and effectively browbeaten into acquiescence in such organizations as the Council for Mutual Economic Assistance or COMECON.

The European Community must resist the temptation to transform itself into a new mega state. Its strength must be its looseness, but as it grows in size, it inevitably becomes less coherent and manageable.

One of its continued weaknesses is that its most important constituent part is still the nation-state. It is upon this foundation that voting rights are based and funds are allocated. Although certain principles such as subsidiarity have been developed in an attempt to empower outlying areas, it must remember the vitality of its constituent regions, which are not always the same as the interests of its constituent member states. It would be unfortunate if nation-states such as Ireland, Denmark, Finland, or areas such as Catalonia or Baden Wurtemburg found themselves stifled by external interference and over-rigorous regulation. The EU proclaims its desire to pursue competitiveness. If it is really serious about making Europe more competitive, it should look to those areas within its borders that have achieved and maintained competitiveness. The Irish government, in particular, has opposed any attempt at tax harmonization. Italian townships have also risen above Brussels' bureaucracy—let alone Rome's.

The achievement of a single market in Europe among the Union's members has had significant advantages. It is now much more cost-effective for a company to invest in distribution within Europe. To do this, it needs to set up only one center of distribution or logistics for the entire European Market area. It also needs to set up a single multilingual CRM or call center for the entire EU operational on a 24-hour basis every day of the year. These are a remarkable improvement on the national CRM/SCM models, which had been one of the handicaps of Europe compared with countries such as the United States or Japan.

Perhaps the most important element that has been developed in the EU has been the euro, the common currency central to the community's Economic and Monetary Union. This was first spelled out in 1992 and finally became a reality in January 1999. Two years later, it replaced the national currencies of 12 of the EU's members. This was a further weakening of the dead hand of the nation state.

Remember that four of the external symbols of sovereignty were a distinct national currency, a separate central bank, a distinct defense capability, and an effective constitution and legal system. Now, the first two have been absorbed by the European Central Bank (ECB) and Euro respectively, while the third operates under the umbrella of NATO or the Partnership for Peace (PFP) program.

The writing had long been on the wall for European currencies, even those with some international leverage like the French franc and the German mark. How could they effectively compete in a world dominated by the dollar?

But sitting around a table and deciding "a common currency is a good idea" was never enough. There had to be rules and criteria for which currencies could join. The various central banks had to be absorbed into a single European Central Bank with the power to set interest rates.

Unfortunately, it would not have the luxury of dealing yet with one big economy, but with a host of different ones, of different sizes and shapes. This will hopefully change in time. As the various economies are so dependent on each other, there has to be some effective "bad-boy" deterrents to prevent unruly and irresponsible economic behavior by an individual member state. Members are prevented from running budget deficits bigger than 3 percent of GDP. It is regrettable that two of the biggest members of the Eurozone successfully defied this during 2003. Ultimately, the credibility not only of European Monetary Union but also of the wider European Union will depend on how far the Union's economic "Big Boys" are prevented from rewriting the rulebook as they play the game.

The euro has had a bumpy start, but it has now settled down. Some of this was due to sluggish economic performance in the Eurozone area. It may very well come to rival the U.S. dollar as an international reserve and settlement currency. Providers of goods and services to U.S. customers, whether based in Europe or elsewhere, might start to demand settlement of debts not in good old greenbacks, but in euros. This is unlikely in the short term, but it could happen: As Exhibit 4.7 shows, there has been a shift away from European currencies over the last decade for fear of their instability. This is now changing, and many central banks and financial institutions will shift to more balanced portfolios. This represents a major shift from the dollar toward the euro and, possibly, the yen.

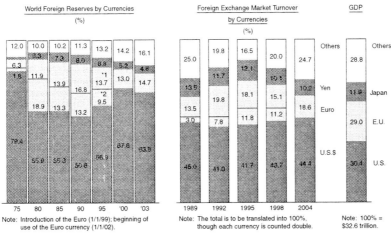

World Foreign Reserves by Currencies (%)

Foreign Exchange Market Turnover by Currencies (%)

GDP

Note: Introduction of the Euro (1/1/99); beginning of use of the Euro currency (1/1/02).
*1: Deutsche mark.
*2: Sum of French franc, Dutch guilder, and ECU (European Currency Unit).

Note: The total is to be translated into 100%, though each currency is counted double.

Note: 100% = $32.6 trillion.

Source: World Economic Outlook, September 2004, IMF; Annual Report 2004, IMF; Triennial Central Bank Survey of Foreign Exchange and Derivatives Market Activity in April 2004; International Banking Statistics and Securities Statistics (BIS), JETRO.

Exhibit 4.7 Foreign exchange reserves and turnover by currencies compared with GDP share.

This might lead to a period of furtive feuding, perhaps an economic cold war, with victory for any side uncertain. Sensing the elusiveness of final victory, both sides might decide to come together in a transatlantic currency, the Doro.

Other Unions

So far, the EU is the only group to have gone so far along the road of currency union. But in a world where it often does not pay to be small, other countries are moving in the same direction. The APEC countries have instituted greater trade freedom, particularly bilateral free trade agreements, among members.

Small but important steps are already being taken to achieve this goal. The finance ministers of the ASEAN + three (China, Korea, and Japan) have discussed plans to establish a central agency for monitoring foreign exchange holdings of other member countries' central banks. This not only would lead to greater currency stability, but it also would allow outsiders some important inputs into domestic economic policies. This step, though apparently insignificant, is tremendously important. The notion of watertight sovereignty is one of the great redundant obstacles in the world blocking effective economic growth. We have seen how important the decision of the European Court of Justice in 1962 was: It explained that when the member countries came together, they gave up a part of their sovereignty for the greater good of the whole. A further move toward a common Asian currency is mooted in the form of a common unit for denominating bonds. This unit would be based on a basket of member countries' currencies. These are early steps. As one ASEAN official has noted, "You've got to have countries secure enough in their sovereignty to give up some of it. It took Europe two world wars and centuries of religious conflict to get to that point."[1] But then, as Chairman Mao once said: "A journey of 10,000km starts with a single step."

The APEC nations have recognized the need to adopt a two-speed approach to trade liberalization. The economies of countries such as Laos, Myammar, and Cambodia are still fairly primitive, at less than $1,000 per capita, compared with countries such as Japan, at $35,000. In reality, ASEAN or ASEAN + three is still in the pre–Treaty of Rome phase, trying to line up at the starting line to discuss an Asian Common Market. This built-in fault line might make the ideal of the common market, let alone a common currency, less realizable in the short term.

The African Union, established to replace the Organization of African Unity, is pledged to the creation of a common African currency. The continent of Africa has already had some experience here, as a number of former French colonies were joined in the early 1960s in the African Financial Community (CFA) and still use a common currency, the CFA franc, pegged initially to the French franc. The decision to use a common currency was a response to the lack of financial and technical resources available to the former French colonies that were granted independence in the early 1960s. A combination of natural and man-made calamities have not improved the situation of these countries, most of whose economies are still primitive and based on the production of primary, mainly agricultural, commodities.

The nations of the Caribbean, mainly former British colonies, were too minute to develop independent central banks or currencies, so from the 1960s on, they opted for a currency union based on the use of the Eastern Caribbean Dollar pegged to the U.S. currency.

The possibilities offered by greater freedom of trade at regional level have been realized in theory by many countries. The World Trade Organization has reported no fewer than 150 free trade agreements that are in operation today. But the vast majority of these are bilateral agreements, binding only two nations to differing commitments and levels of trade freedom. Some political leaders favor bilateral agreements over more general multilateral agreements, believing that these give more scope to protect sensitive "national" interests. Apart from the time and energy that must be spent in establishing individual agreements between the 189 nation states in today's world and each other's, broader free trade, especially at regional level, makes sense. In Latin America alone, there are three large trade areas: the Central American Common market, the Andean Pact, and Mercosur. The potential of the latter was severely dented by the financial and economic difficulties that Argentina experienced in the late 1990s. The United States will have to play a key role in supporting the stability of Latin American currencies if the Americas are to move toward a common market and eventually a common currency. Unlike the European Union, the United States will have to offer the dollar as a de facto common currency. This requires a greater fiscal discipline not only on the part of member countries, but also on the United States itself.

Free Trade Area or Fortress?

The challenge is to keep established unions from becoming economic fortresses, offering freedom to member states but also a wall of tariffs and restrictions to those from outside. The EU maintains some very high barriers on imports from beyond its borders. For decades, it pursued the Common Agricultural Policy, a scheme that rewarded waste and inefficiency in the production of agricultural goods in a misguided defense of the member states' rural sector. Not only was this policy based on the costly purchase of food that nobody in the EU wanted, but it also kept prices artificially high. It excluded producers from less developed parts of the world from selling their products and thereby stepping away from perpetual poverty.

The Common Agricultural Policy has been drastically reformed, though not dismantled totally, in the teeth of bitter hostility from Europe's well organized but declining farm lobby. There have always been attempts by the EU or its predecessors to appear less unfriendly to developing nations. There was the Lomé Convention, signed between the European Community (as it then was) and nearly 50

ACP (African, Caribbean, and Pacific) nations. Here the EC removed duties imposed on industrial products entering the community from ACP states. Because the industrial sector in most of these countries was either minimal or non-existent, it was not a move of great generosity.

The Lomé Convention was succeeded in 2000 by the Cotonou Agreement, whereby the EU (as it has become) made a commitment to removing trade barriers on all goods by 2008. This was only a commitment, and certain agricultural goods were to be excluded.

Like many a nation-state, the EU has sought to implement antidumping measures. Most people agree that dumping is an unfair practice. Many also agree that measures taken against it, while at first a virtue, may become a fault. They are, in fact, contingent protection. The devil is in the detail, and within this may lurk attempts to hinder legitimate trade. Certainly, the World Trade Organization has construed some EU antidumping measures as flowing from such an illegitimate desire. Alas, when the currency exchange rate fluctuates so widely, it is difficult to compare the price of the same good in two countries over time.

In a borderless world, where nation-states no longer hold sway, even the concept of dumping will have to be approached fresh. It occurs traditionally where a product or commodity is sold for less in an export market than its price in the domestic market. But it will become increasingly difficult to distinguish so cleanly between markets in the future. When currency exchange rates fluctuate so widely, it is also technically difficult to compare the price of the same good in two countries over time.

Some of the opponents of globalization decry it as an attempt to impose a particular form of commercial activity on the whole world, at the expense of the varied tapestry of cultural differences. Others argue that globalization is the same as Americanization. Globalization is nothing of the sort. It realizes and affirms our interdependence as human beings and societies. It exposes the fallacy of self-sufficiency, whether economic or cultural. It is a process of global optimization and the best mechanism to help less-developed nations to grow without artificial subsidies from the rich but with the legitimate filter of markers.

What I have observed is that globalization is nothing but liberalization of the individual, consumers, corporations, and regions from the legacy of the nation-state in which they belong. Eventually, the information available to each one of them will give them the wisdom of choice. Whether the consumers buy the best and cheapest from anywhere in the world is also their choice and is not the decision of the government. Likewise, corporate activities will eventually shift to the best host regions. Instead of begging from the center, the regions will polish themselves so that the rest of the world comes to help them prosper. Ultimately, it is a competitive world and one that will discipline all members of the global village because wealth will migrate across national borders. Diplomatic and military powers are now subjugated to the branding and marketing strategies of regions as a unit of operation in a borderless world.

Notes

[1] "Spotlight: ASEAN Insecurity," *Far Eastern Economic Review*, 15 July 2004, www.feer.com.

5

PLATFORMS FOR PROGRESS

Relentlessly Forward

Throughout human history, technological improvements have ushered in many developments that have truly shaped human progress. We may like to think of human development as something gradual, made up of small, comfortingly manageable incremental improvements. But the reality is that sudden bursts of energy, often unleashed by or in tandem with technological breakthroughs, have moved mankind forward. They are groundbreaking at the time of their inception, but then they are added to the aggregate of human progress that we call the everyday.

The wheel was once such a development. Much later, the Industrial Revolution enabled the concentration of industry and manufacture, and led, in turn, to gigantic improvements in production. This was made possible by a number of technical innovations, not least of which was the invention of the steam engine. A whole range of products—food, clothing, and shoes—was made available to many more people.

More recently, technological breakthroughs in data transfer, in the materials through which such data must pass, and in the format in which large amounts of data can be efficiently stored, have revolutionized our world. They have made many products cheaper. They have provided many millions of people with access to information that would previously have been beyond their reach. Greater amounts of information can be acquired, stored, manipulated, and retrieved than ever before, and data can be transferred more quickly and effectively.

The reach of technology has become global. No longer is it confined to specific and discrete locations in business and industry. The gap between technological crucibles and users has narrowed. The personal computer (PC) is really personal, though its use is constantly shared with friends, coworkers, and family members. Ordinary users have far more sophisticated and powerful hardware and software than ever before, and this contains the potential for yet further growth.

The growth of technology has laid the foundations for the global economy in two ways. The first is its impact on the world's money markets; the second is the extent to which, through the Internet, it redefines the very concept of the market and the types of relationships that businesses must be prepared to develop.

Technological advances have come at a price, as they almost always do. For example, as the spread and penetration of technology becomes greater, so does the danger of pirating and counterfeiting. Visit Microsoft HQ, and you will frequently see posters that display where software piracy is the highest on a map of the world. The provision and possession of robust intellectual property laws are a must-have for any region that wants to participate in the global economy. Businesses will steer clear of areas where they run a danger of being cheated, in the same way that a member of the public will take a long detour to avoid a neighborhood that is the haunt of muggers or pickpockets.

Malaysia is one country that has not only included tough intellectual property laws in its law book (notably, the Communications and Multimedia Act of 1998), but it has followed this up with a well-resourced detection apparatus. Its neighbor to the south, Indonesia, has a doleful reputation as far as intellectual property is concerned. Proudhon might well write of modern Indonesia that intellectual property theft is the rule rather than the exception. No sooner is a piece of software produced and marketed, than it is pirated and its benefits reaped by the pirates; the software developers see none of the benefit and earn no rewards. Although some intellectual property laws exist, they are vague and seldom implemented. Naturally, this has a negative impact on native Indonesian software developers. Few people, unless possessed of a naïve sense of generosity, will make a product or provide a service from which someone else derives all or most of the profits.

Lax intellectual property infrastructure also frightens off potential investors, not only from the field of IT, but from industry in general. There have been attempts lately in Indonesia to persuade software pirates to become legitimate traders. In return for the government's promise to turn its back on software piracy, some of the former pirates are being appointed commission agents for legitimate software producers. The effort has not been entirely successful because some criminals just like the buzz and excitement of working outside legal frameworks. Legitimate toil, no matter how high the payback, never has the same rewards.

Developing Technology Platforms

The rise of technology has demonstrated the importance and power of platforms. Platforms are a means of allowing companies or individuals to communicate with each other to get things done more quickly or more efficiently. They aid communication; they also enhance delivery. They do so by establishing the common standards that come to be the accepted norm.

Although communications platforms are as old as human speech, it is in the contemporary world, with its potential to use technology to enhance the whole spectrum of human activity, that they come into their own. Platforms can be seen as applied technology.

At the heart of a platform are two characteristics: They are open and communal—anyone with the appropriate license (such as the cardholder on the MS operating system installer) can participate; and they are two-way and interactive. Openness here does not mean that they are freely available without payment. It means that the technology that powers them is accessible to a wide range of users. The communality of platforms means that they can then be used by others who have the same needs. They can be adapted, but, their importance relies on their continuous applicability to solve real-life, real-time problems. As we will see, platforms build upon one another, drawing upon the skills and breakthroughs of previous platforms.

To understand the structure and logic of technological platforms at work on the global stage, let us rewind to the development of today's technology.

Large, menacing computers with dials and valves existed from the middle of the twentieth century. In the final quarter of the century, a new creature appeared: the personal computer. This was a nice name and an even nicer idea, but not everyone believed that it could be translated into reality. At first, personal computers were clumsy and slow. Their memory capabilities were, in retrospect, no larger than a postage stamp. A good one could play a very ordinary game of chess. But these were a start. Some of these vintage computers could also use ordinary television sets as visual display units. In this way, the computer was domesticated. PCs may not have been beautiful, but they were not frightening. Their very mundanity contrasted with the mental image many nontechnical people had of computers in the early 1980s. This consisted of huge arrays of humming valves and flashing lights, and was often inspired by spy thrillers and science fiction offerings on cinema or television. They were initially used by hobbyists and arcade-game *afficionados*, not frightening megalomaniacs intent on world domination.

In the mid-1980s, not only was the Microsoft Windows operating system born, but so too were a series of cheaper and faster microprocessors. Personal computers became faster and more were fitted with hard disks, allowing more effective data storage. They could also do more useful things than play chess (however useful that is). They could store and manipulate data in spreadsheets or databases; hooked up to a printer, they could replace typewriters and word processors. In time, computer printers became faster, while computer monitors not only dropped in price but were able to display a wider range of colors.

There was one large difference between personal and corporate uses of computers. The latter were integrated and capable of communicating with one another and with external computers. The personal computer tended to sit in isolation. An increasing number of computers were fitted with communications capabilities and software, but modems were slow and expensive. Anyway, many personal computer users did not see a great need to make expensive calls just to access a bulletin board or central government database of patents.

This all changed with the development of the Internet (see Exhibit 5.1) and the HTML programming platform for writing Web pages. These provided new communications platforms. The Internet protocol provided the means of communicating, while HTML and

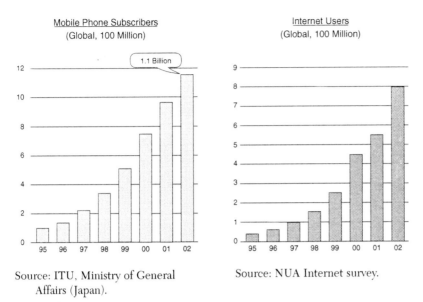

Source: ITU, Ministry of General
Affairs (Japan).

Source: NUA Internet survey.

Exhibit 5.1   Mobile phone and Internet users in the world.

Java ensured that there was something worthwhile for computer users to access. Modems became quicker and cheaper, and the Internet started to be a place where people wanted to go to spend time. It was a source of information, but also a location where products were sold, often at much cheaper tariffs than in traditional outlets.

Businesses also realized that the Internet could be an innovative means of selling products and services. In the late 1990s, the potential to turn the Internet from a plethora of standalone computers and terminals into a virtual market was realized. Among the first to try was Jeff Bezos. He drew up a list of products that could fit into an online selling environment and eventually opted for book retailing. By now, his creation, Amazon, sells many of the items on Bezos' original list. Along the way, a few—such as furniture and apparel—did not work out. These are not suitable for cybershopping because it is difficult to convey the exact information on the Internet. No one has yet found a way of simulating the act of trying on a shirt.

Shopping in cyberspace is like going on a blind date. As such, books and airline tickets were the first on board. There are no two seats with the same code for an airline, and there are no fears of getting the same title with less quality when you buy a particular book. Automobile components are also suitable for Internet retailing. There can be no mistake if you are buying the component of a specific car model of a specific year.

Books and travel tickets became popular online purchases because many users found the traditional means of buying these items cumbersome, tedious, and time consuming. A best-selling title might be prominently displayed in a bookstore, but even then there can be a delay as you stand in line at the cash desk. A more esoteric volume might involve a longer and less comfortable search, which might not even end in success. Compare this to buying online: no lines, no neck straining. In the same vein, purchasing airline tickets might very well involve a trip to the travel agent's, a visit for which the travel agent would happily apply a commission. Using the Internet platform made many activities not only quicker and cheaper, but also less tedious. Internet-compatible mobile phones mean that the screen ticket is now displacing the paper variety.

The rise of Internet usage was accompanied by internal and endogenous developments. One was the rise of the portal site, a three-dimensional signpost on the World Wide Web that could bring together those offering products and services. Platforms were then developed that would allow customers and vendors to trade efficiently and confidently.

At first, there was resistance on the part of some consumers, but they were won over by lower costs and proven safer ways to charge for goods. The Internet enables everyone to be an arbitrageur, taking advantage of the information gap. If you want to buy a product or service, it is possible (and sometimes very easy) to compare costs between online vendors. Some sites even provide calculators so that costs can be converted into different currencies. Savings can be made—some quite small, but they are cumulative.

The Internet is a platform. For most people, it is synonymous with the World Wide Web, but the Web is only a part of the Internet protocol. Most nontechnical users are unaware of this, but there is no reason for them to know about it. That is what a platform is all about.

Platforms work only when they are few in number. The best platform is often the one that has no competition. In the global economy, possession of a platform is essential. Without being able to use the platforms necessary in a business sector, participation is not even an option.

But we must remember what platforms are. Much of their strength lies in their flexibility. A particular platform has to be able, in the medium and long terms, to adapt to local and sector conditions. Maybe the particular platform has to be an asset or skill that, once possessed, gives its possessor the tools to refashion it to meet particular needs. In other words, a good platform gives simultaneously the common ground for two-way communication for the community of participants, and also the capability to develop a space tailor made for its members and users and that is inaccessible to the rest of the community (in other words, to nonusers).

The technical Tower of Babel in the IT world was that the code used on one machine or one type of equipment would not work on another. Many computer developers jealously promoted individuality and lack of adaptability, seeing these as strengths and one way to guarantee some hold on market share. But such an approach forgot, maybe only temporarily, that the customer is the final arbiter. The customer will always value simplicity of use over complexity. So the stage was set for the development of platform standards in all sectors of IT. This did not mean monopoly; often, it has led to oligopoly.

One of the most visible icons of oligopoly in today's world is the Microsoft Windows operating system. As its name suggests, platforms can be further built upon. Windows, for example, is the basis for such platforms as Outlook and Internet Explorer, the Internet browser and e-mail reader, respectively. There are also Microsoft platforms for videoconferencing and Voice over Internet Protocol (VoIP). In the not-so-distant future, there will be developments to incorporate the settlement of e-purchases, or "electronic wallet," transactions; music and video downloads; ubiquitous connectivity (including wi-fi); and search engines, all seamlessly operating on a Windows platform.

Technological platforms are a prerequisite of a wired world. If there were a myriad of software and hardware types, the customer, whether corporate or individual, would be confused to the point of distraction. Consumers have to believe there is a standard, a reference point. They also have to be able to place trust in this and to be able to build upon this trust. Buying a piece of software that promises greater productivity should not incur the cost of changing the whole computer system; it should plug into the system that is already in use.

Robotics is an area of technology that is growing in its applications. It naturally generates irrational fears of the machine replacing the human being. The prospect of humanity becoming a slave to machines is no more than a morbid sci-fi fantasy. Technology is worthless unless it can be implemented by people. When problems arise and are isolated, and when it is realized that certain technological improvements can help, these results can be realized only by employees who empathize with the need to solve them. The automobile industry, for instance, has embraced robotics as much as any other industry and employs as many people as it ever has. People must always be encouraged to work *with* the technology rather than against it or without it. The best technological platform is the one that solves the most problems, but it can do this only by being eminently adaptable to individual circumstances. Otherwise, a lot of time and money is wasted trying to fit square pegs into round holes. Platforms should solve problems, not create them.

Language as Platform

Platforms have been around for a long time; we just haven't recognized them. Any system of writing is a platform. It is a means of communicating and delivering ideas. It can be used effectively by many people. In the West, a system of communicating based on single characters developed, while in the East, a system based on pictograms was established. Both served the same purpose.

Most platforms can adapt themselves over time to particular needs without taking away from their usefulness as platforms for other people. Adaptability and general ease of use are prerequisites of a platform.

I am employing another platform here when I write this book. It is the same platform being used by those who read it: the English language. English has always been one of the world's major vernaculars; today, it is *the* language of the global economy. It is acquired by those who need to communicate with others beyond their borders and cultural niches. English is the most widely used language on the Internet. Let us not dwell upon how or why this has happened.

It is a misfortune of language to have become tied so intimately to the nation-state. A widely spoken vernacular or group of related dialects often has been taken over as a badge of identity, a further aspect of the nation state brand. As a result, any language is associated in some people's minds with those states that use it as a first language. Linguistic nationalists in other nation-states view its widespread use or influence with suspicion. Fluency might betray disloyalty to one's own nation-state. These are all old-fashioned ideas that belong in the garbage can of human development. The fact is, English is the *lingua franca* of the global economy and the *de facto* standard in cyberspace for the storage of information and two-way communication. It has acquired a place that the inventors of Esperanto and other artificial languages have dreamed of occupying.

The phenomenal growth of English as a linguistic platform has been met with skepticism by some commentators, many of who are fluent English speakers themselves. They see it as a further symptom of the dominance of America and American values in the world. If English is the language of globalization, this proves to them that globalization is a cover for Americanization. But such a response is misplaced and historical.

It is true that in certain epochs of history, the political dominance of one state was accompanied by attempts to enforce linguistic conformity. In Europe in the Middle Ages, the power of the church was unchallenged, and the language of its liturgy, Latin, was an international linguistic platform for scholars, diplomats, and statesmen. Perhaps the most recent example was in Eastern Europe during the period of its domination, politically, militarily, and economically, by the Soviet Union. Although the latter was, in theory, a union of dozens of different ethnic groups with their own culture and language, since the end of World War II, there was no attempt to downplay the role of the Russian cultural element within the Soviet Union. Russian was the USSR's language, officially, a means of communication among the various constituent ethnic groups; in practical terms, this was the measure of cultural control. This was extended to states such as Poland, Czechoslovakia, and the German Democratic Republic, which became Soviet satellites. The second language taught in the schools in all Warsaw Pact states was Russian. When the Soviet Union collapsed in 1991 and took with it its control of Eastern Europe, there was a high number of unemployed Russian teachers. Some of the luckier ones knew English. Millions began to learn English as quickly as they could.

The attempt to impose Russian was not generally welcomed in Eastern Europe. As part of the educational system, it was a necessary stepping-stone to academic success and progress to higher learning, so it was accepted with sullen resignation but never enthusiasm. For speakers of Slavic languages, which were closely related to Russian, (such as Polish, Czech, or Bulgarian), it was more of a chore than a challenge. Few students wanted to learn Russian. They realized that it was another form of external domination. Lack of fluency was a form of resistance that could only be indirectly penalized. This is in clear contrast with the role of English in the global economy. Nobody is being forced to learn it. Far from it—there are frequently not enough teachers and classes to fulfill demand.

In Vietnam, I visited a Korean-owned garment factory. The basic means of communication was English rather than Vietnamese or Korean. The management installed a $5 incentive for proficiency in English (on top of a basic monthly salary of $45). Almost all the young women in the factory commuted to after-hours English lessons, riding their bicycles wearing the traditional Vietnamese dress with a slit up the side.

English dovetails nicely with other platforms. Seventy percent of the data transferred on the Internet is in English, while English represents 80 percent of the information stored on servers.

The benefits to world communication are immense. Although French was the "traditional" language of diplomacy, most world leaders now speak English. Whether it is the president of a Latin American republic or a Russian provincial governor, to be heard in the world ,they must speak English.

English is also the first language of the Cable News Network (CNN), which has become a platform (though not the only one) for the dissemination of news throughout the world. It offers news "as it happens," 24 hours a day, seven days a week. It is required viewing for any world traveler, business traveler, or diplomat. Although CNN has subsidiaries that offer its products in a host of languages, such as Turkish, its English-language service was the first and is still the biggest sector. Anybody who seeks international recognition cannot hope to get it without appearing on CNN and being able to communicate with the largest *tranche* of its viewers, in the world's linguistic platform. Need for an interpreter implies, at best, provincialism and a certain lack of sophistication. It is no wonder that the Nordic countries have emerged as the most competitive nations in the world over the last decade. They possess a combination of language skills and Internet literacy that is well ahead of the competition.

English Inc.

Let's leave the world of politics and broadcasting for that of business. We have seen how the board of Finnish company Nokia holds its meetings in English. Look at the success enjoyed by the English-speaking Irish Republic as the e-hub of Europe. We will view India's strength in attracting call centers and cross-border business process outsourcing in the next chapter. This is partly due to the fluency their inhabitants have in English. Put at its simplest, no one can aspire to success (maybe not even to compete in the global economy), unless they do so through English. They should see this not in terms of old-style subjection to an element of the nation state, but as possession and utilization of the linguistic platform of the global economy.

The country that embodies so much about the global economy, China, has woken up to the benefit of the linguistic platform of English. It is by far the most sought-after second language, although in some regions, such as Dalian, it must compete with Japanese and Korean for this role.

This is nothing new. Language schools and teachers of English as a foreign language have been avidly sought ever since the beginnings of reform in China in 1978. But today, this desire has turned into a hunger. In Shanghai, English language teaching begins at primary grade 1, and the city authorities had to prevent some kindergartens from offering English-only environments. There are also estimated to be at least a thousand English-language schools, some charging huge fees. The competition among the schools is fierce and intense.[1] In July 2002, when Beijing's prestigious New Oriental Language School wanted to stage a lecture on spoken English, it had to hire a stadium that could accommodate more than 10,000 people. One of the most popular shows on Chinese television is a five-minute slot called *Go West*. It features Taiwanese American entertainer David Wu who teaches his viewers the latest American-English slang. Li Yang is an English teacher, but with a difference. His style, called "Crazy English," is based on shouting slogans and catchphrases against a background of pulsating rock music, and encouraging his students to emulate him. He visits around a dozen provincial cities every month but only a stadium will hold the 20,000 to 30,000 people who turn up for a lesson. His status is akin to a pop or movie star in the West.

Such scenes remind me of Adam Smith's description of the popularity and the high fees enjoyed by some teachers in Ancient Greece. Li Yang, who proudly describes himself as a loser, defends his mission, saying: "It's not because I love America. It's because English is the standard in the world, and Coca-Cola and Microsoft rule."[2]

China's people have always respected education and educators. It is central to Confucian teaching. We mentioned before the popularity of private education in China; state-provided education just cannot provide the levels and standards of instruction that are required. So education, and especially English-language teaching, is big business in China and elsewhere in the world. All the schools teach English at a very high standard; if they don't, they fail. Many don't just teach

English—they teach *through* English, as in Finland and elsewhere in Scandinavia.

After the economic crisis in 1997–1998 (labeled the IMF Occupation), Korean universities launched a major program to teach subjects in English (part of a program to help Korea become global in the twenty-first century labeled BK21). This does not mean teaching English using English, but teaching all subjects *in* English. Malaysia used a similar approach to avoid the backward-looking discussion about the position of Bahasa Malaysia or Chinese as the nation's "official language."

English seems to turn up everywhere that language is discussed. Many Chinese people, especially those belonging to the numerous expatriate Chinese communities of Southeast Asia, lay much store on an ability to read and speak Chinese in the Mandarin dialect. This is what attracts some to private schools in China. According to a report in the *Straits Times* of Singapore, parents there who seek fluency in Mandarin for their children have found that the best way to inculcate this is through English. Singapore is eager to attain the role of the educational hub of Southeast Asia in all levels of education provision, from primary to post-graduate education. It is hardly surprising that this education is provided in English.

Returning finally to those who worry at the spread of English, we must simply repeat what is perhaps a truism. Human beings are remarkably sophisticated, and the ability to be fluent speakers of two, three, or more languages is not particularly rare. Fluency in a language is a desired goal; once achieved, the speaker sees it rightly as a great asset. He or she never considers that their ability in their mother tongue has been lessened. There is anecdotal evidence that the greater a person's linguistic fluency is, the easier the acquisition of another language becomes. The linguistic ideal of the global economy is general and near-universal bilingualism, or maybe multilingualism. Fluency and ease in the use of English is already a prerequisite, but it need not be at the expense of any other vernacular.

What we need to accept is that a global citizen grows up speaking his or her mother tongue as a community member *and* English as a resident and beneficiary of the global economy. So, being bilingual is a norm, not a special talent, as it was previously. This is already normal for children whose parents speak two different mother tongues. Ironically, the key challenge faces native English speakers. Their opportunities to broaden their global view will be less than those for people who are bilingual. This might have an adverse effect on their long-term ability to compete in the global marketplace.

The Platform Profusion

In addition to technology and language, there is yet another platform that is crucial on the global stage: the U.S. dollar. This is naturally the medium of payment for the substantial part of world trade that centers on the United States. It is also the currency used by a considerable number of other trading partners. We have mentioned how dollars are consumed outside the U.S. In countries such as Australia and Canada, savings in U.S. dollars are important. We must not forget the shadow dollars, the trade paid for in currencies pegged to the dollar, such as the renminbi.

The reason for the pre-eminence of the dollar as a currency platform is both historical and practical. Throughout the second half of the twentieth century, the volume of world trade mushroomed. Mirroring this has been the concomitant increase in the volume of U.S. trade with the rest of the world. Along the way, the United States effectively knocked Great Britain off its perch as the economic head prefect of the world. The Gold Standard, which had originated in Great Britain in the early nineteenth century, was eventually replaced, albeit temporarily, by the Bretton Woods agreement. Instead of seeking value and exchangeability with reference to gold, the countries of the Western world were linked to the dollar. The Bretton Woods architecture eventually collapsed due to its own internal weaknesses, but the power of the U.S. as a world trade player not only remained, but increased.

Despite the pre-eminence of the dollar, the U.S. does not consider itself as the vanguard of the global monetary system. During the 2004 Presidential election debates, there was no mention by any candidate of the U.S. economy's role and responsibilities in the global economy. Uncle Sam tends to think only about its budget and domestic economy when deciding on money supply, interest rates, and how many U.S. government bonds to print. This is not a very sound practice because the rest of the world is totally dependant on the U.S. dollar for currency reserves, savings, and trade settlements, as we have seen in Exhibit 4.7.

It has been the habit of the rest of the world, albeit reluctantly, to adjust their economic and fiscal policies when the U.S. unilaterally changes its course. For example, the U.S. has a huge trade deficit with countries such as Japan, China, Canada, and Mexico. This is largely because of U.S. multinationals producing overseas. But instead of fixing this practice, the U.S. fiddles with the currency exchange rate (as in the Plaza Accord). This has tended to weaken the dollar against the yen and the euro. The Japanese Central Bank then buys the dollar to prevent it going into free fall. The result? Japan is left with a huge stock of dollars. This, in turn, is used to buy U.S. government securities, which allows the U.S. government to keep issuing what are, in fact, deficit bonds. There is no discipline in this process, yet it is largely the *modus operandi* of the global monetary and fiscal system. Since all are in this together, no major nations (or even minor ones—their wealthy people are storing dollars in their closets) are willing to discipline Uncle Sam.

The problem is that the dollar has become too much of a global common currency. This can be solved only gradually over the next decades, as the savings and reserves of the world's central banks shift in favor of the euro and a few other key currencies, such as the yen, the Swiss franc, the pound, and eventually, the Chinese renminbi. This will dictate that the U.S. must live within its means. American political and diplomatic popularity will then be even more crucial during this period because its currency is only as good as its CEO.

Other Platforms

Many other platforms have been developed whose implications are often only visible to the most eagle-eyed:

- **Brands as a platform**—The importance of branding in the global economy is a redefinition of a phenomenon that has been part of the commercial world for decades but that has gained amazing vigor with the greater lack of borders that we see in today's world. It has led to a greater commonality in the world. The same brands are available everywhere. An individual might have difficulty recognizing his location if he were basing it alone on advertising signs. The notion of a brand depends on the production and marketing of a product that is both better and different. It must be capable not only of acquiring market share, but also affecting market capture, giving it a pricing ability. It must be recognizable as a product offering certain features, some of which will not even be rational. But it must contain the promise of consistency. In that way, it will gain loyalty.

    Brands are dominated by American companies. Except for Japanese multinationals, most Asian businesses have not enjoyed anything like the same success in establishing brand recognition (see Exhibits 5.2 and 5.3).

Brand Values   Top 10
(2003)

Rank	Brand	Value ($Billion)	Country
1	COCA-COLA	70.5	U.S.
2	MICROSOFT	65.2	U.S.
3	IBM	51.8	U.S.
4	GE	42.3	U.S.
5	INTEL	31.1	U.S.
6	NOKIA	29.4	Finland
7	DISNEY	28.0	U.S.
8	MCDONALD'S	24.7	U.S.
9	MARLBORO	22.2	U.S.
10	MERCEDES	21.4	Germany

Source: *Business Week*, 8/4/2003 by Interbrand.

Exhibit 5.2   Brand values top 10.

Top 100 Brand Values by Country
(2003)

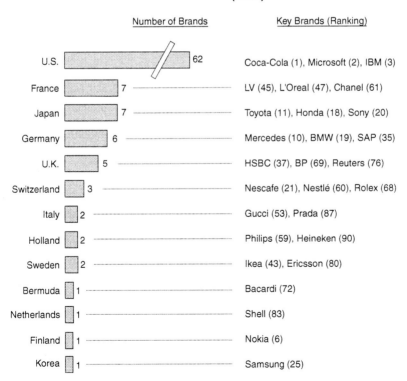

Number of Brands — Key Brands (Ranking)

- U.S. — 62 — Coca-Cola (1), Microsoft (2), IBM (3)
- France — 7 — LV (45), L'Oreal (47), Chanel (61)
- Japan — 7 — Toyota (11), Honda (18), Sony (20)
- Germany — 6 — Mercedes (10), BMW (19), SAP (35)
- U.K. — 5 — HSBC (37), BP (69), Reuters (76)
- Switzerland — 3 — Nescafe (21), Nestlé (60), Rolex (68)
- Italy — 2 — Gucci (53), Prada (87)
- Holland — 2 — Philips (59), Heineken (90)
- Sweden — 2 — Ikea (43), Ericsson (80)
- Bermuda — 1 — Bacardi (72)
- Netherlands — 1 — Shell (83)
- Finland — 1 — Nokia (6)
- Korea — 1 — Samsung (25)

Exhibit 5.3   Brand values by countries.

Doubt has frequently been expressed about the ability of Chinese enterprises to gain market capture when they do not have many recognized brands. They produce many goods for other, non-Chinese brand owners. This seems to be an area in which the Chinese seem content, in spite of the attempts by some, such as Haier, to develop a distinctive brand of low-cost electronics. But it is doubtful that this can be achieved. Brands can be designed and developed on paper in the short term. The transition from the drawing-board blueprint to reality is long and hard. It rests on an ability to focus on a market and dig deep to penetrate it at various levels. But above all, it demands long-term commitment, which can be costly and may well lose out in internal battles for resources.

The position of brands has not come at the price of diversity. The world is not one flat plane, but it is made up of a tapestry of markets, cultures, likes, dislikes, and preferences. In managing the brand on a global or even a regional basis, decisions must be made regarding whether the brand is to be a shield for a range of products that are similar yet different enough to cater to particular markets, or whether the same product is sold and distributed in each but using different marketing strategies, such as a different brand name, a different logo, or even different packaging. For example, the Chinese computer manufacturer Legend is eager to create a global brand for its products, but to do so under the Legend name was seen as difficult. Legend seemed to point too much toward its Chinese background, and its name was changed to Lenovo.

- **A global business culture**—Another phenomenon that can be viewed as a global platform is the emergence of a global business class. Business executives talk the same language anywhere in the world. They are able to communicate fluently and effectively in the linguistic platform of English. The terms that they use are the same. They have the same motivations and professional interests. Many have attended the same business schools, or ones that offer a very similar range of teaching materials, lecturing styles, and placement opportunities. They read the same business magazines. They stay in the same hotels, often enjoying the same range of food and leisure activities, while their children go to the same schools. This truly is a platform. It enables and facilitates communications and the transfer of ideas. This is a global business culture. Although it is very powerful and influential, it should not be seen as possessing an incipient threat to any existing culture. A Japanese, or Finnish, or American CEO may speak fluent English with his colleagues, but that does not dilute his ability to converse and communicate in his native language, whatever that happens to be.

This global business platform has spread outward from the world's boardrooms and five-star hotels. It means that anyone who wants to contribute to business thinking can do so easily and will be understood without difficulty. When I was in Spain, where six of my books have been published, 3,500 people came to hear me speak. When I was in Peru, 700 people came to hear me in Lima. This is a global business culture. It is also a platform for global expansion with the new jargon-heavy language of business—CRM, EBITA, BPO, and so on—being understood across borders.

- **The ATM platform**—ATM is a platform that allows cash to be dispensed to bank customers from locations distant from traditional banks. Naturally, banking hours have never fitted exactly with consumers' demands for money. In a more security-conscious age, consumers might not want to carry huge bundles of money, for fear of attracting the unwelcome attention of robbers.

The ATM platform is operated not by one provider in the world, but two: Plus and Cirrus. These companies operate the ATM technology, even though the cash-dispensing machines are operated by separate financial institutions.

When ATMs were first introduced in the 1970s, they were not greeted with unalloyed happiness. As with all technological innovations, some people cursed the inconveniences of the old world, while decrying as fanciful novelties any technology offering a palliative. Yet a quarter of a century later, they have become an accepted part of street architecture throughout the world. Many businessmen and women are not yet fully aware of these capabilities and queue up at airports and at hotels to exchange their currency. Japanese ATMs are designed to both dispense and accept deposits of cash. They also act like a PC to make payments and transfers. This means that the ATM network has the international capability to become a cash-based global platform containing two-way communication.

- **The credit card and smart card platform**—Credit cards are a platform for paying without cash. The prevalence of ATMs shows that there is still a demand for cash, but in time, traditional modalities of payment for most items may be replaced by electronic cash, or e-cash; already, some attempts to establish an e-cash platform have taken place.

The platform of encoding retrievable information on a "smart" card has grown beyond the realms of credit cards. In Scandinavia, programmed identity cards are used for accessing a wide range of services.

In South Korea, the government introduced credit cards in an attempt to boost consumption. Prizes were randomly given to holders of a certain processing ID number—for example, to the thousandth customer. Transactions were automatically recorded and became a useful and effective way of boosting tax collection. In Japan, Sony's EDY (euro, dollar, yen) card is now spreading rapidly as an electronically rechargeable prepaid card for calculating and collating data associated with customer loyalty schemes, such as airline mileages and shopping points. Given its popularity and ease of operation (POP—point of purchase, Internet connection through a handy card reader), it might yet become a global e-wallet, covering payments and receipts in the three "big" currencies.

- **The GPS platform**—Global positioning satellites (GPS) are a means of using geostationary satellites to indicate the exact position of a person with the necessary equipment on the ground. This may be in the form of bald latitude and longitude statistics, or it can be wedded to other earth-relative information, such as a map. This consumer platform was developed in Japan, where most cars now have built-in GPS units. These are useful in providing information to motorists on travel routes. They are also invaluable when traditional visible clues about location are unavailable because of fog or heavy precipitation. In Western Europe, hobbyists first seized upon this, especially hill walkers, ramblers, and hikers, to whom they offered the same benefits over traditional map and compass movement.

As a platform, GPS has potential far beyond the mist-bound motorist or the disoriented hill walker. A GPS unit in a car is a built-in security feature. The car can be easily traced if it is stolen. GPS units in cars can also be used for assisting car parking. The system can track those who have used a parking place, and this can be invoiced to the car driver. A means of tracking road usage from the sky also has potential for road taxes and tolls. Once a motorist drives along a stretch of highway upon which a toll was traditionally charged, the GPS system would note this and then bill the motorist for the road use. There would no longer be a need for tollbooths, with their associated traffic tailbacks. An additional use in road traffic management would be more anonymous and less intrusive. The traditional means for constructing roads and highways throughout the Western world is highly inefficient. Much use is made of political lobbying to a central government, urging the construction of a highway to aid economic development. Such arguments are largely based on inaccurate information. The government may respond that although such a highway would be a good idea, they have no money for road construction, but once "happy days" return, it will be a top priority. The project becomes politicized. Yet a system using GPS technology would be able to track road use in particular areas, even on particular roads at discrete times of the day. Where road use is heavy the need for new infrastructure would become apparent immediately. There would no longer be any need for anecdotal evidence. GPS, therefore, could become part of an objective public assessment.

A number of Japanese car-makers are working with consumer electronics companies to wed GPS with mobile phones. Although GPS is a wonderful device to "receive" information, it is inefficient and expensive to emit or send it. But by combining the cell phone, which uses a ubiquitous packet network, and GPS, a new interactive and Internet-compatible system can be developed. A cell phone will also act as the key to ignite the engine once it is plugged into the GPS module. This is another way of making car theft very difficult. Phone conversations will be carried out hands free and voice activated. A voice asking for a restaurant's phone number will be entered into the GPS, and the navigation system will start guiding the driver to the location. In Japan, most phone numbers are already entered into GPS equipment. (This labor-intensive data-input process was carried out, incidentally in Shenyang in China, a typical example of cross-border BPO.) It is a matter of years before the two digital islands of GPS and mobile phones will form a single, much larger, digital platform.

An array of platforms is in existence—or set to exist in the very near future. The challenge for all of those operating on the global stage is twofold: to understand the importance of platforms and to be able to utilize them as effectively and as early as possible.

Notes

1 "English, a Language You Have to Learn?," *China Daily*, 1 April 2004, www.chinadaily.com.cn.

2 "Pumping up the Volume," *Asiaweek*, 30 July 1999, www.asiaweek.com.

6

OUT AND ABOUT

Border Crossings

The next issue shaping the global stage is business process outsourcing (BPO). Put simply, BPO is about optimization. Activities that were traditionally carried out in a high-cost environment are switched to one in which lower labor costs apply without any loss in the quality of the process provided. The business community is accustomed to relocating sources (suppliers for new materials and components and for manufacturing). The most important change over the last decade has been the emergence of cross-border business process outsourcing (x-BPO). This originally took place using fixed telephone lines, both public and leased, but now it predominantly uses the Internet protocol.

Two types of x-BPO exist. The first transfers functional operations overseas. Think of the relocation of call centers to locations such as Ireland, Holland, and India. The second relocates support and indirect white-collar work. General Electric, Citibank, and Amazon in India are examples of the second category made possible only through extensive use of business process standardization (BPS) combined

with the digitization of the workplace (see Exhibit 6.1). Less sophisticated companies will have difficulty shifting parts of their business
overseas if jobs and functions are not well defined electronically.

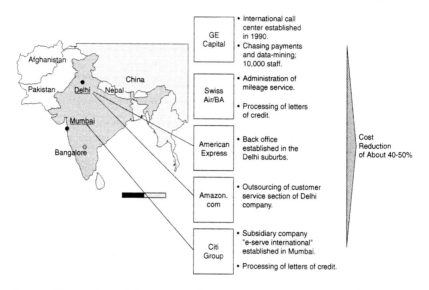

Source: Electronics and Computer Software Export Promotion Council Reference:
The Economist, 3 May 2001.

Exhibit 6.1   Back offices of European and American companies in India.

Beyond these bare statements, there is no disguising that the rise
of cross-border BPO is one of the most controversial aspects of the
global economy. It is viewed by some commentators as entirely negative. Indeed, for some, it is probably *the* most negative aspect of the
global economy. But this view is often based on misconceptions.
Some of these may be deliberately selfish, for cross-border BPO can
and does spread the benefits of prosperity into areas of the world that
until now have been mired in destitution and poverty.

Cross-border outsourcing is an extension of a phenomenon that
has been going on for decades. Within the United States, there has
long been a migration of business processes to less expensive areas for
computing, document processing, and customer contacts. BPO has
been taking place across city limits and state lines. With the help of the
global platform of the Internet, it is now crisscrossing national borders.

This can provide substantial savings. An example of these comes
from the British travel company ebookers. It established a back-
office facility in India that saved an estimated GBP 1.4 million in a

three-month period during 2003. Such paybacks are not unusual and are highly persuasive.

When reference is made to BPO, people instinctively think of India. BPO is important in India, without a doubt, but as we shall see, it is not important throughout the whole of the country. If anything, its success is patchy and uneven. Companies and investors come to locations such as Bangalore, New Delhi, and Hyderabad because of their regional and commercial attractiveness, combined with the efforts of regional governments in India to attract outside investment.

Not only India benefits from BPO. In fact, if we look at a map of the world, it is hard to find large areas that do not have some type of BPO activity (see Exhibit 6.2). It brings real benefits, in terms of good wages for local workers, technology transfer, and the development of improved infrastructure.

At the same time, it should be emphasized that there is nothing inevitable about BPO. We are not going to witness a whole-scale migration of service-sector jobs from the United States and Western Europe to India, China, or any other low-cost location. Cross-border BPO suits some sectors better than others. For some, it can be very successful; for those who are badly prepared, it can spell disaster.

My first experience of BPO was in Ireland in the early 1990s, in the wake of the Irish Industrial Development Authority's endorsement of Ireland as an e-hub. Call centers were established along with back-office facilities associated with the Financial Services Center in Dublin's former docklands.

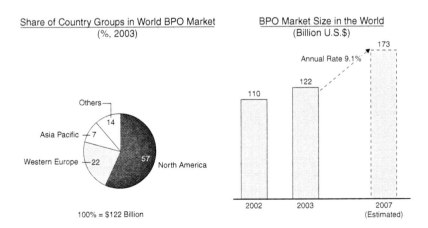

Source: Gardner Group.

Exhibit 6.2   BPO market size and share of country groups in world BPO market.

Contemporary BPO is different than previous incarnations. First, it is cross-border: It doesn't occur within national borders—it seems to defy them with glee. In fact, technology means that it is borderless. Second, the old trade-off between low wages and low skills does not hold anymore. In many regions in the world, the old economic theories about factor endowments in labor do not hold true. According to these, a country might not have vast mineral or landed resources, but it might compensate for this with a large reservoir of labor. This would inevitably be low cost and low skilled. In certain regions of India and China, high skills *are* available for low wages—low by Western standards, that is.

To put this in historical perspective, the most critical resource to create wealth during the nineteenth and first half of the twentieth centuries was agriculture (as in Argentina, Australia, and Canada with vast, seemingly inexhaustible supplies of land), but it changed to industrial resources, mineral extraction, and oil during the second half of the last century. It is now obvious that in the first half of the twenty-first century, wealth can be created by human resources, as long as they are sufficiently intelligent and educated. Wealth and jobs can be imported and exported using the Internet protocol across national borders.

Technology: The Fairy Godmother

BPO would be unthinkable without present-day telecommunications technology. India, for example, has witnessed a near revolutionary improvement in its telecommunications infrastructure. There are still places in the country where making an ordinary long-distance phone call is expensive. It can also be something of an ordeal, demanding patience, stamina, and a degree of spirituality. Data transfer both within and beyond India's borders via existing fixed lines in these areas is physically impossible. Yet investment in the improvement of phone lines, as well as provision of fiber-optic cables and satellite connections, has revolutionized the possibilities open to all Indians, though admittedly only in some fortunate regions.

India is a large country, and provision of landlines to all areas is expensive, time consuming, and often impossible. Cellular telephones are therefore an inexpensive alternative. There are estimated to be 59 million cellular phones in India today, and the number is growing by around 2 million every month. (In China, the growth is an astonishing 5 million per month and, at the end of 2003, the number of cell-phone subscribers passed 300 million—twice the number in the United States.) In 2003, mobile phones surpassed land-line installation in India for the first time. Because of buoyant competition, bills and subscriptions are kept low. One analyst observed that India is the best place in the world to be a telecom customer. This, combined with growing affluence, allows cellular phones to be more than a status symbol. Traders in Mumbai are developing home-delivery services using their cellular phones to contact potential customers and take orders.

Ireland is another country whose telephone system has improved in a revolutionary way, thereby making call centers and back-office provision possible. Until the early 1980s, the nation's phone service was archaic, not dissimilar in some ways to India's. Many areas had telephones, but to make a call beyond a short distance was arduous. Telephone lines stretched over mountains and into remote valleys, often connecting to one isolated house. Furthermore, the lines did not always function properly. The telecommunications system was then opened up; new structures and strategies were injected into a previously moribund public utility monopoly. With the growing involvement of the private sector came new investment in fiber-optic cables and digital exchanges. People in all areas and of all ages also eagerly embraced the mobile telephone. Irish people are reputed to be the most avid senders of text messages in the world.

As in India, the improvement in telecommunications infrastructure has benefited the economy, enabling the establishment of call centers. But in both countries, the winner has also been the general public.

BPO: India as a Launch Pad

Before looking at the fears engendered by BPO, let us go back to India and examine the reality of x-BPO in more detail.

Cross-border BPO may not solely be an Indian phenomenon, but it has put India on the global economic stage. What is being done today in India through English will spread to other centers attracting x-BPO tomorrow.

India owes a lot (but by no means all) of its position within the x-BPO arena to call centers, especially ones dedicated to providing technical assistance or customer response management (CRM). People in the Western world may visualize these facilities as rows of tightly packed operators, each tied to a telephone line, working for long hours in a humid environment for a meager wage. The modern reality is different. The person answering the call is not a robot. He may have a position similar to a manager of one person's account, responding to queries and imparting information.

The Indian call center is equal to call centers in the West. Some may denounce the latter as dehumanizing. The same attempts to inject vitality into the call center working environment are pursued in India as are implemented in Ireland or Great Britain. This is also true of call centers in China and other locations (see Exhibit 6.3).

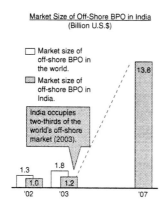

Source: Gardner Group.

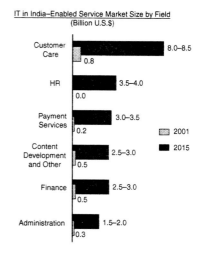

Source: NASSCOM, McKinsey, & Company.

Exhibit 6.3   Market size of off-shore BPO in India.

BPO in India is much larger than call centers. Indian call centers make up only about an eighth of cross-border BPO value. BPO facilities include a range of back-office functions, such as data entry, facilities management, auditing, accounts receivables and payables tracking, payroll management, technical writing and editing, and professional and technical services. India also has a huge reservoir of technical talent that can be employed in a range of R&D roles, such as product design.

The reality of BPO is brightly lit, well-ventilated offices with computer terminals on every desk. They are the equivalent of offices providing professional and technical services in the West. They operate at only a fraction of the cost of their Western equivalents, of course. Such places are attractive places to work and offer attractive salaries. Already, Indian professionals (doctors, lawyers, accountants, engineers, and so on) who offer their services in a BPO environment are emerging as an employment category. These are people whose skills and expertise are in demand worldwide. Rather than feeling exploited by customers in the West, they see their work as a career, capable of providing them with a lifetime's employment and personal development, not to mention a very desirable quality of life.

Professional careers have long been a part of Indian society, but entrance to them tended to be restricted. Many graduates of Indian universities, whether technicians, doctors, or other professionals, often had to look forward to spending years—maybe decades— abroad, in Europe, North America, or the Middle East, after which there were some, but by no means generous, possibilities available on returning home. Such a return, even when possible, often involved a considerable financial sacrifice. Yet the growth of x-BPO in India means that well-paid (by local standards) jobs are now available. What is more, it is possible to enjoy a bigger slice of the good life within India's borders (see Exhibit 6.4).

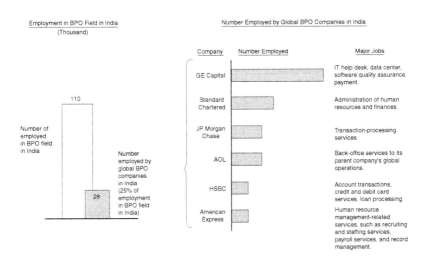

Source: Various news articles.

Exhibit 6.4   BPO employment and global company employment in India.

More challenging for some in the developed world are the inroads being made by x-BPO providers into professional services. Recently, it emerged that a company in the United Kingdom that was seeking a software audit had been quoted a figure of GBP100,000 by a British company. An Indian firm staffed by qualified computer professionals carried out the task for GBP30,000. The vice president of

WIPRO, one of India's leading BPO providers, recently commented that BPO has potential in areas such as medical diagnosis, where X-rays could be taken in the United States or the United Kingdom and then transferred for analysis by a specialist in India, and the findings could be delivered back within a few hours for considerably less cost.

Considerable strides are being made in high-tech BPO. Many major U.S. companies have already taken the plunge into the waters of technical BPO. Motorola is building a large research center in India, partly as a result of winning a tender to supply more than $300 million of equipment to the fast-growing Indian mobile-phone sector. General Electric established an R&D center in Bangalore, which serves not only the Asian market; it has become a center of R&D excellence worldwide and has applied for a sizable number of U.S. patents.

Some commentators look at India and compare it with China. They say that it is nearly as dynamic of an example of the new global economy as China. True, its growth rate may not be quite as high yet as in China (somewhere between 7 and 8 percent, compared to 9 percent for China). They also point to the fact that so much of India's growth has been led by the private sector. The government, whether at national or state levels, has helped by doing less, by removing barriers, and by deregulating and denationalizing. India toyed with socialism for many years after its independence in 1947, but it never had a centralized communist government as in China, although the state of Kerala (now a leading location for attracting BPO) had the first democratically elected communist government. But even though the two countries have very different histories, there were many publicly owned companies in India. These have largely been privatized. The national government does not play a significant role in the economy anymore.

Dormant India

It is important to grasp one important reality: India *as a nation* has not yet woken up to the global economy. So, 8 percent annual growth is a result of certain regions doing extremely well, while the rest of the country is still lagging behind. Outside the promising areas of growth, India is a very poor country, where telephones don't work and where businesses and consumers have to struggle with power outages and ramshackle infrastructure. In many areas, parents are unemployed, so they send their children to sweatshops to earn money. Parents confiscate children's earnings only to ease their hunger. It is far easier for children to find these types of jobs than adults. So, the poverty of India and the lack of minimal education to children in poor areas are still a continuing and chronic problem.

Two-thirds of India's population are employed in agriculture, but many of these are engaged in subsistence or near-subsistence cultivation. They do not grow for the market because they cannot get any surplus produce to market. They do not have access to dependable water or electricity, while sources of credit even for the smallest improvements are lacking.

India's central government does not understand the global economy. It cannot figure out why certain areas are succeeding so phenomenally and why they are able to attract investment from the rest of the world. This does not stop them from engaging in some self-aggrandizing self-congratulation. In the general elections of 2004, the governing Bharatiya Janata Party (BJP) attempted to adopt India's prosperity by using the electoral slogan "India Shining." (In the end, it did them little good.)

The Indian government takes credit for economic growth and for the success of places such as Bangalore, claiming that this is due to its far-sighted macroeconomic policies, such as lowering interest rates. Yet government policies have contributed in no way to the success of the prosperous region states, where growth rates may exceed 20 percent. Thanks to the country's federal structure, there are regions like Andhra Pradesh, Maharashtra, Kerala, and the vicinities of Mumbai and New Delhi, which are eagerly embracing the global economy and are looking outward to the rest of the world for investment and prosperity. They are truly behaving like region-states, and the central government is content to let them and do nothing except take some unearned credit. The good news is that the prosperity of these regions will encourage others to imitate them.

Consider West Bengal, which has been governed since 1977 by the Communist Party of India (Marxist), or CPI-M. Not surprisingly, businesses avoided the state and its poverty-beset capital, Kolkatta (formerly Calcutta), like an outbreak of bubonic plague. Many sectors of economic activity were in public ownership, and a powerful trades union movement used strikes to extract generous pay settlements and working conditions for members. The CPI-M is still in power there, so it would seem an unlikely area to expect much recognition for the global economy. Yet when the current state premier Buddhabev Bhattacharjee took power in November 2000, he adopted as his slogan not an aphorism from *Das Kapital*, but three words made famous by Nike: "Just Do It." Since coming to power, he has attempted to attract inward investment, including BPO providers. He knows that he and his state have a bad reputation to live down, but as he asked in an interview with the *Far Eastern Economic Review*, "If you can do business in China, why not in West Bengal?"[1] He realizes that the greatest competition he faces comes from other Indian states eager to attract outside investment. His role is that of a chief marketing officer for his state, though he does not warm to the term. In the same interview, he described a light-hearted exchange he had with the former chief minister of Andhra Pradesh, Chandrabubu Naidu, who has been to the fore in successfully attracting investment into his area, particularly Hyderabad. The West Bengal premier joked that he looked forward to overtaking Andhra Pradesh.

It is significant that Indian political leaders of all political stripes support a commitment to pursuing wealth from the rest of the world instead of promoting domestic poverty. Andhra Pradesh's chief minister, Mr. Naidu, was swept from power early in 2004, but there is every indication that his replacement will pursue the same far-sighted policies as his predecessor.

The experience of one area is leading not to jealousy, but a desire to emulate. Policies that bring wealth will not be suddenly reversed, so continuity can develop. Prosperity will therefore spread, albeit slowly.

There will undoubtedly be backlash. The economic progress made possible under the leadership of the BJP was perceived as unfair in the poor rural districts. This, of course, has been the favorite game of the National Congress Party ever since the days of Ghandi and Nehru. So, when the NCP took over the government again in May 2004, a chill ran through the international business community, in which the NCP has a bad reputation for overly socialist policies and overpromising redistribution when few companies were generating wealth. But overall, I believe that some of the regional leaders will continue their connectivity to the global community, and progress, albeit at a slower pace than in the BJP days, will continue because many enlightened people have woken up to the potential of x-BPO in India. Once people have enjoyed prosperity for a time, they are very reluctant to give it up.

Already the benefits are visible in those regions that look most avidly to the rest of the world: Indians own more new cars instead of near-vintage models. Shopping malls selling everything from the latest fashions to consumer electronics have sprung up. This pattern is also found in the more prosperous region-states of China.

For much of the twentieth century, India was a byword for chronic poverty and deprivation. It was a land of contrasts. At the pinnacle of society, there were princes and courtiers living in unimaginable luxury. Most other people either lived a hard and bitter hand-to-mouth existence or lived in abject penury. They saw the luxury of the first group on cinema screens in the often-surreal setting of Hollywood blockbusters. It fashioned their dreams, but more felt unable to taste the good life themselves. But some of the descendants of these people now own their own homes and their own cars. They no longer worry about starvation, though some do worry about overeating, especially Western fast food.

Frightful poverty remains, sometimes in the midst of prosperity, but maybe even this, considered for so long endemic, may change, if only gradually. In this regard, the aspirations of the Indian government to end poverty by 2020 are probably misguided. BPO can help, but it cannot get rid of deprivation on its own. Currently, more than one million Indians are employed in the BPO sector, a figure that is expected to double in a few years, but this must be set against a total Indian working population of more than 450 million. Nevertheless, the contribution of BPO in poverty alleviation in India should not be underemphasized. What is important to note is that the global economy is helping India come out of the chronic malaise of poverty, which New Delhi could not solve in half a century.

If the Indian government really did understand, it would do everything possible in its power to educate children. The only hope for poor countries such as India is to have the best human resources to attract employment from the rest of the world.

The Indian government also aims to slash illiteracy by 2020. Such a goal is probably equally unreachable, but it shows a realization that greater prosperity can be attained through literacy. Improvements in education cannot be merely wished into existence. The massive and inefficient state educational sector has to be reformed. Already there is a growing realization among Indians that the government must not be looked to as an automatic provider of education. The role of private education, so long dismissed as the preserve of the super-rich, has grown exponentially. Among the traditional providers of private education in India have been Roman Catholic religious orders. Their high standards of excellence are once again attracting parents, many of whom are not even Christians.

The *Harijans* were the lowest members of India's caste system. In some parts of southern India, they used to alert their presence from afar by shouting, for fear that a member of a higher caste would even see them and thereby incur defilement. These practices died out in the twentieth century, but still Harijans earned the lowest wages and had the shortest life expectancy. A number of aid projects in the Pondicherry area in south India are providing literacy education to Harijan children, but it is not traditional words and numbers literacy: It is computer literacy. These children, for so long mired in poverty and destitution, may very well be the BPO employees of tomorrow, earning more than they could ever hope for and enjoying a quality of life they felt to be permanently beyond their reach. If this is made possible, the world will experience visibly the positive side of the global economy.

Some industry insiders in India see BPO as having the potential to transform India's economy from a third-world to a first-world outfit.

Although in the short term, such aspirations might be over-optimistic, there is no doubt that x-BPO, together with technology transfer and the development of Indian business, has the long-term potential to improve the lives and incomes of the vast majority of India's population (see Exhibit 6.5). Today, only certain regions and certain sectors of the country have proven that x-BPO is profitable. But it will be a long time before they are called a resource-rich superpower of the cyberage.

Cross-border BPO can help to distribute and spread wealth in the world in a way that is more effective and efficient than the disbursement of development aid. The money goes directly to individuals rather than to often corrupt government agencies. It offers societies in the Third World the chance to enjoy the standards of living of the developed world that are truly sustainable. India has a long way to go before it can ever deliver such standards to its one billion citizens, but some regions have come a very long way over the last decade.

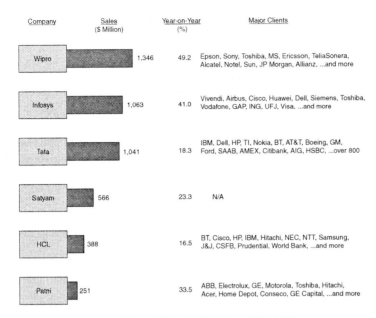

**Indian Companies Are Diversifying Their Business
from Their Traditional Software Development to BPO**

Major Indian BPO Companies

Company	Sales ($ Million)	Year-on-Year (%)	Major Clients
Wipro	1,346	49.2	Epson, Sony, Toshiba, MS, Ericsson, TeliaSonera, Alcatel, Notel, Sun, JP Morgan, Allianz, ...and more
Infosys	1,063	41.0	Vivendi, Airbus, Cisco, Huawei, Dell, Siemens, Toshiba, Vodafone, GAP, ING, UFJ, Visa, ...and more
Tata	1,041	18.3	IBM, Dell, HP, TI, Nokia, BT, AT&T, Boeing, GM, Ford, SAAB, AMEX, Citibank, AIG, HSBC, ...over 800
Satyam	566	23.3	N/A
HCL	388	16.5	BT, Cisco, HP, IBM, Hitachi, NEC, NTT, Samsung, J&J, CSFB, Prudential, World Bank, ...and more
Patni	251	33.5	ABB, Electrolux, GE, Motorola, Toshiba, Hitachi, Acer, Home Depot, Conseco, GE Capital, ...and more

Note: HCL, end of June 2003; Patni, end of December 2003; others, end of March 2004.

Source: Web site IR report of each company.

Exhibit 6.5   Major Indian BPO companies.

More Than a One-Country Wonder

Cross-border BPO is not just a process involving U.S. and U.K. firms outsourcing parts of their business to India. Its reach is much more extensive. There are companies whose traditional language of operations is Spanish, or whose market is made up of Spanish speakers, in either Continental Europe or Latin America. For them, the establishment of x-BPO facilities in Central America or the Philippines is worthwhile. Similarly, those whose targets speak Portuguese have outsourced elements of their business to Brazil. In East Asia, Taiwanese companies have found that BPO is available on the Chinese mainland. The providers speak Mandarin, and their wage levels are probably one-sixth of those in Taiwan, so they are very attractive. Once again, good business can dissolve any political hostility. The magnetism of the Chinese mainland to Chinese-speaking businesses in Hong Kong and Singapore is the same. In some areas of China, call-center operatives speak Japanese instead of English, so they are a useful tool for Japanese companies. About a million people in the province of Jilin, in northeastern China, are fluent Korean speakers. Again, some Korean financial institutions have started to tap into this attractive resource pool.

Exhibit 6.6 shows the geographical perspective of Dalian in Liaoning Province. The distance from Tokyo to Dalian is about the same as to Okinawa and Hokkaido, where the Japanese government is trying to set up call centers with 50 percent subsidies on operator wage. But this is to no avail, as the wages of the Chinese workers who can do data entry in Japanese and/or answer simple questions in Japanese on the phone are one-tenth that of the equivalent Japanese workers.

BPO providers in China also supply extensive back-office facilities for companies in Japan and Singapore. Singapore has benefited from BPO, though not surprisingly, at the technical "high end." In particular, one of Hewlett-Packard's computer servers was designed there.

The Philippines has most of the advantages of India in call center provision. Fluency in spoken English is high; what is more, many Filipinos speak English with a slight American accent. This can be an advantage. There are many qualified health-care professionals, especially nurses, who cannot find work in the Philippines and who face emigration to Europe, North America, or the Middle East to find work. However, many are now employed in the provision of medical BPO services. Manila, the capital, has been the main location of these businesses, but due to lack of sufficiently qualified workers, their attention has moved increasingly to the nation's second city, Cebu. Because of the availability of highly skilled computer programmers in the Philippines, there are a number of computer-science research laboratories. Many of these youngsters would have become hackers or software counterfeiters were there not legitimate x-BPO work for them, such as developing antivirus and firewall applications.

Using *Historical Ties*, Dalian Could
Become the "Backroom" for
Japanese/Korean Corporations

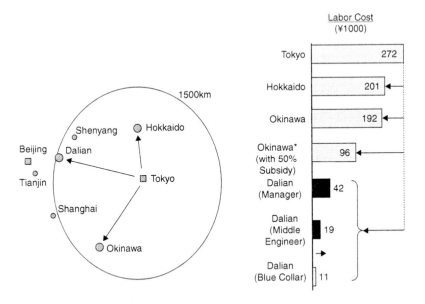

Labor Cost (¥1000)
Tokyo	272
Hokkaido	201
Okinawa	192
Okinawa* (with 50% Subsidy)	96
Dalian (Manager)	42
Dalian (Middle Engineer)	19
Dalian (Blue Collar)	11

*Japanese government subsidy to encourage siting in Okinawa.

Source: JETRO, Ministry of Health, Labor, and Welfare.

Exhibit 6.6 Dalian could become the backroom for Japanese/Korean corporations.

BPO is not solely an East Asian or a low-cost environment phenomenon. Ireland's success as an e-hub owes much to its ability to attract business from American companies wishing to take advantage of the time difference between Europe and North America. The Netherlands is also establishing a reputation as an efficient and effective provider of BPO products. Its central location in Europe is helpful, while its multilingual workforce can provide services in fluent English and German. The new members of the EU, particularly the Czech Republic, Hungary, and Poland, provide a fertile ground for recruiting English and German BPO operators for continental European countries, as well as for R&D facilities. See Exhibits 6.7 and 6.8.

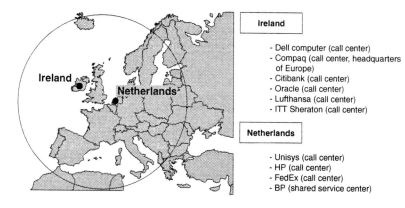

Source: *The Economist*, 26 April 2001, Nikkei.

Exhibit 6.7   Back-office clusters in Europe.

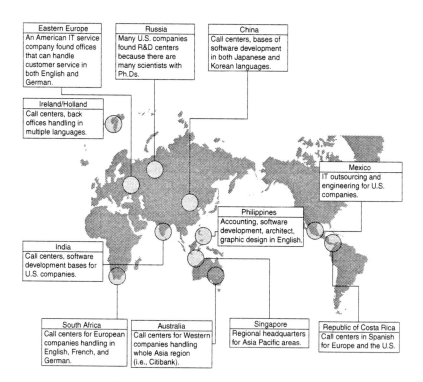

Source: *Business Week*, 3 February 2003.

Exhibit 6.8   BPO off-shore operations.

BPO as a Platform

In Chapter 8, "Reinventing Government," I talk about the important role technological platforms play in the global economy. A platform can be defined as an application or technology that allows both individuals and companies to do things better and more efficiently. Business process outsourcing clearly conforms to this definition.

For example, the airline Lufthansa has frequently had problems with seat allocations. There is often a mismatch between seats demanded and seats available on flights. It is not always possible to mop up the demand for places by putting on extra flights. There is little commercial logic in providing a fully crewed, fully fuelled plane to fly thousands of miles with only a few passengers. Similarly, it does not make much sense to turn away potential full-fare passengers on flights that are supposedly fully booked. The traditional means of matching seat demand and supply used computers employing linear equations to solve the problem. Seating can be rearranged by means of human and manual reallocation, providing the two or three extra places needed.

Lufthansa found that this was complex and repetitive work, unattractive to workers in Germany or Europe. However, India and especially the hinterland of Mumbai had numerous qualified engineers and specialists who were both eager and able to do this work. It might be boring, but it was far from repulsive. So Lufthansa established a facility in Mumbai whose employees are dedicated to seat reallocation on flights that the traditional, computer-based systems describe as full. These Indian workers are, in effect, human linear programmers.

Another example of work that is both complex and repetitive but that demands highly skilled employees is the compilation of indexes and abstracts databases. These are a necessity for scholars, especially in scientific disciplines, who must be able to find out as quickly as possible the work that has been done in their discreet area of inquiry before they can carry out further worthwhile research and experimentation. Dutch publishing houses have traditionally specialized in producing indexes of scientific abstracts. The work of compilation was carried out in Western Europe: It is now occurring in India. Such indexing is also applicable to other disciplines, such as law. Common law systems, such as those in the United Kingdom and United States, rely heavily on precedents, and these are contained in indexes of cases with references to legal reports. Legal success may depend on being able to access such cases and, of course, use them through effective argument. Although cases from other jurisdictions might not have the same power of precedent, they may be of persuasive value, especially when dealing with new areas or factual scenarios.

Lawyers already are using legal BPO, especially in the area of intellectual property law. This usually depended on granting patents to protect rights in new mechanisms or processes. But gaining adequate patent protection is a long and very expensive process. The developer of a process in, say, the United Kingdom can gain patent protection in his own jurisdiction, but this will be of little protection in Australia and the Far East. To gain full patent coverage, it is often necessary to apply for patents in a string of countries, using highly paid legal services each time. A legal expert in Mumbai has recently developed a service that is less time consuming and less expensive. If a client supplies him with an American patent, he researches the jurisdiction in which it is worthwhile or valuable to seek copyright or patent protection, and then translates the patent into the necessary languages before filing it in the respective countries' patent offices.

BPO is being used for compiling corporate research material. For some time, investment banks in the United States have used Indian backroom operations to supply company analyses. This has gone one step further: Not only is the analysis carried out in India, but it is also collated and even processed into a bound volume in India before being sent to the bank's clients.

I have mentioned the possibilities for BPO in the medical sphere. Its back-office capabilities are also valuable. Already some consultants in U.S. hospitals are using back-office dictation services in India. Using Voice over IP telephony, they dictate prescriptions for patients that are then completed and sent back either to the consultant physician or to the hospital's pharmacy department. The workers in India who take the dictated prescriptions are fully qualified as medical secretaries.

Possibilities also exist for outsourcing in the pharmaceuticals industry. Before any new medicine or preparation can receive approval in Western countries, it must undergo long, rigorous, and expensive testing procedures. This can take many years and add substantially to R&D costs. Indian laboratories can provide the clinical expertise and the equipment for these tests at a fraction of the cost. India's vast population is a very effective source of volunteers for drug testing. This does not mean that ethical standards in drug testing are in any way compromised. Iceland, on the other side of the world, is offering a test bed for certain types of drug development because of its DNA "purity" caused by long years of isolation. The country has possibly the lowest rate of inward migration in the world.

Accounting services for x-BPO are being offered in India and the Philippines. The latter is also the source of designers and architects. In what may be a peace dividend of the end of the Cold War, Russia's contribution to x-BPO comes in the form of aerospace engineers who provide their expertise in design to international clients outside Russia. Some of these engineers gained their training in the old Soviet military and suffered redundancy in an era when their talents had no foreseeable outlet.

Home Sweet Home

It is easy to think of the providers of BPO as inhabiting a dedicated building or office space. The reality is that many BPO providers work from their own homes or in a small office/home office (SOHO) environment. This return to a nonindustrial, often domestic environment is the single most important difference between the manufacturing age and the cyberage. Many BPO workers can turn on the switch of a PC when they are ready to work. How long they work is up to the networked individual, as they can adjust their work hours according to their families' demands on their time and other factors.

This is the reason why some corporations want to shift their full-time/full-scale operations to outsourced providers first within the same country and then eventually to other countries. This way, they can offer 24-hour, year-round services to customers. A round-the-clock call center can be built by utilizing similar people in London, New York, and Los Angeles. Companies can achieve seamless 24×7 operations without paying overtime. When it is 5 PM in Tokyo, it is 9 AM in London, so the call-center work is passed on to the pool of resources in London. When it is 5 PM in London, work is passed on to Los Angeles, where it is 9 AM.

Improvements in telecommunications and especially lowered costs for telephone lines and installation mean also that the providers of BPO services need not leave their homes. The "switchback" technology used in modern call centers means that important and relevant client information can be accessed by call center operatives from their own home. For example, a call center based in Dublin dealing with Western and Northern Europe would employ a number of fluent speakers of the vernacular languages of their market. If someone were to call from Sweden, they would be able to talk to a fluent

Swedish speaker located in Dublin. If during the call from Sweden there were no or insufficient Swedish speakers, the call might be switched to an operator in Sweden working from his or her own home. The original caller would be unaware that the person dealing with their query was either in Dublin or elsewhere in Sweden.

Domestic call centers have mushroomed in East Asia and Australasia. Many of these domestic workers are Japanese, sometimes the spouses and partners of Japanese employees working overseas. They are highly educated but unable to break into the local labor market because they are not fluent in English. With the lower price of leased lines, it is possible for them to work from home for customer-service management companies based in Japan and deal with the Japanese market. They speak fluent Japanese, far more fluently than even the most dedicated Japanese-speaking Chinese call-center operative in Dalian. They are also inexpensive; their rate of pay is far less than that of a worker in Japan.

Nobody can sincerely believe that such call-center workers are exploited. They work only for as long as they desire.

Myths and Half-Truths

Despite the manifest success of BPO in parts of India, as well as in Ireland and elsewhere, BPO remains clouded in myth and sepia-tinged images from the past. It summons up pictures of sweatshops manned by serried rows of badly paid and badly housed operatives. Some of these images may come from television news reports aired in the 1970s showing textile workers in overcrowded workshops in Southeast Asia. But they have no place in today's world. The gleaming offices of Pune are a far cry from the imagined sweatshops, but belief in myths is often comforting. It provides some measure of justification for irrational beliefs and actions. There are those who would like to decry x-BPO for supposedly humanitarian reasons, who want to prevent the exploitation of people in developing countries.

These fears and apprehensions about exploitation are misguided. BPO brings prosperity and, more important, hope to countless millions of people. In reality, much of the controversy about BPO is inspired by basic fear and insecurity.

The side effects of the x-BPO phenomenon are increasingly felt by educated Western white-collar workers and professionals. Contemporary BPO is a middle-class, middle-income issue. It affects those whose lifestyles were traditionally comfortable and secure:

office workers, administrators, and increasingly members of the professional classes. Membership of these groups was for years seen as advantageous over manual labor: Pay was considered to be better (it wasn't always) and workers didn't get their hands, or any other parts of their body, dirty. White-collar work was respectable. It was also secure. White-collar workers did feel a certain threat from automation, but they consoled themselves and their families with the impossibility of a computer doing their job better than they could. But now x-BPO seems to be undermining this cozy scenario. For some in the United States, its impact is catastrophic, for among those who are losing out are technical operatives, including computer programmers and college graduates.

It is estimated that in the next decade, six million American jobs will move from the United States to low-cost environments such as India, peripheral European countries, and China. These will not be manufacturing jobs, which have been accustomed to competing with low-cost labor markets and being exported to countries such as Mexico. Professionals and technical workers, unlike blue-collar workers, are not unionized. When this happens, it will be a quiet process, often not even noticed by the news media.

Losing skilled jobs is viewed in a different light than the loss of manual work. It is one thing to make a donation to a Third-World charity, but quite another to surrender your job to the enrichment of people many thousands of miles away. Of course, a job is a significant feature. It is a rock of stability upon which so many elements of daily life depend—financial well-being, status, and self-belief being only three. Loss of a job is a serious blow, but for people in the West, it is far from being the end of the world. The workhouses of Charles Dickens's days are no more. It is possible for the retrenched worker in the West to get another job. This may involve relocating or even taking a drop in salary, but starvation is not a threat. Government-provided welfare makes sure of that.

The job is then transferred to a non-OECD nation; let us for the sake of argument suggest that this is India. It enables someone who has the same level of expertise as the Western worker to have a comfortable lifestyle, to not have to worry about moving maybe to the other side of the world in search of work or, failing that, returning to a life on the margins of existence.

One of the Americans who did lose his job is Zach Hudgins, who lives in Washington State. He worked for both Microsoft and Amazon.com but found that employment in the computer arena was uncertain. So he went into politics, gaining election to the state senate. He is the sponsor of a bill that would outlaw the use of BPO by those that hold contracts from the state for the provision of goods or services. A similar legislative initiative was tried in Indiana, but it was defeated on the floor of the state legislature. It was felt to be too hostile to inward investment. Nevertheless, the state governor annulled a contract that had already been awarded to an Indian company specializing in BPO.

The hostility to BPO in the United States has a ring of populism. Many politicians, at least the smarter ones, know BPO makes sense. If a state decides to outsource its work, it cuts costs. Similarly, a company outsourcing work to a lower-cost environment can cut costs and, no doubt, offer their goods and services at a cheaper rate. Whether the government or a government supplier does it, it should mean savings in government spending, probably lower tax rates and more money for schools and highways, not to mention the gains accruing to the societies benefiting from BPO and a more healthy economy for the world.

Many American jobs and families will be at risk, and any holder of elected public office in the United States knows that he ignores such fears at his peril. Even if a senator, congressman, or gubernatorial candidate was courageous enough to support companies that outsourced either production or back-office operations, he would know that, in the election, whenever it comes, his opponent will be a diehard defender of American jobs and an opponent of outsourcing. He may be an opportunist, having previously been a devotee of free trade, but when there's a campaign to be fought and won, consistency is a luxury that can seldom be afforded for long. As one-time vice presidential candidate Lloyd Bentsen said, "In America, politics is a contact sport." Put at its bluntest, the people of an African or Asian country may be starving, but they don't have votes in a Western country's elections, and they don't pay any taxes into its coffers.

The View from India

There is an uncomfortable feeling in India that some American companies are reacting to a backlash and are citing vexatious reasons for reversing their earlier decisions to invest in BPO.

At the end of 2003, Dell pulled much of its business customer management from its call center in Bangalore. It cited a rather quaint and old-fashioned reason: Its customers could not understand the call-center employees' accents. This was greeted with disdain and derision in India, where commentators reminded Dell that Americans were not the only customers of Indian call centers and that their employees were mostly college graduates. In other words, you may not understand them, but at least they know what they are talking about. The *Economic Times of India* made a tongue-in-cheek question that underlined the interdependent world in which we all live: "Imagine what would happen if we moved our techies out of the U.S. back into India? Oops, there went Silicon Valley."[2]

Shortly after Dell's announcement, Foimamco, a services company with investment bankers Lehman Brothers, cancelled a contract with an Indian BPO provider that was dealing with its computer help-desk services. The reason cited was unsatisfactory service. However, the company's IT director seemed determined to play down any hint of walking away from India or BPO, estimating that Indian call centers would soon account for 40 percent of Lehman's IT business. GE announced in December 2004 that it planned to sell a majority stake in its BPO business. This, too, had the same politically motivated overtone.

An alternative view is that the American services vector has taken in jobs in software development, financial services, and many other professional services. Many countries are outsourcing high-end services to the U.S.!

However, patriotic sentiment and a desire to protect domestic jobs doesn't make much of a positive contribution to a firm's balance sheet. A decision by a company to outsource is never based solely on lower labor costs. As we've seen with Ireland, labor costs do not come into the discussion at all. Processes are outsourced to environments that can provide the same level of service and expertise as in the "developed" world, but at a lower price. BPO makes economic sense, so it will inevitably derail its critics.

Moving away from knee-jerk reactions, jingoism, and politics, the reality is that it is in the American corporate chromosome to seek the best location for production and to sell to the most attractive markets in the world. They do so, regardless of their industry and size of the company.

I am often called by Americans asking for my advice on the best production partner in China. "How big is your company? And how many units a month do you need to produce?," I ask. The answer is sometimes embarrassing. Before they start production in the United States, these business people are thinking about production overseas.

Before they start up a company, some entrepreneurs plan production in China as part of their prospectus. The United States is not losing jobs to overseas. It is not exporting jobs. Instead, Americans are using the entire world as if it were their backyard. They are simply not conscious of national borders when it comes to managing a company.

American consumers are accelerating this trend. Back in the 1980s, while the politicians were pushing Japan to produce in the United States, consumers were specifically looking for cars made in Japan rather than cars made in the United States (particularly on a Monday). This is no longer the case. In 2003, Toyota sold 2.07 million cars in North America, of which as many as 1.28 million were locally produced. This number was 582,000 in 1992, when former President George Bush came to Japan with the CEOs of the Big Three automakers asking Japanese producers to produce 300,000 more cars in the United States. Over the last two decades, Toyota and other Japanese auto producers have taken more than 100 Japanese auto component companies to the United States—especially the Mississippi Valley. The United States now has a major auto production cluster. This also helped American auto producers to become stronger as they were able to procure from the Japanese transplants. Toyota and Honda have become honorary American citizens.

Lou Dobbs and others cite American corporate greed as the motivation for x-BPO.[3] I disagree. If anything, it is the greed of American investors that pushes American companies to optimize their operations worldwide. Despite the huge outcry against the Japanese and others in the 1980s, and the obvious decline of home-based manufacturing, American manufacturers have remorselessly increased their global presence. IBM, HP, and GE are in all of the world's key markets, while Motorola has an impressive presence in the world's fastest-growing mobile-phone market, China. Along the way, the United States has increased job numbers faster than any other country in the world. This is because American companies are compelled by competition to do better, to optimize their global operations, to re-examine their business systems, and to redistribute elements of them throughout the world. If they do not do so, their competitors will eat them alive and their stockholders will abandon them.

Of course, people can and will vote for protectionist politicians. Before doing so, they should consider how ineffective they have been in protecting old manufacturing jobs. In Japan, the politicians and bureaucrats are highly effective in protecting old jobs and killing opportunities to create new types of job. Japanese companies are so comfortable at home that they do not even think about x-BPO. This explains Japan's lost decade. My preference is to have blood circulating in the business system, so that anyone in the world can come into Japan, or get out of Japan, to offer Japanese consumers, the second-largest consumer market in the world, the best and the cheapest products and services possible through the better use of the global economy.

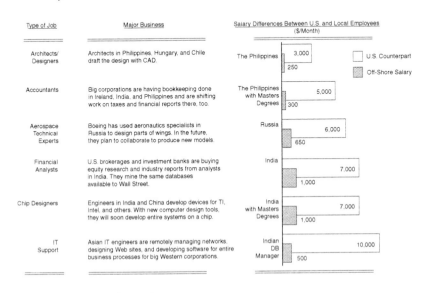

Source: *Business Week*, 3 February 2003.

Exhibit 6.9   Major outsourcing businesses and salaries of local employees.

Concerns about x-BPO aren't the sole preserve of the United States. In the United Kingdom, x-BPO has had a bumpy ride, too. Among those most eager to take the plunge are banks and insurance companies. There was a mild national outcry when Barclays' Bank announced that it was investigating outsourcing some of its back-room functions to India. Students' groups threatened a boycott of the bank. The biggest union among the bank's employees was less than happy, too, but rather than throwing down an industrial relations gauntlet, it adopted a realistic approach, entering into negotiations with management on the reallocation of work to BPO centers. Employees of the bank in the United Kingdom who are to be replaced will be told of the move three months in advance and will be entitled to a three months' salary severance deal.

Other concerns that have been voiced about BPO involve data confidentiality. Whereas companies operating in the United Kingdom or the European Union must sign up to fairly rigorous strictures on data protection, these do not apply in countries such as India or China, and some of those handling BPO functions for these firms are not company affiliates, but independent BPO providers. Worries have also been expressed about the confidentiality of medical data.

My own experience concerning data confidentiality is that there are a lot of technological solutions to this problem as well as human discipline and compliance procedures. An effective solution can be easily built into a system responding to inputs such as a doctor dictating a prescription or a lawyer dictating either a letter or a contract. If the computer terminal in India is a "dumb terminal" without a cache facility, it will be impossible for any record of the information to be stored there. It is the equivalent of speaking into the microphone of a tape recorder that hasn't a tape in it.

I have also developed a system for my own BPO operation in China. This basically breaks up a set of data into components. For example, a handwritten credit card application is read by an optical character recognition (OCR) scanner. Each line is broken into different packets. So an operator in Dalian reads the name without other information, such as the address or telephone number. Each of these detail packets goes to different operators. In this way, the security risk is greatly reduced.

Any regulations would be adhered to rigorously by all concerned: After all, compliance would be in the BPO service providers' vested interests. BPO is too big a fish to let slip out of the net.

Reaping the Benefits

As in all forms of human endeavor, there is a right way and a wrong way of approaching business process outsourcing.

The first step for a company thinking about x-BPO is to ask whether it will really benefit from it. Will the benefits accrue if the whole business process and value chain is outsourced? Or is it something from which the company can derive benefits by outsourcing individual components of business activity? The former can be a very risky business because it involves breaking up the business and rebuilding it again. This reconstruction may be theoretically possible, but whole ranges of issues have to be considered. For starters, there has to be in-depth, intuitive knowledge of the organization and what makes it work, and of its internal, sometimes indefinable synergies.

Business process outsourcing can bring benefits, but the attitude of some companies, especially in the United States, might be summed up in a paraphrase of the Roman writer Virgil: *"Timemus BPO et dona ferrentem,"* "We fear BPO even when it brings gifts."

BPO is a development that is based on perceived advantages, not always just financial ones. Once those advantages disappear, the process will move to where they are available. BPO has no room for sentiment. Areas that are successful in BPO marry their cost advantages with skills that they already possess and that the recipients of the BPO services have not contributed to building up. The fact that hundreds of millions of fluent English speakers are able to staff call centers is not the result of any actions taken by companies like Dell. It is the product of the Indian education system and the place that English has traditionally enjoyed in it.

Beneficiaries of BPO provide their workers with short-term training to enable them to carry out their tasks. Staff at Indian call centers dealing with queries and calls from the United Kingdom receive extra tuition in British popular culture, including the current story lines of popular British soap operas. They are also encouraged to "adopt" British personal names for identification purposes. But such instruction costs little in overall terms. When and if the advantage of one area begins to decline, companies will search for alternative locations, confident that they can re-establish BPO relationships and facilities quickly, cheaply, and painlessly. In this regard, BPO is fickle. It knows of no binding ties greater than economic ones. In the early part of 2004, there was shock and horror when the operators of a call center in the Irish Republic announced its closure and relocation to Poland. Accenture moved its British BPO center to Prague and GE from Germany to Hungary. In this regard, the receiving end of the x-BPO should know that relocation is far easier than for a manufacturing enterprise.

BPO can bring real advantages, but those who enjoy them should make the most of them while they possess these advantages. They should try to prolong them for as long as possible and not do anything to threaten them. Fatalism may be misplaced, but it is not inevitable that the BPO caravan will leave town. In India, a stock of expertise is being accumulated in technical BPO. This is innovative and is on the lookout for new areas in which the BPO model can be applied. It is hard to imagine that other regions can effectively compete in the short term. At the same time, India's universities and technical institutes continue to provide a reservoir of ever more skilled workers.

BPO in a Borderless World

Cross-border BPO is yet another example of the borderless world. Indirect work is constantly reduced by business process redesign (BPR) and is also absorbed into computers. Many clerical jobs have been replaced by computers, and even some professional work, such as accounting, has been absorbed by applications such as Quicken. Then there are companies that outsource key functions such as procurement, personnel management, executive education, and even sales or marketing to a third party. It is one of the key roles of the CEO to constantly look for the next chunk of his business process to push outside when better and cheaper skills are available, and a seamless, virtual single company is possible through the use of networks. It is, therefore, only natural that some of the better and cheaper operators should be found across national borders.

The politicians may have a different view, but it is a natural extension of corporate evolution for companies to seek more competitive ways to grow on the global stage. Because technology makes x-BPO possible, it is fundamentally irreversible. As such, the nation-states on the losing end of highly paid jobs need to further accelerate the upward migration of skills in the areas of creativity and innovation, as well as sideways migration to increase and improve service levels. Survivors will be those able to realign their business systems by globally optimizing their capabilities.

Notes

[1] "Cheerleader in Chief," interview with Buddhadeb Bhattacharjee, chief minister, West Bengal, in *Far Eastern Economic Review*, 29 April 2004, www.feer.com.

[2] "Call Centre Pull-Out? Kya Bolti Tu!," Economic Times Online, 23 November 2004, http://economictimes.indiatimes.com/.

[3] Dobbs, Lou, *Exporting America: Why Corporate Greed Is Shipping American Jobs Overseas*, Warner Books, 2004.

7

BREAKING THE CHAINS

The Portal Revolution

The final element in the script is execution, how things happen on the global stage. That involves buying and paying and, most important, delivery. Here, too, revolution is in the air.

Three functions have become exceptionally important. To place an order on an e-commerce site, we need to be able to first find the best site to buy from, the one that is offering (all things considered) the best deal. Then we have to pay the bill. Finally, the supplier has to ensure delivery of the item we've purchased.

The first need is catered to by the notion of the portal site. The competitive battle over the last few years has been fought to secure pole position on the desktop screen. Companies such as AOL, Yahoo!, and MSN competed for portal services: They have now reached a stalemate. Over the forthcoming years, competition enters a new stage: the battle for control of the search engine.

The search engine is *the* best travel guide and helpmate for Internet users as they move through billions of pages (and growing) in the cyberjungle. Google currently leads the pack, but companies such as Yahoo! and Microsoft are not going to throw in the towel.

The Search

From a corporate point of view, the reality is that no matter how well your home page is designed and decorated, unless it gets visitors, there are no prospects of sales. It is all mere ornamentation, a farrago of bells and whistles. So, use is made of advanced tools of detection in search engine optimization (SEO).

The customer visits the online shop once he or she looks for directions by punching in a few keywords. Your site must then be among the top three to be clicked because, chances are, a simple search request will result in hundreds, maybe thousands, of pages being called up. On their first tentative search of the Internet, the inquirer tends to browse through several pages, but on his next visit, he feels more confident; he has a slightly clearer idea (or so he would like to believe) of where he wants to go (or where he doesn't want to go), and this is beyond the first page of Google's findings. Chances are, he will click and read only the top three—at the most, the top five. On the second visit, the searcher also starts refining the search by keying in a few words to focus on the target. A person who engages in this narrowing or refining is more likely to buy the product when eventually found than is someone who simply searches in a general and ill-defined manner. For example, someone who punches in "wooden bench" is more likely to buy than someone who simply keys in "bench." Likewise "short-sleeved men's shirt" is better than "men's shirt." This is a result of psychology. The first person has already made up his mind to buy a concrete product. He may well have visualized buying it, taking delivery, and using it. The second person has not gone so far. As a result, the advertising at the end of the search, known as keyword advertising (usually in the form of a banner attached to the destination page of the search) is definitely cost effective.

This trend is more pronounced in the United States, but it is becoming increasingly clear throughout the world (see Exhibit 7.1). People no longer respond to advertisements in newspapers and magazines; they tend to ignore them, even blank them out of their perceptions altogether. I have several different businesses in Japan, and they have all taught me one lesson: Newspaper ads do not pay. The response to an ad informing readers of the opening of my school has declined by a factor of five in as many years. But luckily for the school, students do come in via the Internet. Prospective students who come through the Web also have a much higher percentage of conversion potential into actual students.

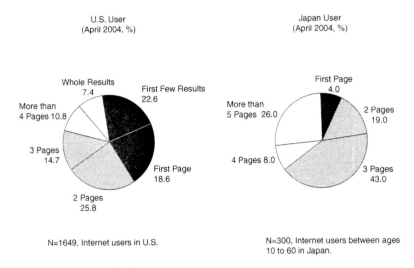

U.S. User
(April 2004, %)

Japan User
(April 2004, %)

N=1649, Internet users in U.S.

N=300, Internet users between ages
10 to 60 in Japan.

Source: iProspect. Infoplant.

**Exhibit 7.1   Search engine user attitudes: How many pages do you actu-
ally need?**

Have You Been Googled Recently?

I have also noticed something else that's new. When I was in Spain recently, the gentlemen I had dinner with talked to me with a degree of familiarity. It was as if we'd known each other for years. A few weeks later, I had the same experience in New Zealand with a group of businesspeople. The subjects and comments were very similar. It struck me that they must have "Googled" me just before the dinner— that is, entered my name into the Google search engine and read all the results. Indeed, this kind of *déjá vu* experience continues almost every week as I travel around the world.

We are living in a small and intimate global community where all sorts of information, even rumors, runs through its residents in a matter of seconds. But in reality, this village is not small at all. It has a population of 800 million at the end of 2003 (that's the number of

people with URL addresses) and is increasing every day. These 800
million people could be treated as a single race or a tribe. In my 1985
book *Triad Power*, I called the 700 million residents of JEU (Japan,
Europe, and the United States) "triadians." Their behavior as consumers
was becoming similar because they possessed a large, surplus discre-
tionary income and the aspiration and commitment to have a good time.

Now we can see the emergence of *cyberites* or *netians*, with
slightly different constituents. The tribe has certainly spread outside
the JEU region and is no longer limited to the $10,000-plus-per-
capita GDP club. The new tribe includes the enlightened and curious
in developing and underdeveloped countries. They have a tendency
to follow three rules in Internet behavior, which I call, at least in
Japan, Ohmae's theorems:

- **Theorem 1:** Cyberites who have used the Internet for five
  years or more tend to think, act, and behave similarly.

  Those who are living and breathing on the global stage tend to
  share information with each other and, over time, may come to
  belong to a separate cybercivilization than their mind-locked,
  nation-state heritage. This is not so obvious in the first couple
  of years after they first plug into the Internet. For example,
  Chinese and Americans tend to access different sites. The
  interactions they engage in tend to be quite local in nature. But
  from their third year on the Internet and onward, the cyberites
  become more adventurous. They tend to go to Amazon; they
  acquire digital cameras and start using them to compile pictures into albums. They also download music and fiddle with
  the Excels and PowerPoints of the world.

  In their fifth year of online experience, they exhibit amazing
  mobility in the cyberjungle and acquire skills to orient themselves with cyber "GPS," such as Google. Consequently, they
  develop confidence and start ordering goods from online sites,
  such as Victoria's Secret. They then have them delivered by
  courier and are fully aware of their own national governments'
  idiosyncrasies and petty attempts to stifle or at least hamper e-
  commerce. They eventually become more global in outlook
  than the narrow nationalists they may have been at the start.
  They want to buy the best and cheapest from anywhere in the
  world: They are confident that they can live well under the liberated regime of a truly global environment.

- **Theorem 2:** (Age – 10) ÷ 10 is the number of years it takes for anybody to become a true cyberite. It takes longer to "unlearn" accumulated twentieth-century assumptions and myths, depending on how long you lived in that century and were exposed to them. The young generation, who start playing on the Internet at the age of five or six, do not have the same problem. They have less to unlearn and fewer problems learning the rules and games of the cyberworld. For example, a 20-year old will become a perfect cyberite in a year or so—(20 – 10) ÷ 10 = 1—whereas a 40-year old will take three years at least—(40 – 10) ÷ 10 = 3. This is a rule of thumb and nothing scientific, but it fits with my observations of people around me.

- **Theorem 3:** Cyberites are proactive consumers. This has profound implications for marketing and media strategies. People are basically passive when watching TV. They want to be entertained, whether the program is entertainment or not. They do not want to take notes or act on what they see, even when good advice or information is broadcast. We remember portions of certain useful tips and hints, but seldom write them down or otherwise record them. This is one of the reasons why TV advertising, while effective, costs dearly and often does not pay adequate commercial returns. The overall impact may be a little better when a newspaper ad catches a reader's attention: The reader may tear out the page, make a clipping, or call the number, if necessary. But such a response rarely hits 1 out of 10,000 or 100 responses per million subscribers.

  But if a cyberite types words into his favorite search engine, such as "pants big waist," "bad sun burn," or "Japanese management guru," his chance of actually making the discovery or buying the product is quite high.

So the cyberites who have become the *de facto* residents of cyberspace take a very proactive stance, regardless of their nationalities, cultural backgrounds, or upbringing. As a result, narrowcasting on the target page of the search engine's findings or search engine–triggered advertising is a far more effective promotional method than advertising in traditional broadcast or print media. During their first or second year of surfing, visitors to the Internet do not take such a proactive stance with confidence, but a true cyberite does. That is why search engine synchronized advertising (SESA) is now a crucial practice for marketers and why using the latest SEO technologies is key.

Paying the Bill: The Payment Revolution

The payment system is important because Internet purchases must be settled in some way. In Japan, cash payment upon delivery is still dominant because people do not want to release their credit-card details into the cyberuniverse. Ever since the cashless Mondex experiment took place in Swindon, in the United Kingdom in July 1995, just about everyone of importance in the cybercommunity has tried to come up with an e-commerce payment system or electronic wallet. But to date, there is no established global platform of settlement. The credit-card companies, Visa and MasterCard, are still the most frequently used payment instruments, though they are not tailor-made for e-settlement.

One of the problems is that if you browse through a number of different Web sites, you don't want to punch in the same information over and over again. For large portal sites such as MSN, Yahoo!, Amazon, and AOL, credit-card information is carried over from site to site after a single password-enabled sign-in. This concept is close to the idea of an e-wallet, but it still lacks portability from one portal to another.

Sony's EDY (euro-dollar-yen) is a non-contact IC card–based technology where airline mileage and real money can be stored in its prepaid chip. A low-cost terminal can be attached to the USB port of any computer, and payment is easily made as with Mondex. A significant number of retail outlets in Japan are already equipped to accept the card. However, like any other system, it faces a big hurdle unless the card reader and money loader terminals are installed literally in all corners of Japan and eventually the world. Sony has made the technology available to any company. As a result, more than 50 companies participate, including banks, credit-card companies, manufacturers, telephone service providers, and amusement parks. Since its inception in April 2002, the operating company, bitWallet, has acquired 3.8 million customers and 3,700 outlets (as of January 2004). A significant breakthrough was achieved when NTT DoCoMo and KDDI, two of the three Japanese mobile phone operators, joined the group. Both companies are eager to increase revenue in a field that is already nearing saturation. One way of doing this that they have identified is to make use of the concept of the "smart phone," capable of doing far more than merely making calls or accessing the Internet.

In the summer of 2004, DoCoMo unveiled a number of smart phones that use EDY technology. A customer pays for goods using the smart phone that, in addition to storing credit-card information, can store "cash" in electronic form on its chip. Fortunately, mobile phones are more popular than PC-based e-commerce in Japan, due to the high usage of the Internet through packet networks. Because all Japanese cell phones are equipped with infrared ports, they can make payments through the PC as well. Of course, if the PC does not have an infrared port, the mobile phone can make the payment by accessing the PC's site through Internet mode communications. DoCoMo has come to agreements with nearly 40 retailers, including All Nippon Airways and convenience store operator AM-PM Japan, who have agreed to accept payments by smart phone. It is to be hoped that this will finally work and that EDY can become a platform for e-commerce settlement.

On the Rails

Japanese railway companies are not standing still while Sony takes over the e-wallet battlefield. The East Japan Railway Co. has introduced a noncontact IC-based payment card to go through the passenger gates at stations. This is known as Suica (Super Urban Intelligent Card) and is similar to the Octopus card now provided in Hong Kong and is used by tens of millions of commuters who have season tickets. Suica can also be used to purchase goods and services within the premises of railway stations. This opens up huge possibilities—stations such as Shinjuku in Tokyo have more than five million people passing through them every day. Add on more services, and it becomes even better. A card that allows passengers to pass onto the platform is one thing, but a card that allows them to do this in addition to, say, buy a newspaper or some candy, has convenience built into it.

The Suica card does not have a credit-card function, but a similar card in the Kansai area of Osaka, known as Surutto Kansai, does. In fact, the "Suru-Kan" offers three functions: a prepaid card (as with Suica), a credit card, and a post-paid card. It is the last function that is going to be the mainstream of future payment systems. Already most Japanese public utility bills are automatically debited from customers' bank accounts at the end of the month or a few days after their salary is paid. This is inherently a frictionless arrangement because there is no credit-card company holding the position of a middleman.

If you go one step further into cyberspace, most people are ubiquitously interconnected. So, if you need to check a person's creditworthiness, it is easily verified through a mobile phone, PC, or PDA by accessing the person's time deposit account or some equivalent instruments. I patented a system, known as Debit with Float, along with Dr. Kazuma Tateishi, founder of Omron, in 1982 in both Japan and the United States. If the amount of savings far exceeds the purchases, the individual can get a personal credit line by agreeing to have the deposit collateralized—in effect, locked—until the payment is made. In other words, in a ubiquitous society, you are able to prove your own creditworthiness no matter where you are, as long as the system is built to look up one of your accounts. This is the most friction-free system of settlement that can be used in real-world shopping and in e-commerce. We no longer need a credit-card company to represent our creditworthiness with respect to the merchants and compensate them if we do not make the payment.

The late Dr. Tateishi and I spent hours trying to think through the implications of the cashless society. Many of the visions we had 20 years ago have become reality, thanks to the advance of the networked society, but many are still at the embryonic stage because of regulations, reluctant industry associations, and sector domination by cozy companies.

Delivery: The Logistics Revolution

The final part of the revolution is taking place in logistics, the physical distribution of goods. Traditionally, this was thought of in terms of chains. These include supply chains, a line of discrete but interconnected and interdependent processes leading from the acquisition of raw materials to the delivery of the finished product, to either the customer, the retailer or another manufacturer for further processing. In the 1980s, Harvard Business School's Michael Porter added to this concept with his theory of a value chain.

Behind it all, there is still a physical chain apparently determining what can be moved and how. In the United States, 68 percent of freight is still moved by road, 12 percent by rail, and 7 percent by water. A hundred years after the Wright Brothers' pioneering flight, air traffic still accounts for less than 0.1 percent of American goods transported.

Once again, much of the revolution stems from the availability of new technologies. This revolution is ongoing. It is a response to a major reorganization of the whole trading environment. The traditional division between wholesalers and retailers, embracing everything from billion-dollar companies to mom-and-pop stores, is anachronistic. Warehouses and inventory are still important, but more decisive are distribution centers. The relationship between the product provider (who may also be the producer) and the end consumer has been simplified, even collapsed, by e-commerce.

The need to move components in industrial and manufactured processes, as well as the need to transport finished products to market, has had a significant impact on both the logistics industry itself and on some far-seeing and sensitive sections of the business world.

One of the corporations that epitomizes so much of the global economy, Dell, realized the importance of optimal logistics in its overall operations. It manufactures computers to individual orders, received either by traditional telephone contacts or in response to form-based questionnaires on the Internet. It uses its own platform for assembling and processing orders. This has been so successful for Dell that one of its biggest rivals in providing PCs to the home market, Gateway Computers, has devised a similar platform for order acquisition. In the case of Dell, the orders are received, but then a lot of the remainder of the process, both the delivery of the components to the final assembly line and its shipment to the customer, is dealt with by a logistics company, FedEx. Orders arrive, by whatever method, from anywhere and everywhere. Not all orders then go to a central Dell warehouse. Some go to a warehouse managed by FedEx, where key computer components (processors, motherboards, input devices, monitors, and so on) have been temporarily assembled in JIT inventories for packaging to customers. FedEx's staff deals with the shipment of modules according to Dell's specifications and rushes the product to the customer in one box. UPS is establishing a similar seamless service.

Dell and FedEx have given birth to a new type of business entity, one that seems peculiarly suited to the global economy. We can call this a virtual single company (VSC).

In the Dell model, an operator (customer relationship manager) who receives a call from the customer plays multiple roles, ranging from order-taker to procurement order issuer, to vendor and subcontractor. There is no longer the value chain in a system like this because a pivotal customer interface is actually triggering the production process and JIT component delivery, while alerting the logistics partners about the forthcoming delivery schedule. The CRM then ensures the delivery of finished products, usually in a week's time after receiving the order, and follows up for cross-selling printers and other peripheral systems.

Many Japanese companies have tried to emulate Dell but have concluded that it is simply not possible to change their existing business systems. In a way, Dell was created on a green field location in 1984. The fact that it was not imprisoned by the legacy of old value chain thinking was why it was able to create a VSC on the enterprise resource planning (ERP) platform. Had it established a long value chain of distribution, it would have been very difficult to bypass the wholesale/retail outlets. The fact that more than 70 percent of Dell's sales are to corporations is also a factor that contributes to its efficiency. Had it been focusing on consumers (as Gateway did), it would have needed a much heavier customer support function. Because of their affinity with existing customers, and vice versa, Dell's CRMs can now sell printers and other appliances without middlemen or distribution agents.

Dell gets the headlines quite rightly, but it is no longer alone. There are many more logistics revolutionaries. Inditex, a Spanish apparel giant located in La Coruña, is another example of exceptional just-in-time supply chain management. In this case, the company's largest global brand, Zara, receives orders not directly from customers, but from 2,000 store managers twice a week. The CRM operator then delivers the products within 48 hours to any location in the world. Its delivery process uses trucks within continental Europe, but outside Europe, the company uses DHL as its alliance partner. The logistics center in La Coruña alone has an area of more than $500,000m^2$, and its sorting system (apparently learned from FedEx) looks like an express train spitting out items into the boxes destined for each of its stores. The products on hangers, such as dresses, go into a container with handles, so there is no need to press before display at the stores. Zara stores do not have inventory space, nor do they need it, because the products are delivered as they are sold. This is a remarkably different business system from that used by anyone else in the industry, where orders are placed in large quantities a few seasons ahead; they often miss the target by a huge margin, and the excess stock ends up on bargain floors.

These developments have had a major impact on the logistics industry itself. Federal Express has become far more than a delivery service: It is now a major logistics partner of Dell. In such relationships, the partners work so closely together that they appear almost to be a single corporate entity. The traditional demarcation lines have been blurred.

FedEx calls its strategic section the Logistic and Electronic Commerce (LEC) division. Although it still earns a great deal from its "traditional" parcel delivery activities, it aims to make money by insinuating itself in a vital way into other companies' supply chains, not just Dell's. By utilizing new technical platforms, FedEx can offer a whole new type of service to customers. A further example of FedEx's movement away from its traditional core is provided by one of its subsidiaries, FedEx Trade Networks, which collates information on matters affecting cross-border trade, such as Customs duties and tax information. It can also identify the location of any package all the way from the taking of the order, through the assembly of components, to the delivery of finished products.

Companies such as FedEx, UPS, and DML are becoming a platform in themselves. Smaller, less resourceful companies than Dell can plug into FedEx's LEC division and become as competitive as a larger corporation.

What all this means for senior managers is that an increasing part of their role is to determine which core skills to keep and nurture inside the company, and which services can be procured from outside. The key is to keep the customer interface strong. When the service is delivered, the customer does not know the identity of all the members of the coalition.

The Arrival of the Micro Tag

The issue of logistics will be further developed by the micro tag. A micro (or *mu*) tag is, on average, only 0.5mm square. It can be buried in products such as books, clothes, or anything that is not going to be eaten. In a few years, most items, except perhaps for fresh food, will have *mu* tags built into them. This will represent the products' ID card, with a radio frequency capability so that it can be remotely detected. The *mu* tag will be read at the point of sale by dedicated equipment that will also be able to pass on to the chip the details of the person to whom the item is being sold.

This will revolutionize physical distribution and merchandising. It will change the point-of-sale system and inventory control, and make the cost of reuse (as in rugs and laundry) cheaper.

For example, the operator of a laundry will read the chip and know immediately whose shirt he is washing. A lot of the book publication industry will change. There will no longer be a need to deface books by writing one's name on the flyleaf. Shoplifting will become increasingly difficult, if not impossible. A book (or any item), once stolen, will be a marked item. Few people will want to try to resell it because it will immediately identify itself as stolen. This technology can also be applied to rental videos and DVDs.

These *mu* tags have the potential to radically change retailing, through point-of-sale co-ordination, as well as inventory management. Once a person picks an item from a shelf, this is immediately recorded and fed into the store's stock control software. The purchaser then need only walk past a point-of-sales checkout with the requisite equipment. There is no need for each item to be individually checked out. As a result, passing through the checkout can be as simple as walking by with a shopping trolley. Payment can then be made remotely, the amount being automatically extracted from the purchaser's account. There will be no delays and no long queues. The act of shopping will become quicker and less stressful.

The introduction of *mu* tags will also revolutionize e-commerce because it will allow individual items to be monitored. This has long been a problem in the world of logistics, which deals with the movement of large volumes of goods. The larger the individual item is, the greater the prospect is of individualizing its relevant data, but books and clothing are too small and too numerous to be individually monitored. With their embedded *mu* tags, each book, each sweater, or even a can of fruit-juice, can be followed. Once *mu* tags are installed in products, a company can convert its manufacturing system to Just-in-Time more readily, as they know exactly what models, size, and color are selling where and when. This further reduces the need for large inventories.

One area that might be resistant to the application of *mu* tag technology is the fresh-food sector. The tag is, by its nature inedible, so it cannot readily be inserted into an item that is to be wholly consumed. This could be overcome with certain food items such as fresh fish, where the tag could be inserted into the tail or some other part that traditionally is not consumed. The tag could also be inserted into packaging of semiprocessed food items. Eventually, a smaller chip will be developed that can be glued to the price tag or label. This is precisely the area Professor Ken Sakamara of the University of Tokyo is working on with his group, known as the e-TRON project. The logistics industry is very excited by these developments, though their full implications are not yet clear.

The *mu* tag is the invention of the Japanese company Hitachi and will first make an impact in Japan, where, within the next three or four years, its use will become widespread. Its first widespread application is now contemplated for the Expo fair in Nagoya in Aichi Prefecture, where the chip will be mounted on an entrance ticket. This will enable the organizers to tailor-make service for each of the 15 million expected visitors during 2005.

Cool Chains and Fresh Food

On the global stage, much of the logistics process is now containerized and standardized into homogenous chains, depending on the items being transported. These might be cool chains, in which the temperature in the containers is maintained at 7°C the world over. For perishable items such as food, there is a frozen chain and then a normal temperature chain. This guarantees a seamless transportation from point A to point B.

In the Shandong peninsular on the southern shores of the Yellow Sea, there are farmers who grow fresh vegetables for delivery to the Tokyo market. Thanks to logistics, they are able to deliver their produce as quickly as suburban market gardeners in the Tokyo area. The distance between the Shandong peninsular and Tokyo is now as short as that between Chiba and Tokyo's central markets.

This is not completely novel. The world has for many years been exposed to the phenomenon of shipments by plane to the four corners of the world of the first wines from the Beaujolais area. Each November, hundreds of enthusiasts from around the world descend upon eastern France to carry on board crates of the young wine for delivery to the world's finest restaurants, or simply to a small circle of friends. This has always been attended with an element of fanfare and media buzz, not to mention occasional danger. But a similar phenomenon takes place every day between Shandong and Tokyo without anyone noticing.

What was once a spectacle is now common. Look at fresh seafood. Raw oysters are flown from Tasmania and Chesapeake Bay by cool chain cargo air transport for consumption in Japanese restaurants. This type of food transport was once considered impossible. But now, it is common using available logistics platforms. In this instance, one of the platforms developed by cool chain specialist Nichirei was able to bring fresh-food products by this means using air cargo to Japan. Products now literally come from the seven seas. The Japanese are the world's greatest consumers of shrimps and fresh fish. It is as easy to fly raw oysters from Tasmania to Tokyo as to fly them in from Atsukeshi, Hokkaido. The only constraint is that it must be capable of being carried out within 24 hours. A sushi restaurant in Taipei, Taiwan, imports raw fish from Fukuoka, Japan, every morning so that it can have fresh *nigiri* for lunch and dinner on the same day. The success of this chain lay in convincing the Customs office in Taipei about the importance of just-in-time delivery.

Such shipments, no matter what the product, are impossible without a very good and efficient platform for taking in orders and feedback to the client about the product's progress. With the transport of food, there must also be rigorous control of hygiene throughout the system. The route will probably cross many borders and time zones. Seamless physical distribution chains now have been established by specialist logistic companies.

This causes some conceptual changes, including how we view the world around us. There has been a change in the notion of the suburb. This used to be an area lying on the periphery of a great city such as Tokyo. They grew outward as the city expanded. In a city such as London, the suburbs are residential areas. This is true also of Tokyo, but they used to be the location of a market-gardening zone that grew fresh vegetables for the city. There were also maritime suburbs, whose fishermen caught and sold fresh "fish of the day." This phenomenon is not confined to Japan: It is to be found in any large city on the coast. If we hold on to the definition of a suburb as a fresh-food production belt for the larger city, the applications of logistics mean that Tokyo's suburbs have become any point on the planet within 12 hours' flying time. So the restaurants and diners of Tokyo and other large cities can now enjoy fresh food from around the world. If you visit a sushi restaurant in Tokyo, you will find that less then 10 percent of the fish served is Japanese. India is the largest supplier of tuna to the Japanese market. It, too, is transported by air. This was impossible five years ago. Now it is, thanks to the development of seamless logistics platforms. This is a real, fundamental change to lifestyles.[1]

Deliverance

Another area that will increasingly be impacted by the logistics revolution is the mail. Postal services have strangely tended to be divorced from thinking about logistics. After all, they are dedicated to the delivery of items of postage: postcards, letters, and parcels. A "national" postal service with its own postage stamps was considered yet another of the fetishes of the nation state. Many have responded to deregulation by spawning logistics companies and other services, such as fast delivery options. But by being tied to old and misplaced loyalties, postal services are one area of logistics that have not always shown revolutionary improvements.

It is hard to make money delivering parcels or letters within the confines of the nation-state. There may not be enough people, or they may live in awkward places. No matter how remote their location, they will usually demand personalized delivery, whether it is a large parcel or a single letter. Individual post offices have to be located throughout the state's territory. Sorters and other postal staff are sometimes wedded to antiquated and outmoded work practices. And the post office has to provide its services at a price level that often demands heavy government subsidization.

In Japan, the standard rate for domestic letters is 80 yen. In real terms, it is possible to send a letter from Hong Kong to anywhere in Japan, by airmail, for the equivalent of only 13 yen. Not surprisingly, an enterprising group of individuals set up a business flying bulk postal items from Japan to Hong Kong and individually posting them back to Japan. The Japanese government responded in a traditional nation-state way: It banned the practice. Now items of mail are sent using e-mail to Hong Kong, where they are printed, put in envelopes, and mailed back to Japan. Such a practice cannot be interfered with because the most important part of it takes place using the Internet protocol of e-mail.

"Traditional" postal services face many challenges. The advent of e-mail is obviously one of them. But there is still a tendency to see postal services as part of a communications matrix. In Japan, the same ministry that deals with IT matters oversees the postal service. This dates from a time when postal services were lumped with telephone and telegraph deliveries as part of the one communications sector. Yet nowadays these are two very different animals, belonging almost to different universes. Postal services must be seen much more in terms of logistics and governed more by the same trends.

The success of Deutsche Poste has been due to the foresight of its CEO, Claus Zumwinkel, in breaking its operations into three discrete units: mail, parcels, and banking. While the bank has been spun off to outside investors to generate cash, DP is now focusing on parcels so that its subsidiary, DHL, can compete with logistics giants such as FedEx and UPS.

Using Logistics to Solve Bigger Problems

The revolution in logistics and food distribution can have a major impact on "domestic" food production, if we allow ourselves to be liberated from traditional stereotypes of the nation-state and what constitutes "domestic" production.

We can import land for food production. No, this does not mean transporting large swathes of turf and heathland, but rather a shift in emphasis away from fixed borders and mindsets.

In Japan, rice is produced at ten times the cost of production in parts of Australia, California, and Thailand. This is uneconomical, but due to a dense raft of protection and tariffs, it is possible for the domestic rice producer to go on gathering his rice harvests from his uneconomic paddy-fields and selling it to consumers who seem ready to consume it, albeit at a high price.

Japanese farmers are fanatically opposed to importing rice, even though this would be cheaper for Japanese consumers. A solution might be to shift the discussion to land importation. The Japanese government pays billions of yen in subsidies to rice farmers. They could be given this money on condition that it is used to buy land in, say, Australia, which could then be leased or rented to local producers for growing rice acceptable to Japanese consumers. About $20 million would buy enough land and water rights in Australia to produce 300,000 tons of rice, 3 percent of Japanese rice demand. The Japanese farmers could go to Australia and grow the rice themselves, or they could employ local managers under contract. An investment of $1.2 billion would be enough to acquire sufficient land for satisfying the entire domestic demand for rice. This may seem like a huge investment, but the Japanese government has already subsidized its rice farmers to the tune of $400 billion over the last 10 years. The Japanese government could say that it has imported the land because it has been bought by Japanese farmers, although it still forms part of the sovereign territory of another country.

It doesn't matter that the land is far away. There is still food security, a major worry of those supporting protection to Japanese rice farmers. The rice is secured until eternity for Japanese consumers. There might be worries about concentrating so much of Japan's food source in one country, such as Australia, but part of it could be produced in California, Arkansas, Ukraine, or Thailand. Ten million tons of rice would be imported into Japan: It would be the type of short-grain rice preferred by Japanese people. Because precious land would no longer be devoted to uneconomic rice cultivation, there would be an increase in the amount of land available for house construction. Presently, many people cannot afford their own homes because land values are too high. Consequently, land prices would fall and there would be opportunities not just for more houses to be constructed, but for bigger and more comfortable homes. The country would have imported land and would have more land to use.

There would be opponents to these policies both in Japan and in the source country for the imported land. They would say that this is a form of "colonization by cash." But such a process is effectively happening with items such as iron ore, coal, and oil. Rather than being seen as colonization, it should be viewed as a clever use of money and available resources. It is a natural process of optimization on a global scale. The land mass of Japan cannot be increased. Japan is not the Netherlands, with possibilities for large-scale reclamation from the sea. Japan can dictate the quality of land it imports.

This is a twenty-first-century paradigm for solving many problems: expensive food and shortage of resources. It also improves the quality of life for many people. It is preferable to trying to solve a country's problems by tweaking "solutions" that are known to be doomed to failure. This is what I mean by the global economy.

This is a solution not just to Japanese problems. It could also be of assistance to countries such as France and Switzerland. If we accept that land can be imported in this way for growing crops cheaper than they can be grown at home, a solution is at hand. It exists on the global basis, not within the narrow confines of a nation-state.

This is a *de facto* redistribution of wealth to the rest of the world. The provision of subsidies to inefficient sectors of a nation-state's economy is a waste of wealth. It is also a selfish use of wealth when a portion of it could be used to the benefit of other countries. So the global stage can be expanded not only in manufacturing and cross-border BPO, but also in the use of land for agriculture and fisheries.

The logistics revolution has had an impact on many areas, bringing them closer together, collapsing traditional barriers such as time and distance. It has compelled many people to look at concepts such as space and difference, and ask, "Are they really barriers?" But we are not yet able to speak definitively about the impact of the logistics revolution because it is ongoing. It has the potential to have some startling and positive effects on our world—and on our psychology. The extent to which these potentials will be fulfilled lies with human beings. Technology has supplied the answers. Are we brave and imaginative enough to apply them?

For Dinner

To answer, all you need do is to look at your dinner table. This is the global stage, full of food from the four corners of the Earth. You may not know it, but in addition to the salmon coming from Chile, flour from Canada, and broccoli from Australia, the sauces and spices come from an array of countries—pepper from Brazil, Worcestershire sauce from the U.K. (its constituent ingredients from China or Southeast Asia), and so on.

The table mat may come from China, your favorite Herend china from Hungary, Christofle silverware from France, and Bohemian glassware from the Czech Republic or Waterford Crystal from Ireland. Thanks to the low cost of logistics, the shortening of the distribution chain, and easing of Customs restrictions, the price of all these items in Japan or in the United States is not very different than where they were produced. If that is not the case, the cyberites are going to arbitrage and discipline old-fashioned incumbents until they stand to proper attention. Although that is not a good excuse to eat and drink more, it is one of the net benefits of the global economy.

Notes

[1]   One of the top Japanese restaurants in New York's Tribecca area, MEGU, is doing the reverse. It imports fresh fish and certain vegetables from Japan on a daily basis.

PART III: THE SCRIPT

8

REINVENTING GOVERNMENT

The global stage demands a new script. This new script requires that the major players change how they act and think. This applies to individuals as well as institutions, whether they are corporations, unions, campaigning groups, investors, regional governments, or national governments.

Disappearing Power

First, let us consider how governments must change on the global stage. There can be no escaping the reality that on the global stage, the role of governments is completely different. Governments have conventionally considered themselves as repositories of power. Now, however, central governments will find that a lot of their power has gone. They may even believe themselves to be totally impotent without the powers that they once thought were vital. In a borderless world, the strong, powerful central government will be a thing of the past. Some governments may still try to hold on to the lingering delusions of this power, but they will appear increasingly ridiculous. The more they try to exert pressure on the no-longer-working pedals of power, the more pathetic and impotent they will appear.

Governments and politicians need to ask themselves these questions:

- Does the government constantly encourage people to think positively in terms of interaction with the rest of the world?

- Is there too much bureaucracy preventing government and regions from taking initiatives?

- Are the right incentives in place to promote such initiatives?

- Is the nation-state hindering such initiatives?

- Is the rest of the world bringing in fresh capital, new technologies, and dynamic companies into regions because they are attractive in comparison to other regions?

- Can enough companies succeed and impetus be created?

- Is there a good, clear, unobstructed, unhindered chain of command?

- Are there "brokers" in the center giving different orders and sending contradictory messages?

- Are any specific special-interest groups (traditionally, national trades unions) or political lobbies (farm groups and many others) opposed to the regions taking initiatives?

Inevitably, some governments have more answers than others. In some countries, the relationship between the center and regions is historically looser and more accommodating to the global economy. In the United States, a president who tells a particular state what to do would be considered a bad president. (Worse, he would be an unconstitutional president.) Americans would resist such interference. In Japan, by contrast, people are told from early on to look to and respect central authority. This is a conditioned obedience. Listening to Tokyo, doing its bidding, and not annoying it offers better short-term results. That way, more resources are distributed from the center. The obedient dog is rewarded with more bones; the disobedient one is punished. This punishment can take the form of reductions in budget allocation from taxes or a lack of approval for new projects. Roughly 40 percent of taxes in Japan are collected by the regions; 60 percent is collected by the central government, but the central government spends only 40 percent of the tax taken and provides 20 percent to be redistributed to the regions. This is where the power of the central bureaucracy lies. The redistribution of this 20 percent is at the discretion of the central bureaucrats. This tranche is, in overall terms, big enough to make each region pay obedient attention to central government.

Japan's government structure clearly needs to change. There are 47 prefectures. Each of them is too small, except for Tokyo-to, which has 13 million people. Some of the smaller prefectures have only 600,000 people; they are too small to be autonomous and to interact with the rest of the world. The amalgamation of some of these prefectures into larger *Doshu* regions would make more natural regional units of maybe three million to six million people (with the exceptions of Kanto and Kansai). Japan could be divided into 11 *Doshu*, each one of which would have an average of 10 million people. The Kanto region (embracing Tokyo) already has a GDP that places it ahead of France, while Kansai (around Osaka) has a GDP higher than Canada's. Even the second smallest of the *Doshu*, the island of Shikoku, is the size of Denmark. The smallest of the cohort are the Okinawa islands, with 1.2 million people. (Because of its historical ties with China and geographical location in the East China Sea, I propose it should be an autonomous *Doshu* rather than joined with the island of Kyushu.)

Although strong central control contributed to the rapid growth of Japan from 1945 until 1980, many of Japan's problems can now be traced back to its leaden-handed centralized system of government. It is hard to see how Japan can effectively emerge from the economic doldrums without making significant reforms in its governance structure. Already the borrowing ratio compared to GDP is 140 percent—higher than any other OECD nation (even Italy's). Because the rest of the world doesn't invest in Japan and taxpayers are not willing to carry the burden, the Japanese government has been borrowing from the future by issuing national bonds against which there are no complaints from the current generation. So, it is no wonder that, according to *Moody's* (May 2002), Japan's national debt bond is rated at A2. This is the lowest level for a developed country and the same level as that of Botswana. With respect to Botswana (probably Africa's most stable country), this is not impressive for Japan.

In Japan, as elsewhere, there is an appetite for change. But not surprisingly, there is no will to change where it is needed most: at the center. The classic attitude of "If it ain't broken, why fix it?" prevails.

Demands for change require an intellectual *coup*. In the absence of a unilateral declaration of autonomy or an armed rebellion, there must be dialogue between the center and the regions. Who is to initiate this dialogue? The center is hardly likely to do anything that it senses will lead to a loss of its powers. Maybe if a political party were to make such regionalization the plank of its electoral manifesto, there might be some progress. But although some politicians might understand the importance of these reforms, they usually lack both the courage and the intellectual creativity to take the much-needed next step.

Beyond Distribution

Today's intellectual battle is between old government and new. Put simply, the traditional role of government is concerned with the distribution of wealth and prosperity. Governments are wealth *distributors*, not wealth *facilitators*: They do not create wealth. This wealth is acquired through taxation, and it is in this form that many people experience governmental intervention in their lives.

In terms of taxation, I believe that ultimately the region-state should be the source of tax raises; concomitantly, taxes raised in a prosperous area should remain there, as far as political expediency allows. We have seen how advances in technology and new technology platforms have the potential to make raising taxes much simpler and less expensive. But the fact remains that some taxation is still necessary (though, to be successful, it should appear as just as possible).

The best way to achieve this is through simplification. Throughout the Western world, taxation appears to taxpayers and corporations as a minefield of gargantuan complexity. It can appear chaotic, its secrets known only to the initiates who control its operation, whom many people suspect of making up the rules as they go along, with the result that they always win and the taxpayer always loses.

With this complexity reduced, the taxpayers would be responsible for paying their share, but this would be more straightforward. It might eventually be possible to eliminate the intermediary role of the taxman altogether.

As distributors of wealth, governments have gone down the road of developing welfare states and welfare economics. They see their role as protecting domestic companies, their home population, and certain regions that are considered vulnerable or disadvantaged.

These industries are usually globally weak. Large governments worry about protecting home-grown industries, and they use taxpayers' money to do this. At a global level, strong companies, whether from America, Europe, or the Far East, have become stronger than ever, often taking advantage of new borderless opportunities. The cyberites are impatient and won't accept second best. They want to buy the best and cheapest, wherever it is in the world.

Efforts by big governments to tempt the cyberites are as hapless as they are hopeless. For example, in 2003, Japan launched an "Invest in Japan" campaign, which had the blessing and active support of Prime Minister Junichiro Koizumi. This program is ironic, given that Koizumi's government (and its predecessors) have spent so much money protecting the weakest sections of industry and the economy in general. In 2003, Japan, the world's second-largest economy, received only $6 billion in foreign direct investment (FDI). China received $54 billion (see Exhibit 8.1). From the point of view of global investors, Japan appears to have ceased to exist. Today, China is the largest recipient of foreign direct investment, a position it took over from the United States under President Clinton (see Exhibit 8.2). It is clear from this that President Bush's policies, such as tax cuts and lower interest rates, have not been well received by the global FDI community.

China: Almost a Monopoly of Foreign Capital Inflow to Asia
Foreign Direct Investment

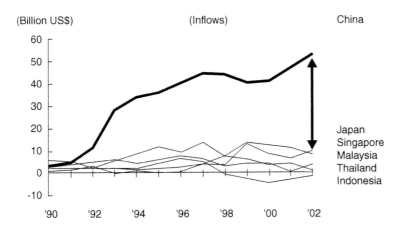

Source: UNCTAD.

Exhibit 8.1   FDI in Asia.

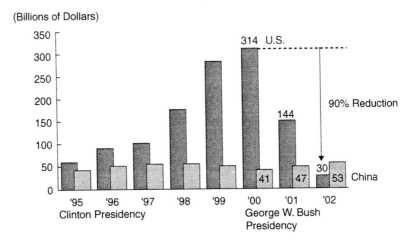

Foreign Direct Investment

Source: UNCTAD.

Exhibit 8.2   Growth in China FDI, compared with the U.S.

Size Matters

Part of the mentality of the distributive state is that whatever wealth is being distributed should be spread evenly and fairly throughout the country. This leads to the dream of the civic minimum, as in Japan, where each region of the country is statutorily entitled to a minimum of public services, no matter how remote and underpopulated it may be.

An integral—perhaps inevitable—part of traditional distributive government is bureaucracy. Bureaucracies are wedded to strong, central government. Without it, their *raison d'être* becomes shakier. We can look at China and the schizophrenia that often reigns in its regulatory sphere. On the one hand, there are the dictates from Beijing, the center. These can then be compared with the actions of mayors and governors in areas such as Qintao and Dalian who often do things that are contrary to the letter—and to the spirit—of government policy (which may be pretty vague anyway). Some might see this as anarchy, as evidence of lawlessness, nothing less than a breakdown in government control. Others would see it as pragmatism and flexibility in action.

Governments of the future that want to remain vibrant and relevant must accept some hefty changes in what they do. They must seek to facilitate rather than frustrate. They must also start to examine time in a new way. The public service of any country must be prepared to work more on short-term projects with identifiable goals than to enter into a permanent employment regime.

Much governmental activity in China is pragmatic, as I have said, and governments throughout the world should learn the value of flexibility. They should never be imprisoned by ideology or old ways of thinking. This pragmatism has to seep out into the acts of governments themselves so that governments think about new ways of governing. None of this brainstorming should be left solely to governments; other agencies and inputs must be sought.

Downsizing and Resizing

Only an anarchist advocates the dissolution of government altogether. There are still areas in which governments can work effectively, sometimes hand in hand with private sector involvement, but even here they must face a radically changed landscape. The simple bottom line is that governments should not try to do things for business, but should allow business to do things for itself.

The cornerstone of the reinvention of government is that the dimensions of government must change. It is a truism in economics that the best government is small government. It is so much of a truism that its true relevance to the global economy may be lost.

The role of central governments in the global economy is the opposite of what they are used to doing. Their best service to their people is to invite in capital so they don't have to use taxpayers' money, to welcome corporations so they bring in jobs and take over weak companies so the government does not have to subsidize them.

The most important reason for why diminutive status matters is that this is the way to interface with the rest of the world. Wealth is abundant in today's world. The developed countries cannot possibly use all the money piled up in pensions and savings within their home countries. They could waste it on public works, as the Japanese government has done. The return on investment is so poor that the pension program itself is going to be dumped, only to arouse popular ire. The region-state that aspires to be prosperous in the global economy should be organized to attract some of this wealth from the rest of the world.

The smaller the government is and the more open it is to wealth and investment from outside, the greater the payback will be for the region-state. Its people will also be better off. In the era of the traditional nation-state, a political entity might be wealthy because it inherited this bounty from its predecessors. It might be factor rich, with abundant fertile land and mineral resources. Alternatively, it could rob the wealth from others, either as a pirate, as a colonist, or through military conquest. During the Industrial Revolution, wealth was augmented by hard work, and the advent and ownership of technology allowed some states, such as Germany, to become prosperous without much robbery.

This might be termed the British route to prosperity, which was then adopted and pushed much further in the United States. This industrial growth model was dependant on trade with other countries because none possessed all the requisite natural resources for the domestic industrial complex.

Today, the situation is different. It no longer matters if a country or region-state does not have its own well-established domestic industry or home markets. What is important is to have an educated and motivated workforce—on the factory floor, in the computer room, or in the provision of professional services. This is now more important than mines. It is also a prerequisite to attract wealth from the rest of the world, which will always seek optimum locations for investment in the global economy. A region must also have good infrastructure, in both technology and logistics. It has traditionally been the role of government to provide physical infrastructure. In the last two decades, there has been a rise in public-private partnerships (PPPs) as a means of injecting efficiency into their provision. But behind the planning and the decision-making must be the goal of providing the best infrastructural solutions order to help generate prosperity. In particular, they must facilitate inward access to the region and outward access from the region to the markets by land, sea, and air. There have been far too many large-scale infrastructure projects of dubious use, whose only "benefits" have been to promote local contractors and other special-interest groups.

A Vision for Change

Change to a smaller, more dynamic form requires governments to do a number of things.

First, they must possess vision. The development of a long-term vision is one of the things that governments can—and must—be good at. I believe that having and communicating a vision is the most important thing that a government can do. This need not be, and no doubt should not be, the work of government alone. A vision should not be afraid of looking well into the future. Neither should it be afraid of being brave, possibly reckless, in its goals. The future is an uncertain sea to chart at the best of times. But it must not, and never should, remain in the realm of the speculative. There must be a vision that informs at all levels; at the level of government strategy and policies, how the government deals with its people and with other governments. It should inform even the smallest and seemingly most insignificant of official activities. This vision may well have a price tag, as in Singapore becoming the *de facto* capital of ASEAN, or Malaysia's Multimedia Super Corridor. A vision can be built around a concept, such as Ireland's e-hub idea. Sometimes, it does not need to be formalized in a policy, a slogan, or a set of documents.

Whoever is charged with the task of implementing the vision must not keep any secrets. It must be open and transparent. It must educate all sections of society on what they can and must do to make the realization of the vision a reality, and why they should do it. It should demonstrate what is "in it" for these people.

A vision must not be a mere collection of words and aspirations. It must contain clear, practical goals that can be pursued. Only by means of long-term commitment can it be affected. It demands from government a visionary approach, one that looks quite far into the future, farther than the next round of elections.

Coming up with a valid vision can be challenging. It has been made difficult in three ways. First, we now live in a borderless world, and no longer can we overemphasize the national interest first. Second, we are deeply married to IT and live in the labyrinth of cyberspace. Third, wealth creation is increasingly leveraged. A steady state growth rate of savings is no longer good enough to guarantee a safe and fun retirement at the end of your career. Borrowing from the bank, as in the previous century, is bad news for a corporation. Governments must come up with and deliver a vision that attracts a lot of global investors, resulting in high multiples.

The Japanese Vision

Japan's post–World War II "economic miracle" was the result of a vision called value-added trade (*kako boeki*). Japan has few minerals, so it had to import natural resources and add value and then export. The difference lies in the "value-added." Those who do not add value do not eat. The concept is simple and its direction clear. That is what Japan did for decades after its land was brought down to ashes.

Indeed, even after Japan achieved the second-highest per-capita GDP in the world, it kept its export engine at full throttle. It has not shifted down a gear, to "give people a better life with a lower cost of living"—a phrase I coined in my citizen's movement, the Reform of Heisei. This cannot be achieved unless we truly open up to the rest of the world.

If we aspire to have a good life, we would, in fact, increase economic growth in a country like Japan, where there is $14 trillion in savings frozen in low-interest-rate iceboxes. If this money is thawed, the money supply to the market would certainly be far more than the government could provide by borrowing from future generations.

Mapping the Future

Although it is not possible to spell out the exact map of the future, there are ways to develop a viable vision for a country along the already-known fundamentals of the global stage:

1. **It must empower individuals,** as it does in art, music, and sports. Although teamwork and group work will remain important in the future, it is clear that the wealth of a nation, region, and company is more dependent on how many "tall poppies" we can generate. As we have seen, not only the shift of wealth, but basic economies develop around towering individuals such as Michael Dell, Bill Gates, and Jorma Olilla. We have also seen certain educational institutions breed more entrepreneurs than others: Trinity College, Cambridge; Stanford University; Helsinki Institute of Technology; the University of Limerick in Ireland; and Qinhua University in Beijing. Exhibit 8.3 shows how universities have contributed to the creation of new enterprises. Here again, China is leveraging academia to boost knowledge-intensive industries in key cities with prestigious universities. Whereas the private sector is very dynamic in promoting innovation and entrepreneurship in Japan, its universities remain academic and have not emerged as a crucible for new businesses.

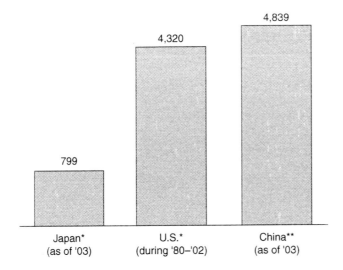

* Total number of start-ups. ** In operation.

Source: Ministry of Economy, Trade, and Industry, "AUTM Licensing Survey FY 2002," www.cutech.edu.cn/.

Exhibit 8.3   Ventures created by universities.

2. **It must invite capital from the rest of the world.** A region, not the nation, is the port of entry for prosperity. It is the strategic business unit for attracting and creating capital and corporations in the new global economy. A region must be like a first-class, five-star hotel. Singapore's prime minister, Lee Kwan Yew, told me in an interview in 1992 that the reason he had to discipline his countrymen was precisely because his country wanted to be the most desired "hotel" for global corporations in Asia. This means the hotel employees had to be trained, skilled, and disciplined so the guests could do business, relax, and enjoy their stay. He defended himself against Francis Fukuyama's accusations of operating a "benevolent dictatorship." If his people were relaxed and chewing gum in the lobby, the guests would leave. Whether the penalty for chewing gum or spitting in the street is justified can be debated, but there is no argument about the importance of being the best host for global corporations and consumers if a region wants to prosper by inviting capital and technology from the rest of the world.

3. **It must maintain an even keel.** A role for the central government is clearly that individuals are allowed to grow and shine, and that regions interact with the rest of the world. So the most important role for the center is to ensure that such a policy continues. After 9/11, the U.S. government has made the entry of foreign nationals very difficult by requiring a lot of personal and biometric information. Although there is a great deal of support and sympathy for the U.S. in its war against terrorism, it has nonetheless become a less desirable place to operate for multinationals. It was once the best and most comfortable modern hotel in which to stay and from which to operate.

Visions Versus Mirages

Many politicians say they have a vision. It is a good line—perfect for a sound bite on the evening news. It allows them to be associated with people like Martin Luther King. But, in effect, their visions are often verbal window-dressing and semantic long-windedness. A vision needs courage because it demands that all of the pieces of furniture that have traditionally been a part of the economy and political systems be looked at afresh and maybe subjected to some tough questions.

Government Vision

Governments at both the national and regional level can do a number of things to help ensure prosperity. Their visions will vary, with differing emphases, but they should remember the following.

- **They will be ambassadors for new technology.** We saw in Finland how computers with Internet access were introduced into many public places. In the Irish Republic, a concerted effort was made in the early 1990s to provide all primary schools with personal computers and to ensure that teachers could pass on knowledge about their use.

- **They will diminish hindrances to the inflow and outflow of capital.** Much of the financial sector has been deregulated, but there will always remain a need to monitor capital flows in the interests of battling organized crime and money laundering.

- **They will eliminate obstacles to companies attracting the best people to work for them, at the level of either skilled workers or managers.** These may be recruited from far away, and there should be no organized or administrative difficulties placed in the way of their relocation and absorption.

- **They will minimize bureaucracy.** Since the middle of the nineteenth century, governments have involved themselves in business activity by creating rules and procedures for establishing companies and assessing liability in the event of the enterprise's failures. This can (and ought to) be a simple process, involving no more than filling out a clearly worded form and maybe handing ver a nominal fee, or it can be an arduous task beset by difficulties and technicalities, and often demanding professional assistance. If a country or region already suffers from the latter, it knows well the barriers to investment that exist, so it should remove them before even thinking of inviting investment from the rest of the world. Otherwise, it is just wasting everyone's time.

- **They will specialize.** The most critical aspect for the government is to decide what specialization it wants to attract and promote, be it in the service sector, the traditional manufacturing industry, or even value-added processing of agricultural products.

Getting Noticed

Regional strategy is today far more important than ever before. If this strategy is well developed and communicated, the particular region will make it to corporate investment short lists and be in the minds of CEOs when they come to make investment and location decisions for their next operation.

This is a dramatic change from the past, especially for attracting manufacturing industries, when boards of directors were bombarded with pleasant eye-candy brochures singing a region's praise and maybe even lauding its scenery. They might even have been invited to pay a visit, where they were entertained lavishly.

Today, companies such as Dell can manufacture, even for the American market, using just-in-time production methods and logistical arrangements with operators such as FedEx. Corporations such as GE can use back-office and call centers throughout the world. In the cyber, borderless world it is vital for regions to get ready for these types of decision makers, who are looking for the optimum location for each of their functions on a global basis. Protective governments are usually on the unpleasant short list of locations to avoid. Governments whose commitment is considered as less than total are also ignored.

Only Educate

A truly visionary government is dedicated to education. Indeed, the provision of education is one area in which government involvement in society and the economy is still desirable. Even in countries such as Ireland, where much education was provided by religious organizations, the government paid teachers and had a responsibility for curriculum development.

The government role in education will have to change, as education's identity changes from a process through which citizens pass at a certain time of their lives, to become a far less centralized or even institutionalized resource available to citizens of all ages and tailored to individual needs.

Education has very tangible benefits: A highly educated workforce is a necessary part of any economy because it adds intellectual value to whatever it produces or provides. One of the major strengths that any economy, and the people making up an economy, can possess is versatility. In Japan, the long-accepted norm of the "job for life" is recognized now as a museum piece. Even the most highly trained individuals can be overly rigid. They may refuse to recognize that their vocational specialty has a sell-by date. The world changes, and with this come changes in job markets. There may be internal developments in particular skills or disciplines; there may be applications of new technologies. The traditional impermeable barriers between jobs may start to break down. Just as developments can lead to the sudden death of an industry, they can also cause the sudden or even gradual death of an occupation. A rather crude but effective example is the old-style stenographer who refused to recognize that word processing was revolutionizing the job. But then, even the most skilled word processor operative now knows that he is competing with equally qualified workers on the other end of a VoIP line in India or the Philippines. The day is near when voice-pattern recognition software can convert most of the spoken words into digital sentences as easily as optical character recognition (OCR) can digitize handwritten documents.

Some arenas of human expertise will be eventually replaced altogether. This may be due to cost or efficiency factors. For decades, science fiction of an unsophisticated kind has frightened blue- and white-collar workers with a vision of a future staffed by robots. The robot has been a figure inspiring hate and disdain ever since it first emerged in the pages of Czech playwright Karel Capek in 1920. The prognostication of science fiction has failed to be realized, but research into the application of robotics in highly repetitive or dangerous manufacturing activities is continuing. Robots will never rule the world, but they will carry out a lot more actions previously felt to belong to humans or too dangerous for humans (as in highly radioactive environments).

Workers in all sections of the economy, including the professional sectors, should be taught to be open-minded and versatile. They should realize that education is not a closed, once-off process (maybe lasting many years) that leads to the goal of a job, but rather an ongoing process that lasts a lifetime. They must be prepared to make career changes in response to oscillations in demand. Some might see this as disruptive; others see it as dynamic.

I have seen surveys of MIT graduates (of which I am one) that show that after five years, slightly less than half of the technology graduates are working in a different field from the one they studied at MIT. Specialization has always had a short half-life. Possession of disciplined thought processes and the ability to approach problem solving are always useful because they can be built upon and applied in many different areas.

Governments can also help by facilitating life-long learning, by ensuring that the technological backbone is in place, and by establishing a sympathetic regulatory system for providers of retraining. There had traditionally been a pattern of governments providing such help only when a crisis breaks, such as once a number of industries move out of a sector. Only then are packages for retraining provided. This is akin to attempting to put out a raging forest fire with buckets of water after it has burned down half the forest. Governments can provide financial and fiscal incentives in this area to encourage employees to seek greater skills Retraining options should be available to everyone at all times. In fact, it should not be seen as retraining at all, but as skills aggregation and consolidation.

Further education or skills acquisition should be as easy to acquire as possible. We're not talking about ease of course content—that should never be watered down, but for someone teaching school who wants to retrain as a lawyer or an IT specialist, it should be possible to do so without having to give up an existing job. The Internet protocol, and especially broadband technology, makes it possible for a person to attend and participate in seminars and teaching modules from remote locations.

Closing Down Distance

I am very excited about the potential of distance learning. It provides a new way of acquiring perspectives and information throughout life.

A long-standing obstacle to new skills acquisition was that the provision of teaching or training was often inflexible. A person might well have to leave home to spend long spells away from family and work. But the advent of broadband technology means that much instruction can be provided to remote locations—indeed, to any location with suitable hardware and software. Because both are now widely available and affordable, there is no reason why providers of education should be imprisoned in university lecture halls, seminar rooms, and laboratories that are inaccessible to those who are hungry for knowledge.

I am involved with an MBA course taught by Bond University in Australia in which the students do not attend classes and seminars at the university, but study from their homes. I use a remote education system that I developed called Air Campus. My course is a one-year course in strategic management that contains two units out of the 12 required to receive an MBA. I meet with my students electronically every day. Every month, I give them a video to watch, containing both text and video footage. It may also contain excerpts from entrepreneurs talking about a topic, or my own remarks with presentations. This video streaming is distributed by Internet to students wherever they may be in the world. I have created 4,000 hours of television-quality teaching content, some of it in English.

For communicating with my students, I use a platform called Air Campus, supplemented by a live 1:N discussion tool called Interwise, which was originally developed in Israel. I can stay in touch with my students, discuss points with them, answer their questions, and send them PowerPoint presentations. Using the method I have devised, it is possible to initiate a real in-depth class discussion. The course finishes with an exam, but one with a difference. There is no standard exam paper, but rather 150 individual papers: Each candidate receives a personalized paper. This allows me to challenge candidates who might have "played safe" during the course and to challenge their assumptions. Because each student receives individual questions, there is no cheating. It would be pointless.

At any one time, I might have 130 to 150 students taking my Strategic Management course for a credit toward their MBAs. The course participants are mostly Japanese because Japanese is the language of 50 percent of course content (the remainder is in English). Some students come from as far afield as Brazil. In 2003, 50 students graduated with MBAs. This type of education is far superior to anything that exists in Japan and even to study in some of the world's top business schools. Participants can continue to work in their companies and pursue their lifestyles. Admittedly, it does entail sacrifice in terms of time and money. The physical graduation ceremony in Australia is accompanied by a cybergraduation for those unable to attend the former. About 40 MBA candidates sit in front of their TVs (via satellite) or computers, viewing the ceremony. When their name is called, a prerecorded picture with graduation hat and cape is shown while the graduate might be in his own home celebrating.

In U.S. business schools, the case study network remains popular. But if you look at the cases, half are no longer relevant, and the other half features companies that are now either bankrupt or absorbed into another corporation. My approach to online education looks at on-going, current, and realistic examples.

I chose to do this with Bond University because so many American universities have a fundamental belief that courses and teaching should be provided on-campus and that it is inherently better than distance education. I disagree. On-campus education is good, but there are many different ways to improve the quality and the yield of learning. Distance learning can reduce costs. A program can be structured to provide a much higher quality of education. The benefits are manifest at every level. Not everyone can go to the United States, pay $200,000 in fees, and give up maybe two years of "company life." If they can, they are either very wealthy or very privileged. Our MBA candidates are hungry for both knowledge and success. They are paying their own tuition fees and sacrificing part of their life and experience with colleagues and family. I believe that they are much better students.

It always takes two to tango. There must be a group of motivated, hungry students, as well as an equally motivated, flexible, and broad-minded faculty. Systems should be developed together. I developed the Air Campus platform because I interact heavily with my students.

Existing platforms were unsuitable because they were server-based and meant that I could not use them on the plane or the train. Air Campus is a client-based system in which all the relevant information and contact protocols are stored on my PC. Once reconnected, it will synchronize with the server.

A New Role for Government

Governments have been viewed as the providers of education, but their role should change to being a member of a team. Although governments will still play a significant role in education, they should not be afraid to open up to private sector involvement. In China, there is a growing and vibrant private education sector. Governments should not be suspicious of such developments. They have a responsibility to ensure high educational standards, especially in areas such as computer science, but they should not be shouldered with the responsibility of providing it.

Nor should it be assumed that governmental involvement in education involves big government. Many of the changes in education can be carried out not by a centralized nation-state, but in the region-state. In educational terms, the former has been sluggish and ill equipped to provide for the needs of a changing economy and society.

Education and the school system represent one of the best ways in which government can teach the citizens of the future about changing roles. It can attempt to alter the way citizens should view the government: not as a distributor, but as a facilitator. The schools are also a good place to begin the development of optimal personal skills that are necessary in a changing environment. One of these is self-reliance. Instead of looking to some external source for assistance, the solutions to problems should be sought nearer to home.

Traditionally, the approach has been that these schools cannot teach these skills; they are best learned in the "real world." This may be partly true, but students should be given the skills to learn these lessons.

The questions are difficult and the outlook can appear depressing as we look around the world and see countries trying to come to terms with economic realities by listening to outdated philosophies. So many countries still waste resources by trying to shore up the barriers of the closed economy. They do not realize, or maybe refuse to realize, that such barriers are *part* of the problem, not the solution, and should be allowed to fall.

The reality of the global economy has nevertheless been realized by some countries and regions. Some of these countries are very different. We will look again at China and, staying in Asia, visit Malaysia and Singapore. Then we will travel to northern Europe to examine Sweden and end our travels in Ireland.

China: Governing the Ungovernable

If we look at China, we see an entity that perhaps no longer deserves the title of People's Republic of China, but ought instead to be approached as the United States of Chunghua. China began to open up to the Western world in 1978. At first, the steps were tentative and unsure. Minor services such as taxi driving and photography were opened up to private enterprise, yet by the 1990s, it became clear that such cautious approaches were likely to cause more problems than they solved. Running alongside the thinking on economic issues was a need to decouple economic from political liberalization. While private enterprise and privatization of state industries might be allowed and promoted, there should be no slippage in the Chinese Communist Party's "unique role" in Chinese politics, and no opening up of opportunities for alternative policy perspectives.

The moves of Zhu Rongji in 1998 have had the greatest impact— not only on China, but on the world as a whole. These were codified in terms of the Three Respects, one of which was respect for private property, for so long the ideological bane of Marxism-Leninism. The latter was not abandoned; it was merely moved to a side altar in a dimly lit alcove, while an amendment to the Chinese constitution stated that private property was inviolable. These ideological changes were accompanied by a devolution of more and effective decision making, down to regions of proven success. It was clear that places such as Dalian, Guangzhou, and Qingtao were prospering and that nothing should be put in their way. They must be given their heads, and those on the ground who had power should be told to use it as they saw fit. The people who were granted this *de facto* autonomy were the provincial governors and city mayors. This was important because, in the Byzantine pecking order of Chinese administration, their position was technically subordinate to that of the local Communist Party secretaries. Yet the latter were redundant, and the likes of Bo Xilai in Dalian and, afterward, in Liaoning Province, were given the task of attracting investment to their areas, with no regard for what the center might think. Those mayors who have done well in promoting economic development are kicked upstairs. Both Jiang

Zemin and former Premier Zhu Rongji were mayors of Shanghai before they became party First Secretary and prime minister, respectively; Bo is now the Minister of Commerce.

As we have seen, an economy must remove existing barriers to capital inflows. There must also be a readiness to attract the best skills, especially in management, from throughout the world. Recently, a Chinese company appointed an American as its CEO. The desire—in fact, the necessity—to establish joint ventures shows how the Chinese are willing to learn from others. They are exercising Deng Xiaoping's philosophy: "Whether it is a white cat or black cat, it does not matter. The cat that catches the mouse is the good cat."

China is still not entirely open. The activities of non-Chinese companies in areas such as banking and rail transport are still restricted. Worries persist about the role of government in bankrolling former state-owned enterprises for political reasons.

Even so, China shows a path to a prosperous future. The twenty-first-century economy, as in China, is shaped by the development of IT, by the growth and expansion of borderless thinking and practice, and by movements in capital. Yet few outsiders, whether politicians, economists, or journalists, view China realistically. They persist in viewing it as a nation-state. Others predict the fall or disintegration of the country. Although it is entirely possible that China may eventually break into pieces, I predict that China in the future will be stronger collectively because it has already discovered the formula of prosperity on the global stage. It no longer matters whether it is one country with two systems, or three countries together, combining Hong Kong and Taiwan in some way: It is *de facto* an assembly of many region states. As long as the regions are allowed to interact with the rest of the world, their collective power will become stronger as their entrepreneurial mayors and governors do their best to attract capital and corporations from the rest of the world. These business-minded (and business-appointed) mayors know how to work with the global economy better than most of their bureaucratic or political counterparts in Western countries.

It is my observation that Chinese economic growth should continue even though it is accompanied by an increase in bad debts through overinvestment and overlending by governmental banks. I have spoken of the numerous Cassandras among financial journalists who have spoken of the imminent hard or soft landing of the Chinese economy. Yet investment in China shows no signs of dipping, whether it is from large companies such as Microsoft, Siemens, or General

Motors, or from the providers of business services such as accountancy firm Deloitte Touche Tohmatsu. Measures by the Chinese government are construed in a narrowly Keynesian way, such as a "dampening down" of an overheating economy, and are presented as "early warning" signals. Then there are the U.S. partisans of a Plaza Accord II, who view the renminbi in an identical way to the yen in the mid-1980s, as a currency whose cheapness makes its exports less expensive and those of its competitors, especially U.S. industries, less competitive. Were the RMB to be revalued upward, they say, some form of balance in trade with China would be achieved.

In the short term, the renminbi would appreciate, probably greatly, by as much as 200 percent. It is also highly probable that this would be accompanied by much volatility in international currency markets. The beneficiaries of this appreciation might not be the United States, but economies much nearer to China, such as Hong Kong's. Another beneficiary would be the likes of George Soros who would argue that China actually has serious structural problems and should sell RMB. One result in the medium term would be that China's position in the global GDP league table, currently seventh, would inevitably rise. But over the long term of 10 to 15 years, the effects of this type of revaluation (which is being sought more by vote-hungry politicians than economists) would no doubt mirror what happened in Japan after the Plaza Accord. Domestic industry would stay ahead of the game by becoming ever more competitive. This would be enhanced, rather than stymied, by an expensive currency. Imports would become cheaper, including the commodities upon which Chinese manufacturing industry depends.

Once again, I must add the caveat that looking at China as a totality imposes a mistaken and blinkered vision of what is happening and what will happen in the future.

Malaysia's Corridors of Power

Malaysia is a country that has truly embraced so much of the thinking behind the need for the nation-state to open up to the rest of the world.

Malaysia has a varied economy, with some manufacturing but quite a lot of traditional agricultural activity. It is situated in a strategic location between India and the Far East. Its infrastructure is good, and affluence is well spread throughout the country and its society. Malaysia's opening up to the global economy centers on one project, which was the brainchild of former Malaysian Prime Minister Mahathir Mohamad.

The Multimedia Super Corridor (MSC) is a small portion of Malaysia, close to Kuala Lumpur and its international airport. It is described as a "garden corridor," 15km by 50km (9 miles by 31 miles), dedicated to the creation of an optimal environment for businesses engaging in IT activities. It is fully serviced with the most up-to-date technology and fiber-optic cables, as well as access to satellite communications. In 1997, there were 94 companies operating in the corridor. In April 2004, this figure had jumped to 1,016, with 287 foreign owned, including such giants of IT as Nokia, Ericsson, NTT, DHL, Fujitsu, Microsoft, and Cisco Systems.

Dr. Mahathir was aware of those in Malaysia who would view the opening of the largely Islamic country with disdain. Malaysia is a secular state, but one in which the sentiments of Islam have to be treated with care. One of the concerns that some religious conservatives had about the Internet was its potential for spreading pornography and immodest material. Yet the prime minister was stern in his dedication to the Multimedia Super Corridor vision, warning those who feared the intrusion of new technology that they had the opportunity to control such innovations, in a way that would be denied them were they to choose to turn their backs on it.

Dr. Mahathir was a controversial figure because he spoke freely against the West when, for example, his country was targeted by currency speculators in 1997. He was in many ways a traditional politician, a government functionary, but one who knew the value of carefully nurtured government intervention in the economy but saw it as ultimately inferior to the actions of the private sector. His biggest accomplishment during his 22 years as prime minister was that he all but eliminated poverty from his country by any measure, such as per capita GDP or family housing. This was because wealth came from the rest of the world into regions such as Johor, Penang, and Selangor, while the central government concentrated on the development of the rest of the country to which it was difficult to attract foreign capital.

Singapore's Appetite for Reinvention

Singapore is a clear example of a nation that has attained riches without being blessed by nature. Its position at the southern end of Malaysia is strategic, but it has no mineral resources and its land is indifferent. But throughout its years of independence, it has always been ruled by leaders who have not been afraid to fashion and, when necessary, refashion visions of their country, although they have never been especially tolerant of those who are not in agreement.

At the time of its independence in 1965, Singapore was a rather poor city-state, making its income from passing maritime trade and tourism. The economic thinking of its first premier, Lee Kuan Yew, was dominated by the all-conquering Keynesianism of the day. He considered that Singapore's road to riches lay along a route paved by the manufacturing industry. By the late 1970s, it was obvious that this had not brought a massive increase in the standard of living of average Singaporeans, so in 1982, an ambitious plan called IT 2000 was unveiled. Its aim was to use computer technology, whether imported or domestic, to boost the Singaporean economy. It also set itself the task of raising the per-capita GDP level of Singaporeans above the level of $10,000 a year by 2000, a figure that would guarantee entry to the Organisation of Economic Coordination and Development (OECD). To oversee the project, a National Computer Board was established and computer literacy was promoted at all levels of education and work. More recently, the Internet has introduced the prospect of a genuine "e-society" whose citizens gain information and access to services through their PCs and electronic kiosks placed throughout the city.

Singapore achieved the IT 2000 goal five years ahead of schedule. The National Computer Board had done its work. It was a governmental creation, but once its goals had been achieved, there was no longer a need for it to remain as a part of government, so it was privatized. Since then, it has earned praise and, more important, new business through advising many countries in the developing world about the application of computer technology to everyday life. Its fate mirrors that of the Port Authority of Singapore (PAS). It, too, was a creature of government. It achieved not only an increase in the amount of business passing through Singapore's port, but also some major logistical successes in cutting delay times between ships berthing and the onshore or onboard delivery of cargoes. It has also been privatized and is playing a major role in the improvement of port facilities throughout eastern Asia.

In Singapore, government activity is valued, but its value is confined to the short term and to the completion of a defined project. Once the project has been attained, the justification for the government agency disappears. It is never just scrapped; its value and potential are then made available to the rest of the world. Its employees are aware that they do not possess jobs for life and that, paradoxically, the achievement of their goals hastens a change in their employment status. This is in stark contrast to the Japanese bureaucrats (and those of most countries in the developed world). Once hired, they have a guarantee of lifetime employment. They do not even have to pay unemployment insurance because they can never be laid off or fired (unless they have serious criminal charges leveled against them). This is one of the reasons why Japan cannot change—and why Singapore can. An ability to pursue new avenues and a genuine appetite for change are key factors for success in the global economy.

Alongside the success of IT 2000, Singapore has successfully reinvented itself at least twice. The decline in the manufacturing industry was accompanied by a drive to attract multinationals to base their regional headquarters in Singapore. To facilitate the process, Singapore has created a large-scale, efficient international airport on reclaimed land in Changi. The result was the appearance of many more skyscrapers housing corporate headquarters. Each was a place of employment for a large number of workers. In the late 1990s, Singapore sought, once again successfully, to become a focus for technological research, especially in the area of biotechnology. It has also become a significant base of indigenous technology with companies such as Flextronics, the Electronic Manufacturing Services (EMS) provider.

The country thinks about broad problems. Its sights are never fixed for long on bread-and-butter issues. It is noteworthy that the annual debate on the budget in the Singaporean parliament should be accompanied by worries about Singapore's declining birth rate. Would Singapore have enough citizens to ensure its continued success? Lee Kuan Yew once told me that even if the country loses its competitiveness to countries such as China, he and his heirs must feed their people. When he became chairman of Singapore's Central Provident Fund (CPF), he said, "We now have some money to invest. If we invest this money cleverly, our three million people can live well on the return of the investment. So if China becomes too powerful, we can invest there and get attractive returns. If the U.S. high-techs do well, then we get their returns as well."

Singapore is a paradox. It is a haven and showcase for private enterprise, but the state has had a very direct and "hands-on" influence on its economic development. Deep in the minds of its leaders is the commitment to their own people and their obligation to deliver a better life. They know their solutions do not lie within, so they instinctively look to develop a role and relationship with the rest of the world. Changing their act on the global stage is natural—and necessary.

The Singapore experience may redefine the mantra about government. The best government is short term. Government involvement in the economy has been focused on clear goals. Once achieved, the government moves out. It is rather like the perfect houseguest who knows when he has outstayed his welcome.

Swedish Rhapsody

Sweden appeared at one time to be a very unlikely candidate to showcase openness to the global economy. It has a stable government. Most administrations were coalitions of more than one party, and throughout the twentieth century, the political party most frequently in government has been the Social Democrats. They oversaw the construction of a welfare state *par excellence*, providing generous levels of transfers to cover health and welfare from cradle to grave. The Swedish people were not just comfortable; they were positively cosseted, and they came to see such comfort and security as their birthright. This had to be paid for with very high levels of taxation, at both national and local levels. The high taxes, together with overintrusive regulations, led to a hemorrhage of some of Sweden's best companies. Astra relocated to the United Kingdom, eventually merging into Astra Zeneca, while ASEA and Tetra Lavall moved to Switzerland.

But in the 1990s, this dispensation changed, partly as a result of shocks from the international economy. Sweden also joined the European Community and so had to adopt a more streamlined and orthodox set of economic policies. The Welfare State, with its in-built safety nets and its commitment to social solidarity, started to be viewed as a hindrance to individualism. A new interest in the individual—and especially in entrepreneurial effort—emerged. New business schools mushroomed. The realization was reached that the world was changing. Mining and traditional manufacturing, the mainstays of the Swedish economy, were in decline, as was the case in many other high-cost and aging societies.

There were sectors in which Sweden still held a comparative advantage, particularly in the technology sector. Sweden was the birthplace of many global enterprises, such as Electrolux, ABB, Astra, Tetrapak, IKEA, Saab, OM, Volvo, H&M (Hennes and Mauritz), Scania, and Ericsson. In particular, Swedish involvement in telecom-

municions had to be expanded, but this could occur only by opening up to the rest of the world. Success in the relatively small Swedish
market of about eight million people was not enough, and the world
was recognized to be the only marketplace worth winning in. In 2003,
according to WTO/IMF figures, Swedish exports represented 33 percent of GDP (see Exhibit 8.4).

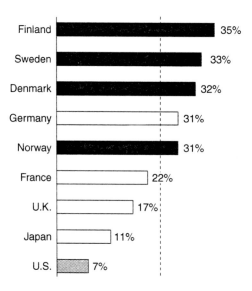

Source: WTO, IMF.

Exhibit 8.4   Export/GDP ratios.

This was accompanied by a restructuring of the Swedish economy. Tax rates, especially those affecting the corporate sector, were
reduced. Deregulation and privatization, especially in telecommunications, were pursued much more vigorously, resulting in the
formation of companies such as Telia and Tele2. The government
supported efforts by the private sector to establish technology
clusters, sometimes embracing specialist technical and scientific
institutes. These provided not just research insights, but also
qualified staff. Many research institutes have developed special
incubation units where startups are given the opportunity to gain
experience and contacts. But space in the incubators is not open
to all comers: It is given only to those that have a real technical
and, most important, global potential.

Among the most notable clusters is Kista Science City, on the outskirts of Stockholm. This is home to 250 high-tech companies. This 2-million-meter-square site had created 27,000 jobs by the end of 2003 and is a mecca for R&D in wireless systems, broadband and mobile communications.

Swedish firms continue to dominate the world in specialist areas of high-tech engineering. These include Autoliv (airbags and safety equipment), Cardo (industrial doors manufacture), and Gambro (world number two in the manufacture of equipment for dialysis treatment).

At the beginning of this decade, Sweden had achieved some admirable results. It spent 3.7 percent of its GDP on R&D. Two-thirds of this occurs in the private sector. This was higher than in any other country, including the United States. The OECD also calculated that Sweden was one of the most "knowledge-based" economies in the world. Bringing together investment in R&D, in education by both the government and private sectors, as well as in software development, it was calculated that 6.6 percent of Swedish GDP was invested in knowledge acquisition and development.

The Swedes are very proud of their country, but this does not prevent them from having a very high level of fluency in English. Swedes traditionally have been good linguists, but in the first half of the twentieth century, the second language most frequently acquired was German. The growing success of Swedish popular culture on the international stage, in addition to the strengthening of ties between Sweden and the descendants of Swedish migrants in the United States, led to the phenomenal growth of English learning. As in neighboring Finland and Denmark, a growing amount of education is provided through English, and a high percentage of Swedes are not just proficient in English, but truly fluent, sometimes nearly accent free. The integrity and leadership of the Swedes was symbolized by Dag Hammerskjoeld (1905–1961), a Nobel Prize laureate and UN Secretary General, and Hans Blix, who led the UN Weapons Inspection Team in Iraq and did not yield to the pressures from the superpowers. The tradition of producing globally compatible leaders is a strong plus for Sweden on the global stage.

Sweden still remains a high-cost economy, but it is able to justify high costs as the price to be paid for cutting-edge innovations, especially in areas such as wireless communications and biotechnology. The government set this development in motion by deciding to sit back from heavy-handed intervention. It is noteworthy that this new departure from Swedish government policy has not been the result of a seismic shift in the country's political landscape. Sweden's political stability is as calm as ever, and the Social Democrats remain the largest party in government.

The Craic of the Irish

We have touched on the historical experience of Ireland already. Previously, it was a poor agricultural country in which there was a long tradition of seeking scapegoats for the country's many problems. Some blamed the outside world rather than seeking amelioration from it. Nationalism, in a variety of forms, developed to the extent of a state ideology. The difficulty that occurs when nationalism meets economics is that the former breeds a damaging myopia. The country's problems are usually someone else's fault; their solution exists internally and can be resolved only by the nation's people working together without outside help. Ireland's economic policy in the 1930s and 1940s was dominated by Listian principles of native industry being propagated behind high tariff walls. Import substitution was the ideal; as long as the imports were replaced by home-produced goods, there was no need to try to export them. This would have been impossible anyway because the industries were uncompetitive. The domestic population was told that not buying the more expensive, often inferior, domestically produced item was unpatriotic (and there are many countries in which politicians still preach this dogma).

Nearly everyone who stayed in Ireland came to look to the government as a source of help. Farmers, small industrialists, businessmen, the Catholic Church—all were clients of official help in the form of grants and cash handouts. The government usually responded by dividing scarce resources among the succession of supplicating interest groups. Ireland's public service was very similar to England's, from which it had emerged in 1922. There were some superficial differences: Irish public servants usually changed their name to their traditional Gaelic forms, and if a Gaelic form did not exist, it was frequently invented.

In the 1960s, a new realization dawned. There *was* an outside world after all, which could be a source of prosperity for Ireland. Naturally, it was a government agency, the Industrial Development Authority (IDA), that was charged with the task of attracting investment; initially, however, there was little realization of how to do this effectively or realization that outside investors had to be shown some solid financial reasons for investing in Ireland. Even though mechanization of all sectors of industry was growing apace, the IDA seemed to be stuck in a world dominated by old-style manufacturing. Politicians wanted to claim credit for the establishment of a factory in their locality employing *x* number of workers. All that the IDA could offer by way of inducement was a preferential tax code and, after 1973, a back door into the European Union. Neither of these two advantages could overcome serious infrastructural flaws and low levels of competitiveness and productivity. Some Japanese companies, such as Hino (trucks), Fujitsu, Noritake, and Yamanouchi (pharmaceuticals), established plants there, but they and a few dozen American companies were not enough to lift the entire economy.

From the middle of the 1980s, the tidal wave of computer and information technology crashed with ever-increasing fury on Ireland's shores. The IDA (retitled as an *agency* rather than an *authority*) increasingly pursued IT companies that were attracted to Ireland by a growing crop of well-trained white-collar workers. In 1992, it was realized that Ireland's prosperity must come from this wired world. The concept of making Ireland a European e-hub grew from within the old IDA. It was adopted as government policy by then *Tanaiste* (deputy Prime Minister) and Minister for Public Enterprise Mary O'Rourke. In 1992, SIGNA, a New Jersey–based American insurance company, opened a back-room operation in Ireland, primarily to shift time and reduce costs. This was the first time the Irish saw the potential of importing jobs on the end of the telephone line or through cross-border BPO. The rest is history.

These countries all have different historical traditions and differing political systems. In all of them, there was a tradition of interventionist government action, especially in the economic sphere. In each one, this has given way to a philosophy of government doing more by doing less, often providing the initial impetus and the right background conditions, but thereafter sitting on the stage's sidelines.

9

THE FUTURES MARKET

All Change

Governments must change, but on the global stage, change is both necessary and inevitable at three fundamental levels:

- **Technological**—The future will be very different in terms of technology. Indeed, technological progress has the capacity to speedily reshape and even wipe out entire industries.

- **Personal**—At a personal level, the global stage means that we have to become more adaptable and more willing to proactively take part rather than remaining a spectator.

- **Organizational**—At an organizational level, the emergent corporation will be homeless, at least in the traditional sense of having a base that can be called and viewed as home. It must be adaptive, focused on innovation, and unencumbered by needless hierarchy or the psychological baggage of its past.

The Technological Future

Complacency is an evil and pernicious state: We must never become self-satisfied, but must always strive onward and upward. One of the ways we can do so successfully is to realize and build upon our current strengths. This is especially true of computer technology.

I have referred in passing to the tiny amount of memory available to the first personal computers. A maximum of 32KB was not uncommon. We now have hard disc units containing 32MB as standard. This is more than enough for most people, yet many computers offer disc storage in excess of 1GB. This is probably one of the reasons additional disk drives are so inexpensive. Some industry specialists argue that a disk drive of around 240GB will be necessary before we can use downloadable video technology. This is the equivalent of the space necessary to store about a dozen standard-length movies.

The reality is that an operating system such as Windows XP (or even Windows 98) contains far more features than most ordinary computer users even know of. They are sitting on a treasure trove of capabilities, most of which they may never need, but if they do, these can be accessed without much difficulty. This may include the operating systems' video-editing tools. These may not be sophisticated enough for professional or semiprofessional users, but they provide a technological entrance level for interested and committed novices.

Computers are becoming ever more sophisticated. Traditional and surviving technology chasms are starting to narrow. One of these is the traditional difference that many users believe to exist between their computers browsing the Internet and the bank of server computers held by their Internet service provider. It is conceivable that this gap will grow still narrower in coming years with improved semiconductor performance. The first beneficiaries of this will probably be the corporate sector. It will mean that medium-size enterprises will be able to fully manage their Web sites and Web content. They will also be able to utilize business applications, such as CRM/SCM based on ERP, using servers priced at the same level as the PC in the mid-1990s.

Technological Progress Means Death Is a Fact of Business Life

For those in the corporate world, technology brings fears as well as opportunities. It means that industrial death is increasingly a fact of business life.

The rise and fall of commercial enterprises, once vibrant, dynamic, and even dominant but brought to the brink of bankruptcy (and beyond) in the space of a few decades, is a fact of business life. In more recent days, we have also witnessed mammoths such as Enron and Worldcom rendered prostrate as a result of falling afoul of regulatory restrictions and what could politely be called internal accounting inconsistencies.

It has never been uncommon to see whole sections of industry wiped out by technological progress. We need only think of the impact that the automobile had not only on the carriage industry, but also on saddle makers and the providers of feed and stables for horses. Each new technological wave usually has its victims, those who were unable to change in time.

But time has now been compressed. In the past, there was usually some time lag between the discovery of a new process or processes, and their complete victory over their predecessors. The new might have been far better but was seldom cheaper, and it took a long time, perhaps longer than a generation, for the novel invention to percolate downward as its price declined. Think, in the recent past, how long it took video cameras to move from an expensive luxury to an affordable mass-market product. In the world of the interconnected global economy, such time lags are very rare. A technology may become dominant in the world while knowing that its usurper is already baying at its heels.

As we have seen, the cast of players on the global stage includes cyberites. They are ready for the new script, and their readiness and enthusiasm is the key accelerator to winning over the rest of the cast. As once-dominant actors are displaced with new heroes and heroines, it is as if a tactful stage director has changed the scene from Act I to Act II in a blink.

Consider the camera industry. The days of the traditional analog film camera industry are truly numbered. The traditional camera's nemesis has been the digital camera (see Exhibit 9.1). In 2004, Japanese manufacturers shipped around 70 million units to win market share, thus eroding both price and profitability (see Exhibit 9.2).

This is similar to what happened in the hand-held calculator market in the late 1970s. This kind of cutthroat competition is familiar to Japanese consumer electronics giants (see Exhibit 9.3).

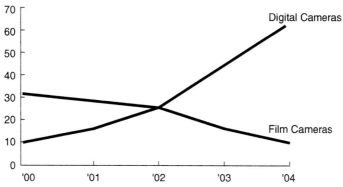

Source: Camera & Imaging Products Association.

Exhibit 9.1 World shipments of digital and film cameras.

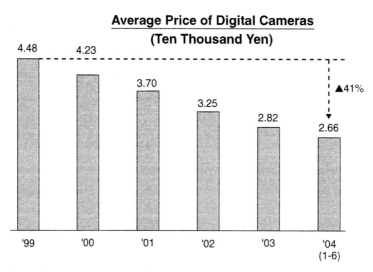

Source: Japanese Camera Industry Association.

Exhibit 9.2 Price erosion.

Digital Camera Shipments
(10,000 Units)

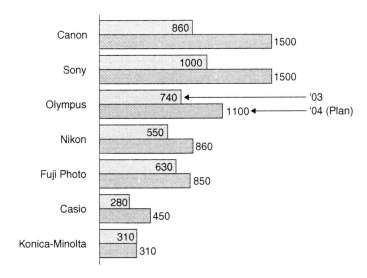

Source: Tokyo Shinbun, April 2004.

Exhibit 9.3 Competition.

When the digital camera first became accessible to a wide public in the mid-1990s it was still relatively crude. The resolution was poor and the number of images that could be stored on the camera before being downloaded was small. Once on the computer, they tended to stay there, maybe arranged in digital photo albums. Their relatively large file sizes meant that they could seldom be shared with other users, unless their resolution was lessened even more. But now, digital cameras are capable of taking pictures with as many as eight million pixels per centimeter, a degree of detail far greater than is visible to the unaided human eye. These can be recorded on rewritable CDs, and improvements in printer and paper technology mean that near-professional quality prints can be produced at home.

Canon is now the world's number one producer of digital cameras. It introduced sophisticated digital cameras in 1995. Nothing much happened, so Canon waited until 2000 to really make a major inroad into the digital camera market. It broadened its product range and lowered the price. The average digital camera price was $450, and the global industry size was ten million shipments in 2000. By 2004, the market had expanded to 60 million shipments, with cameras averaging $280.

At the end of 2004, the digital camera population was 150 million units, or one for every four consumer PCs in the world. In other words, digital camera penetration had to wait until users became ready to plug it into their PC, mostly via conventional USB ports.

This has a number of implications. First, the traditional camera industry no longer exists. It has become a peripheral to the PC, or one of the input/output devices to a PC.

Second, because of the explosive shift to digital cameras, the entire value chain for the analog camera industry is in trouble. This includes films, labs, (silver bromide) papers, albums, and lab equipment companies. The most significant casualty has been the photographic developing laboratory. The shots taken by digital camera users, whether professionals or amateurs, are developed by those same users using their PCs, on which they can be altered or enhanced using relatively inexpensive and accessible software. Then they are printed on special photographic paper using dedicated but far from expensive printers. Alternatively, the photographs may be stored on portable storage devices.

Companies such as Kodak and Fuji are faced with a restructuring challenge throughout the entire spectrum of their business systems. Polaroid, the creator of instant photography, has lost its historical role. After a century-long global battle, they, along with a number of other lesser competitors (such as Konica and Agfa), had established dominance in the photographic industry. Well entrenched and with attractive profit margins, it has been difficult for them to realign in the wake of the sudden shift of the industry. No company can cope with a restructuring demand of 15 percent per annum for four consecutive years when they do not know how much further they have to go.

But is this victory of the new, accompanied by the surrender of the old, merely pyrrhic? Even the digital camera industry may not flourish. In Japan, the real reason for the explosive growth of digital camera sales and use was that J-Phone (now taken over by Vodafone) introduced a built-in camera in their year 2000 model (J-SHO4). This camera had only 110,000 pixels, but it became very popular because it had the "pet name" of Sha-Meiru, meaning "picture mail." Young girls and couples exchanged not only text mail, but accompanying pictures. Subsequently, all the mobile operators rushed into this promising market, and by June 2002, more than half of the mobile phones sold had a camera with a standard resolution of 310,000 pixels. By the end of 2004, the leading-edge model had a CCD lens with a resolution exceeding two million pixels, comparable to that of stand-alone digital cameras. At this stage, the digital camera industry felt the pressure and started to realize that it could become a "compo-nent" industry to mobile phones and that it might not even keep the position of an I/O device to PCs or peripherals. It is foreseeable that it will become an adjunct to other portable equipment, such as PDAs or digital ballpoint pens, or even become part of a credit card.

The message is clear: Technology's onward march makes each and every industry susceptible—even new industries are at risk. If cyberites embrace a new technology, the writing is on the wall.

A similar story occurred with the replacement of videotapes by DVDs. The tapes were inexpensive but bulky. They tended to decline markedly in quality the more times they were played. DVDs offered picture-sharp quality with every scene. In addition, the discs could be used to store a host of additional features, such as background mate-rial on the content and interviews with the cast, or subtitles in a host of languages. They could be navigated much more easily. The begin-ning of the title could be accessed at the push of a button; there was no need to wait while the video player rewound the tape.

DVDs can be played by PCs with the requisite technology, simi-lar to that for reading data CDs. Although standalone DVD players are overwhelmingly more popular as the viewing mechanism in the United Kingdom and the United States, computer-viewed DVDs are preferred in Japan. The reason seems to be hostility to the DVD play-er by Japanese households, whose television sets are usually heavily encumbered by a raft of other equipment, such as satellite tuners. The last glimmer of hope for the videotape was extinguished by the advent of relatively inexpensive DVD recorders, along with software for editing DVDs. The visual display units for looking at DVDs have also been revolutionized, with the obsolescence of displays using cathode ray tube (CRT) technology in favor of units using flat-screen panels, such as plasma display panels (PDP) and liquid-crystal dis-plays (LCD), as shown in Exhibit 9.4.

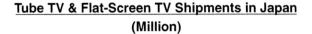

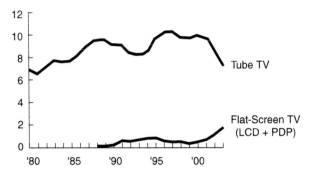

Source: "Data on household electronic appliances 2003," Japan Electronics and
Information Technology Industries Association (JEITA).

Exhibit 9.4   Tube TV and flat-screen TV shipments.

It is an old story, though the pace of the plot is accelerating. The power of technology to reshape industries had already been seen in the field of recorded music. The replacement of traditional vinyl records by CDs is a case study of industry demise known to every business student. CDs were so superior in terms of technology and also in terms of size and transportability that, for many music devotees, the arrival of the CD was the answer to a prayer. The disc, if properly cared for, was almost indestructible and gave near-perfect sound reproduction. They could hardly ask for more. While they might feel sentimental about their vinyl albums, they had to recall the trouble they had wiping off the ubiquitous dust before playing them, not to mention how a slip of the playing stylus could produce scratches and unacceptable noise.

Now the CD is itself declining in sales, as new platforms for music reproduction and distribution take hold (see Exhibit 9.5).

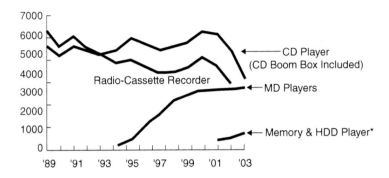

Audio Equipment Production in Japan (Thousand)

* Audio player to save music data on memories and HDD.

Source: "Data on household electronic appliances 2003," Japan Electronics and Information Technology Industries Association (JEITA).

Exhibit 9.5 Audio equipment production in Japan.

The music distribution business is being torn asunder by technology. The starting point was the Napster boom. The technology was called P2P (peer to peer), and the idea was to access your friend's music albums stored in his PC. By doing so, Napster figured that it would be able to avoid paying royalties to record companies. Although this did not work smoothly (and the court case seemed endless), Apple's Steve Jobs introduced iPod in 2001 to transfer music from a PC to a portable device. Subsequently, in February 2003, Jobs introduced a service called iTunes to download music piece by piece for a token 99¢ per music item. Its explosive popularity not only revived the ailing Apple computer company, but it sent MTS (owner of Tower Records) into Chapter 11 protection. Its sales were down only slightly, but the stock market extrapolated the implications of services such as iTunes Music Store on traditional music vendors. In fact, there are already a dozen download sites available, such as buymusic.com, listen.com (Rhapsody), Sony Music Entertainment, and Music Match Downloads.

The sudden death of an industry is brought about because the 800 million (and growing fast) cyberites are ready to accept anything new that is compatible with their Web-connected PCs, and the stock market quickly interprets the far-reaching implications when this happens.

The development of downloadable music files rings a rather mournful chime for the traditional music distribution industry. After all, there will hardly be a need for stores selling CDs or cassette tapes when their contents can be acquired over the Internet. The days of such stores were numbered as soon as e-commerce sites began providing the items at a considerable discount. With the decline in CD purchases, much of the traditional recording industry will disappear. There simply won't be a need for it. It is no longer a novelty for a small band or musical group to record their own album and then upload some tracks onto the Web to aid publicity and name recognition. This may sound the death-knell for traditional labels with A&R men, overstaffed recording studios, and overmighty distribution networks. Some of those specializing in classical music may survive because classical music buyers tend to be more conservative in buying habits and did not seem to be bitten by the Napster/iPod bug. But even this may change.

The fate of the music distribution industry shows how many other sectors may be affected by the rise of the phenomenon of "downloadability." If a product or service can be acquired by an ordinary PC user, with broadband or even on a 28Kbps or 56Kbps connection, it is more than probable that it is being delivered more cheaply and, certainly, more conveniently. The location for downloading can be anywhere because the mechanism used no longer has to be a PC console; it can be a mobile telephone. In addition to surfing the Internet, such a phone can serve as a portable information center and communications platform. In Japan, the number of Internet-compatible mobile phone users is greater than the number of PC-based Internet users (see Exhibit 9.6). This is one of the reasons why Japanese consumer electronics producers are consolidating all kinds of functions and services into a tiny cellphone, ranging from payment chips, games, cameras, iPod–like music chips, and two-dimensional bar codes for ticketing and payment certificates.

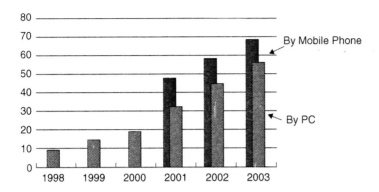

Internet Users in Japan
(Million)

Note: PC users: end of February; mobile users: end of December.

Source: Impress, "White paper on Internet 2003," Telecommunications Carriers Association.

Exhibit 9.6 Internet users in Japan.

The Rise of VoIP and Its Impact on Telecoms

The provision of old-style, land-line–based telephony seemed to lend itself to nation-state-aligned monopolies. Combined with commitments to civic minima—the availability of a phone to everyone in the state, no matter how remotely situated—the task seemed to be of a size and type that only a very large organization could cope with. And so the surface of the land was crisscrossed by an array of telephone lines, while the ocean's beds had telephone cables physically connecting continents. This type of undertaking belonged almost to the military sphere. For a long time, inefficiencies and expensive calls were accepted as the price that had to be paid. In some countries, flat-rate telephone tariffs applied, while in others, a baffling and illogical collection of rates applied. If you lived in the wrong place, you might end up paying the same rate for making a call to a neighbor who lived 5 or 10km (3–6 miles) away as was applicable to a trunk call.

Telecom was one of the areas to attract deregulation in the 1980s as the nation-state monopoly was revised but not removed totally. Although new players were allowed into the schoolyard, they often found that the successor company to the old monopoly was still a power to be reckoned with, and they still had to pay line rentals and fees. Phone charges dropped, but not by as much as they should have.

In the late 1980s and early 1990s, mobile and cellular phones liberated users from land lines. They became especially popular in India, China, Africa, and Scandinavia, where it was difficult and sometimes impossible to lay land lines over vast distances; in some countries, mobile phones have surpassed fixed lines altogether. The mobile phone set soon became recognized as having great potential, not just for making telephone calls. As we have seen, mobile phone operators in markets such as Japan have been compelled to find other platforms using mobile phones, such as using them as portable televisions and developing their "e-wallet" capacity. Third-generation mobile phones are able to access the Internet, and it is from the latter that the next chapter in the development of telecoms has emerged: carrying voice communications over the Internet protocol or VoIP.

Already there are many VoIP providers in Japan and in the United States. VoIP is the next step not only for telecoms users, but also for users of broadband technology, so it is hardly surprising that this is the area from which many VoIP providers have emerged. One immediate contribution it makes to users is in price. A call from Japan to the United States need not be any more expensive than a local call in Japan.

Traditionally, mobile phone calls have been more expensive than calls using traditional land lines, but this price difference will be negated with the use of the VoIP platform. It is already attracting attention in Japan, where the Ministry of Telecommunications has estimated that 7 percent of domestic households have signed up for VoIP.

In the area of corporate and business users, and those who traditionally make high volumes of calls, the impact of VoIP is becoming significant. For organizations, the set-up costs of providing a server, software, and IP-capable telephones are lower, compared to the cost of establishing a traditional phone system based on switching equipment and phone sets. Call costs may then be as much as a half to three-quarters lower. Large corporations such as Mitsubishi Heavy Industry, Hitachi, and UFJ Bank have already moved over to VoIP, while others are adopting a staged approach, perhaps waiting to see what problems crop up with the new platform. Research company IDC has estimated that VoIP telephony was worth 46 billion yen ($422 million) in 2003 but that this will climb by a factor of more than 17 by 2008.[1]

The adoption of this new platform has the potential to revolutionize the telecom industry. Just as the advent of the motor car had a disastrous impact on saddle makers and provenders, VoIP promises testing times for upstream industries in the telecom sector, most notably for the manufacturers of traditional switching equipment. In Japan, one of these companies, NEC (which has more than a third of the Japanese market for switching equipment), has not waited to be swept away, but has actively sought to ride the VoIP tiger. In April 2004, it set up a separate division, and its salespeople now promote its IP-capable equipment (at the expense of older equipment) to existing customers.

VoIP is and should be considered a part of the browser community. Many telephone companies are selling the software to kick-start a phone on IP from the desktop. I have developed a system that is an address book that uses the browser on a PC. As such, if you want to call Joe Smith, you search Smith; his phone is actually activated to be called, using the VoIP interface. The beauty of doing it this way is manifold. First, I can use it like the mobile phone, in which all the past records of calls are kept. I can also send faxes by clicking the activated fax number on the address book. I can include attachments, such as e-mail, which are printed on the other side (at the receiver's fax). I can assemble any number of people in the address book by checking a dialog box in front of their name to form a mailing list or a group, and then by clicking the activated group name, I can talk to all of them in conference call mode. I can also send Christmas cards to any number of the addressees by sending the information and card designs from my browser to an outsourced mail room service company. The same procedure can be employed for sending gifts. This is an explosive expansion of utility from the current e-mail- and search-dominated use of a browser. It opens a universal window and allows me to send mail, fax, or call from anywhere in the world.

Join the March Early

When an industry is faced with eventual oblivion but the execution of final sentence is delayed, what can it do? Does it have any realistic options and alternatives to throwing its hands up into the air in sullen resignation? This depends on the industry, of course, but for some, such as the telecommunications industry, a good beginning for companies is to try to insinuate themselves into the forward march of the new technology.

A telephone company can try to become a content distributor. In other words, it can seek to sell and distribute the products and services that are pulling the rug of security from underneath its feet. A traditional analog telephone company faced with the prospect of Voice over IP telephony could also seek to get involved in the distribution of broadband and of contents and services through the broadband platform. It could seek to develop and offer "one-stop-shop" communications solutions, such as a platform from which all communications media would be available at the click of a mouse button—e-mail, fax, VoIP, and so on. It could also expand into mail room services, gifts, and other types of e-commerce.

To repeat a cliché, forewarned is forearmed. No company should ever become complacent and introspective. It must have furiously twitching antennae sorting out potential trends in its product area. Once a potential threat has been isolated, certain things can be done, but they are seldom painless. One of the easiest is to ignore the threat. Maybe it will go away; then again, it is probably futile to fight against it in the first place. But a more positive approach is to adopt a strategy similar to that used by Jack Welch when he established "anti-units" in various parts of his organization. Such a unit could be a part of the organization that has the role of a "devil's advocate" for the new, potentially destructive technology. It would probably attract the younger elements from within the corporate structure, who could pursue developments in the new predatory technology without fear of offending the susceptibilities of partisans of older technologies considered closer to core competencies.

One company that adopted this approach and that will probably survive in the global economy as a result is Fuji, which has the advantage of breathing the air of Tokyo, the capital of digital consumer electronics. Another traditional camera maker that did nothing of the sort and paid a heavy price was Kodak. When faced with the advent of digital cameras, Kodak acquired a small company called Chinon in Japan to make them. This was too small and too late to compete. In overall governance structures, it was like a subcontractor, even though it elevated the subsidiary's position to a division in July 2004 to call it Kodak Digital Products Center, while at the same time removing the Japanese CEO and parachuting in an American manager. Japan dominates the field of consumer electronics components and systems. An American in the far-away mountain resort of Chino in Nagano prefecture is unlikely to form a critical mass.

The successful company of the global economy has to be adaptable. It may not be able to invent solutions to all its problems, so it should be able to copy and adapt answers from elsewhere. Such a company must be alive to technological developments, for it is technology that has made the global economy possible. But it should not see technology as the only source of productivity improvements or competitive gains. Sometimes, working practices and procedures have grown up and been sanctified by usage. The old adage of "if it's not broke, don't mend it" leads to apathy and ambivalence, as time-honored practices start to impede innovation. Nobody is prepared to speak the unutterable truth and to point the accusatory finger at practices that are wasteful, for fear of offending those who have traditionally controlled them. The employees of the global economy must not only work hard, but they must work smartly. The intellectual value-added, not labor value-added, determines your pricing capability in the cyberage. Often price is arbitraged across the entire cyberworld; indeed, pricing has fallen into the hands of consumers on platforms such as eBay.

Success in the global economy may mean challenging physical constraints—or, at least, the "physical constraints" we think we have inherited. We have to develop a very keen far-sightedness and ability to look deep into the future and perceive clearly. At the same time, we have to develop abilities akin to 360° vision. Our ability to develop innovation depends not only on looking keenly in one specific and unique direction, but on being able to see far in many directions at once. Technology must continually innovate and solve ever more complex problems. This will involve the growth and expansion of new specializations. As these develop, they must not be allowed to become too autonomous from the rest of scientific development. The walls of division between discrete disciplines must not be allowed to grow higher, and where they exist, they must be torn down or seriously downsized.

Much of the recent technological success story, and so much more of the future script for technology, depends on effective teamwork. Some of this will involve multidisciplinary approaches that, despite the title, flout the need and rationale for disciplinary divisions. This teamwork may be formal, although in the best interests and history of scholarship, much of it will be informal. Whatever form it takes, it will be able to utilize the strides already made in communications technology to defy physical distance. A scientist working on the West Coast of the United States can communicate his hunches, his findings, and the results of his experiments directly and instanta-neously from his laboratory or research arena to his colleagues in Europe and the Far East. This approach, called concurrent engi-neering, is not uncommon among leading-edge companies such as Cisco, Caterpillar, and most Japanese consumer electronic and auto-mobile manufacturers.

Discovery will continue to play a big role in technological devel-opment, but a lot of the solutions to problems are already close at hand. The solutions just have to be isolated and applied. Much of the hard work has already been done, and its solutions lie buried in exist-ing hardware or somewhere in the labyrinth of systems stored on the Internet. Teamwork in the solution of problems is important, but not the only solution. Sometimes too big a team in too big a company can be constraining, and as much, if not more, can be done by one specialist working on his own, maybe from home. Imagination is the key word for a new combination of existing solutions, as argued by Schumpeter, or a strong desire expressed by a cutting-edge consumer may be the mother of invention, as in the case of Thomas Edison.

The Personal Future

No matter where they are, individuals will have to learn to adapt. It will naturally be easier for younger people to do this than those in middle age or those facing retirement.

A number of holy cows may have to be discarded. One of them will be the notion of a job or a career for life. Most people make choices about their careers when they are in their late teens. In many instances, these have far-reaching implications. They begin a process or training, education or apprenticeship that will lead to a job in or near their chosen field. Although they may change employers and may even set up in businesses on their own, their career path is set. Such a set path may not be possible in the global economy of the future. Competition allied with technical changes not only may impose substantial adaptation and changes in working practices, but it may entail complete changes of career.

Another change will be the accepted norm that life always gets better and that workers, no matter what their education level, can look forward to an incrementally improving lifestyle, leading eventu-ally to a post-retirement soft landing, in which all or most of their needs are provided for.

People will have to learn to be lifestyle managers. Let us put this another way: People will have to take more responsibility upon themselves if they wish to reap the benefits of the global economy. Individuals will have far more access to information than ever before. Their abilities to communicate with others, no matter where they are, have been enhanced.

There are many opportunities for personal development within the global economy, but they will not be delivered on a plate. This is not a rousing call for a return to the tradition of hard work, as some notions, such as work, may be transformed in the global economy. Flexibility will be central to success, and inflexibility in any area, be it work practices or industrial relations, can only lead to hardship, the lack of the vision necessary to cut through the jungle of the global economy.

Embrace Leadership

Success in the new global economy will also depend on good leadership. This is true whether we are talking about a region-state, a microstate, or a company. There are enough examples of bad leaders around—people who are forever looking over their shoulder, who are reacting, usually belatedly, to events and then trying to pin the blame for their own cognitive weaknesses on others. A good leader needs courage. This shouldn't be confused with gung-ho recklessness, but courage usually signifies the opposite of timidity. A bad leader can usually be defined as fearful of something—or maybe everything. These leaders may be afraid of a disappointing set of sales figures at the end of the next quarter. They may be afraid of losing the next election.

Rather than dwelling on bad leadership, let us try to isolate those qualities that the global economy will constrain leaders to adopt if they want to win.

We have mentioned a number of effective leaders already, from both the public and the private sectors. They have some things in common, one of which is an unwillingness to be imprisoned by ideology and to seek practical results. Bo Xilai came from a "good" Communist family. His father could not be decried as a comfort comrade. He had undergone harassment at the hands of the nationalist government in the early 1930s, followed by the unbelievable horror of the Long March, when Mao Zedong led his followers on a forced migration from southern to northern China, across hostile terrain and under constant governmental attack. Privation was commonplace; shoes and dead animals were eaten. Bo senior's faith in his principles could hardly be questioned. One of these principles was communal ownership of the forces of production. In its Maoist form, it was also tinged with a certain xenophobia: Maoism might differ from "orthodox" communism because it was inherently Chinese. Yet Bo Xilai not only publicly embraced the opening up of the People's Republic to Western-style private enterprise, but he eagerly sought outside investment in Dalian and now throughout the country as the Minister of Commerce.

Singapore's Lee Kuan-Yew, an Oxford-educated lawyer, might seem very different to Bo Xilai. But they both spoke Chinese and English, very important tools to understand what is happening in the world. Lee was a visionary leader, one who was not afraid of formulating a vision and then imposing it on others. He believed passionately in his visions of Singapore—as long as they were successful. Once it became clear that they were no longer working effectively, they were jettisoned. Pragmatism won the day over ideology. If we were to ascribe such a thing as an ideology to either Bo or Lee, it might be belief in success and in accruing the greatest and potentially most long-lasting prosperity for their people. The means to achieve this might lie within ideology, but if the latter proved defective, other ways were to be adopted. The most important thing that Bo and Lee share is that they invited prosperity from the rest of the world with vision, intensity, and a passion for action.

A good leader, like a good government, needs a vision. This has always been true. In the invisible world of the twenty-first century, a vision should also help to set the direction in which to go and the speed at which the goal can be reached. In the jungle or in the fog, such a leader with clear vision helps others to move forward with less fear and confusion. This involves bravery, too. He must have the courage to dare to look into the future, to act according to time scales longer than the present accounting period or the next elections. Vision may not be valued in the short term; it may attract ridicule and scorn. There may be calls to "fix the problems of the present." A good leader has the courage to pursue his vision, to "think big." The more people who, in some way or another, are dependent on him, the more expansive his vision has to be.

We might say that good leaders should have vision, but they should remain pragmatists, never becoming prisoners or mute puppets of their visions.

Good leaders, whether they are in the corporate world or in government, must not be timid. The global economy is a new phenomenon. It does not have the certainties of the past, the mental and psychological crutches upon which leaders in the old economy supported themselves. To paraphrase Shakespeare, perhaps present fears in the global economy are less than horrible imaginings.[2] Uncertainty, like the dark, breeds more uncertainty. In such an environment, the need for a strong, decisive, and brave leadership figure is overwhelming. The leader must be truly fearless. It is no good just pretending because fear is contagious.

Value Information and Innovation

One way of overcoming uncertainty is to gain more information. A good leader in the global economy must be as well informed about the world around him as possible.

To succeed, an individual leader has to be exposed to the world. The global scene should not hold any terror. The leaders of the future will have to understand fully and have an instinctive sympathy and familiarity with the global economy. As things stand, there are many who understand it only partially and incompletely; there are others who are very much still in the dark. Far more worrying for the future is that many in this last group seem to like where they are. Understanding the global economy may be challenging, not to say tough, but it cannot be simply learned in an afternoon's seminar. Nor can it be learned without effort and its handmaiden, the desire to succeed and learn. In many ways, it has to be learned "on the job," but no student learns anything unless he is open to learning and has an inquisitive mind.

Traveling is the first step to learning how the world is and what it is like. It is also essential to develop a feel for how people outside your home base think, act, react, and express themselves. Only then can you really work as a team. Although the Internet can help us better understand the world through our fingertips, it is, at best, a shadow of reality. The deeper knowledge, experience, and input that leaders must acquire themselves before they can lead others cannot be developed on the desktop, nor can it be developed by a whistle-stop guided tour of the world.

I once attended a top management seminar of a large Australian mining company. Its sales spread across the globe, but the reality was that more than 50 percent of its output was exported to Japan. But none of the top managers actually lived in Japan. Many lived in the United Kingdom, the United States, New Zealand, Hong Kong, and Papua New Guinea. Some had visited Japan more than 100 times but had never lived there. There was no Japanese national in the top management group. How could they *know*?

The leader must have a love—in fact, a passion—for innovation. This can be in the form of researching new and better processes in a particular business, or a willingness to do things differently, to try out new approaches and new recipes for business success. Ambivalence in any sector of business is dangerous. It dulls reactions and responses. Just because a company is doing well *now*, in the *present* quarter or the *current* fiscal year does not mean that its success can be extrapolated into the future indefinitely. This is particularly applicable in the environment of the global economy where old certainties can dissolve on contact.

The leader must be able to lead. This may sound like a truism, but if he is unable to stir and provoke others and to communicate his vision and prognostications for the future he will be doomed to be, at the very least, a sad, pathetic Cassandra-like figure issuing prophecies of increasing despair and gloom but unable to persuade anyone to believe him.

A good leader does not have to be one solitary, ascetic visionary figure. It can be a well-defined and integrated group whose members should have good communications skills; unless they are able to interact positively with people, their leadership potential may be squandered. It must never be forgotten that an individual may not have a monopoly on leadership. A dedicated and integrated group can have the same impact, though this is more difficult to achieve in practice.

Of course, there is no universal template for effective leadership. The role of the head of state differs from one country to another. This is often a function of history. In some countries, such as the United States, the head of state really is the boss, the chief executive officer. In others, the constitutional head of state is a figurehead, signing laws into effect but doing little else.

A lot depends on the size of the country. If the country is the same size as the region-state, the task is easier, but if the country is large, such as Japan or the United States, China, Russia, or Indonesia, the role of the head of government should be to ensure that the state is an effective unit of combat in the global economy. The country must have adequate government structures to allow the individual units to interact with the rest of the world and to enhance their capability for doing this. They must learn how to brand their products and services, though preferably not using central funds and taxes. Instead, they should earn their own money from the rest of the world.

The role of the head of government here is not truly active: It is not that of a doer, but it is a catalyst, ensuring that this smooth interaction of regions with the rest of the world takes place.

Embrace Flexibility

It is clear that the role of the leader is changing. In the old economy, in which corporate structure resembled a pyramid, the role of the leader was self-defining. He was the person who sat or stood on the pyramid's apex. He directed those below from on high. Everyone knew where he stood in relationship to those above and below him. It was a neat, geometric, and insulated world. But company structure is changing. What is the role of the leader in an organization such as Cisco Systems, where organization is amorphous, weblike, and virtual, and where there are more than a hundred "other" companies within the matrix of the virtual single company?

One of the most important assets that a leader can possess is *not* having very rigid, preconceived attitudes about his role. He must be flexible and intuitive, able to tune into change.

Earlier, we looked at how latecomers to an industry or business sector can enjoy an advantage over traditional players. This can be true of a nation-state or a business. The newcomer is able to benefit from all the knowledge gained by years of mistakes, but he does not have to carry the same burdens or need to unlearn the outdated legacy. Does this apply to leadership?

If a CEO is at the head of a relatively new corporation such as Dell or Microsoft, it is easy to optimize from a zero base, a *tabula rasa*: Innovation goes with the territory. However, an old-world company has many decades of history as an organization, and change is harder. There may well be vested interests and established patterns of doing business in a particular location. Michael Dell told an interviewer, while visiting Japan in the spring of 2004, that if an outsider happened to peep into his company's board while in session, he would think that the company might fold tomorrow. The discussion is usually on problems rather than accomplishments, and customer complaints rather than satisfaction.

At the level of the probable, an "old-world" company may try to transplant a particular sector in the new world. But this is very hard to get right, and the ideal of straddling the two worlds, with one foot in the old world and another hovering tenuously over the new, is an impossible one. A company such as General Electric can have some amazing results. It is one of the longest-established American companies. Not only has it been around for a long time, but it has also been big for a long time. Nevertheless, it has never complacently sat on its laurels. Instead, it has constantly and consistently challenged its *modus operandi*. General Electric has been to the fore in outsourcing its support base. Much of this was the result of its visionary and brave CEO, Jack Welch. He once told the company to put the letter *e* in front of all the verbs used internally: e-design, e-distribute, e-sell, e-service, and so on—in other words, to try to energize everything through this process of applying the "e-" or electronic concept, and see what happens. Then ask, "Are we the best e-guys?"

When someone of the stature of Jack Welch makes such a statement, that person is taken seriously. That's how GE was able to reincarnate itself in this new world. Its business remains fairly conventional—power generation, medical electronics, broadcasting, white goods, and so on. Its business has not changed, but its way of *doing* business has. Most important, its products and services belong to the old world. You don't have to be a high-tech start-up, a Google, or a Yahoo!. There are many different ways that a leader can give birth to himself or herself, or maybe undergo rebirth—but only if that leader understands what such a process means.

The Corporate Future

The global economy means uncertainty. It also spells giant opportunities for those brave and supple enough to adapt. The global economy really is new. There is no rulebook. Nobody knows what will work. The only solution is to try and, if at first you fail....

Business schools should stop talking about the business models of the past. These belong in the realms of business history and can teach very little about the future. Many students believe that the problems of global business can be solved by cognitive templates and "ready-made" solutions and frameworks. They may be taught to see business in terms of an often-played game, with a bulging rulebook. In such a game, success comes from adopting the right game plan, maybe playing the game according to the well-worn and well-learned rules of the past, though playing smarter than the other guy. Yet this is a recipe for failure. In the global economy, business is also a game: People indulge in it for varying reasons. But nobody is sure what the rules are. They have yet to be reduced to normative prescriptions. This process is unlikely to take place soon, as there is no agreement yet even on the basics of this game—some still stubbornly try to play the game's earlier versions, which only causes frustration and confusion. By the time any rulebook or user's manual appears, the global economy, which is essentially dynamic and fluid, will have changed, and the "new rules" will be already obsolete. Who will listen to anyone saying that the secret of success is to fail many times?

The successful company in the global economy will be—indeed, must be—a new phenomenon, owing little to the precedents of the past. If we were to compare it to a living being, it must largely turn its back on its parentage and ancestry. It must be genetically different from them. I have mentioned in *The Invisible Continent* and elsewhere the need for the new company to have a different set of chromosomes. This difference can be exhibited in many forms, but it is all embracing.

It requires, for example, a root-and-branch rethink of marketing methods. A traditional approach to markets was to see them as self-contained units that could be entered sequentially. This must be discarded in favor of simultaneous penetration of all markets at once, combined with a commitment to *insiderization*.

Businesses will also be compelled to do business in new ways. Notions that were once popular about dealing with customers must be re-evaluated in the light of a changing world. The customer must be reborn as the most important agent in the business world. Whatever business structure is followed must inform customers that they are in control. As far as possible, their involvement must be sought and catered to. It is a paradox that, in a world that is stretching toward farther and less clear horizons, one of the secrets to business success may involve greater attention to the personal and the intimate in customer relationships.

This is one of the reasons why I have serious doubts about the use of case studies in the world's business schools. Companies rise and fall more quickly than ever before, and students need to learn the dynamics of steering the company as opposed to balancing static power. Case studies take a snapshot of a fast-moving car going through a chicane. You may be able—just—to learn something from it, but such a snapshot is seldom useful to a CEO who needs to learn from a Michael Schumacher where to apply the brakes, how much to step on the gas, how soon to steer, and where your eyes should be focused. My good friend Yuichiro Miura skied down Mount Everest. He is also the oldest man to have climbed Everest, at the age of 70. He and his family train people to ski on a steep hill while blindfolded. He tells me that this is the best way to develop a feel for the bumps on the surface and for the slopes. Eventually, learners can "see" the slope by feeling it through their skis. Their entire sensory system is attuned to the mountain. This is a good metaphor to bear in mind when managing and leading a company in the twenty-first century. Instead of logic, statistics, market surveys, the opinions of industry experts, business school templates, and case studies (to name a few), you really need to develop a sensory system for the 800 million cyberites, as well as the 700 million triadians who have become the key drivers of the global economy and key players on the global stage.

The Homeless Corporation

Success first requires that companies accept that their commitment to the global economy is total; there can be no half-measures. It is impossible to act gingerly, to sit on the side of the swimming pool, and observe before taking the plunge. If they do this, companies will find themselves becoming relics of the past. The best they can hope for is to be absorbed by others.

Let me say this once more: The global economy is inherently borderless, and its companies may well be homeless. The traditional company seemed inseparable from the nation-state. Even when its operations covered time zones and continents, the relationship with the old nation-state survived even when the company was deemed a multinational. All commercial enterprise can be traced back to a source. When that source grew into a thriving business, it was identified with its nation-state home, even though it might earn much— even the majority—of its income from export or from business conducted by subsidiaries in other countries. The homeland was the location for the "head office," from which the company's diverse operations were directed and to which regional managers sometimes had to gravitate to with near religious devotion. Even when a company migrates and relocates in another jurisdiction, as we noted with the many examples from Sweden, there is still a tendency to identify the companies as "ex Swedish." That was where they were born. But many "Swedish" companies are already headquartered in the United Kingdom, Switzerland, and elsewhere in Europe. Less than a single percent of Nokia's sales are in Finland. Microsoft is located in Seattle, a gateway to the Pacific. Bill Gates once told me that for the first 18 years after establishing the company, he did not have to go to Washington, D.C. He and his colleagues' world view had Seattle as its center. Had the company been located in Boston, maybe the government contract would have appeared more important (as most companies on Route 128 tend to believe). Had it been set up in San Jose, venture capitalists may have dictated the future of his company.

In the company of the future, the borderlessness of the global economy must inform the thought processes and outlooks of employees. There must no longer be any sentimental attachment with an old nation-state in which the company has its headquarters. The notion itself of a headquarters is giving way to the reality that the market never sleeps, that business is done 24 hours of every day, and every day of every year.

Old, hide-bound divisions of the business world into industrial sectors must also be relaxed. Self-definition can be a dangerous activity, imposing straitjackets and limited vision. The global economy can bring a company into areas where it does not expect to be, where indeed it may feel less than comfortable. This may compel corporate self-denial, which is no bad concept in itself. A company that rests too securely on its laurels risks becoming complacent. The natural state of *homo economicus* is movement.

Innovation, Inc.

Full commitment to the global economy needs to be accompanied by full commitment to innovation. Companies must commit to innovation as never before. This is a simple truth but one that must be absorbed into corporate belief systems. Many companies not directly involved with technology pay lip service to innovation. It is a good thing, they all agree. They would like to do more of it, but either they do not know how or they are afraid to innovate. Innovation can lead them into uncomfortable zones.

But they should look around them. They should learn from Scan-dinavia. In particular, Sweden's approach to innovation is reminiscent of the representations of the Roman god Janus. He was shown with two faces, one looking backward and the other gazing intently toward the future. Sweden never tires of proclaiming its own history and contributions to scientific innovation. It is the home of the Nobel Prize, and the world of botany and physics owes a fundamental debt of gratitude to Linnaeus and Celsius. But Sweden does not rest on its past successes; it aims to be at the cutting edge of technological innovation, particularly in the areas of global telecommunications platforms (as with Ericsson) and also in securities markets (as with OM). This plays a major part in the strategy of the Invest in Sweden Agency.

Observers can look, perhaps with amazement, at the People's Republic of China. China may not be a universal model of success in the twenty-first century. It possesses assets denied to other countries: a large land mass and an inexhaustible supply of inexpensive labor. The success story occurs at the level of the regions of China, the United States of Chunghwa. Its present success is based on its regionalization and on the nurturing and propagation of region units of prosperity.

The Scandinavian economies are probably more useful as guides. They are much smaller than China. They are expensive; they are old and they have well-entrenched bureaucracies. Their national flags are entwined with lots of red tape that developed countries have acquired and once saw as representative of development. But over the past 10–15 years, they have revived their economies and their competitiveness. That is why we can learn so much from Scandinavia's success over the last decade. I mentioned above the two faces of Janus as being a model for Sweden. Let us imagine a variation on Janus, only this time one face looks inward into the domestic nation-state and the other gazes outward upon the world. In Scandinavia, the inward-looking face is proud but at the same time realizes that the domestic market is too small, and that success comes only through competing and winning on the global stage.

As we have seen throughout this book, innovation and competition in the global economy must take place specifically in four areas:

- **Business systems**—Companies must seek to ally with the best and cheapest providers of service across the entire spectrum of corporate functions: R&D, manufacturing, sales and after-sales service, back-office activities, systems development, and maintenance. This can take the form of 3PL (third-party logistics), BPO, x-BPO, concurrent engineering, EMS, e-commerce, and e-finance. Whether they go all the way to a virtual single company (VSC) as with Cisco or combined CRM/SCM on ERP as with Dell, companies must seek ways to make the organization scalable. This way, there is less stress on growing fast. They must bring in partners from all corners of the world to work on the company's platform. Perhaps the only function you would not let the third party do is the customer interface, although a lot of it can also be shifted to the cyberworld.

- **Products and services**—The need for innovation in this field is obvious. But the challenge is also formidable. What were thought to be technological islands, such as audit cards on IC-chips, GPS navigation for cars, mobile phones, PCs, digital cameras, printers, CD players, video games, and IP/LAN/wi-fi, are all converging to form a huge continent. We can no longer define the battlefield in the traditional sense, and yet we must slice off a piece of land for it to produce food for the company today. Though tomorrow is a very different journey, we must define today's territory and make the best of it. Innovation, therefore, is the process of defining the territory and coming up with the best equipment to use in it. New products and services are needed to ensure compatibility within the new bounds, but they must also reflect the potential of utility that this extended and newly opened territory holds in the new continent. Innovation is the survival kit in this global market place.

- **Customer interface**—Innovation is especially dynamic in this area. The introduction of mobile phones in Japan, for example, opened up entirely new ways of marketing through mail magazines delivered periodically to the displays of cell phones. Using onboard functions such as Save the Screen, it can become an electronic ticket, discount coupon, or certificate/ receipt. This is a low-cost and interactive way of maintaining a communications conduit with a large group at once or narrow-casting to a target segment. Likewise, Google and other search engines are no longer a simple guide to the cyberjungle. It is potentially the venue of the lowest-cost promotions, as customers who are interested in your product and services come to ring your door rather than the other way around. Their chances of purchasing your product are also quite high. As explained in Chapter 7, "Breaking the Chains," Ohmae's theorems point to the importance of working with the cyberites (in their fifth year of cyber-exposure). The innovation in the customer interface is really a prerequisite for most corporations in the world. The traditional advertisement through media such as TV, newspapers, and magazines is not only not cost effective, but it is also an inadequate way to keep the customers interested in your service on an ongoing basis.

- **Employees, managers, and staff**—Innovation is needed
  most in recruiting, training, evaluating, and rewarding people
  in companies. As Jonas Ridderstrale and Kjell Nordstrom write
  in their book *Karaoke Capitalism,* power is shifting from those
  who make rules to those who break them or rewrite them. This
  means that corporations need to find ways to recruit dropouts,
  petty criminals (the unfortunates who have broken time-
  honored rules and laws, rather than serious serial offenders),
  children, and retirees.

Companies need to bring heterogeneity onto their corporate platform instead of the homogeneity of the past. The platform has to be
global, participatory, and interactive. At the same time, the means of
delivering remuneration other than salaries, wages, dividends, and
stock options need to be crafted. As there is no hierarchy in the
process of giving birth to breakthrough ideas, a very new mechanism
of generation, detection, evaluation, and improvement of innovative
ideas needs to be installed. That very process of managing human elements of creativity within a corporation is where the innovation is
needed the most and will be abundant.

The Adaptive Corporation

When it comes to characteristics of successful companies on the
global stage, the clearest is that to succeed in the global economy,
any company must be adaptive, with a keen and sensitive set of antennae for picking up and decoding signals, and capable of responding
in an instant.

The global economy, particularly technology, which is its handmaiden, has refashioned time frames. What happens on the other
side of the world at this instant can have an impact here not after the
markets open, not even the next instant, but *this instant*—right now.
There will be no intellectual slack time. Coffee must be consumed on
the job, not in a distant and secure restroom.

Without this ability to discern developments in their sector,
companies are like blind people walking forward without a cane
or any means of support, until they come to an obstacle that stops
them abruptly. Such a company is merely reactive, buffeted by
circumstances.

The past may or may not be another country, but for many successful companies, it is a comfort zone, a VIP lounge to which recourse can be made in times of uncertainty. Just because a company has been in a certain line of business for generations does not mean that it is bound, as if by some hereditary element, to remain there and to keep on doing things in ways fashioned in and by the past. Companies must realize that in the global economy, such comfort zones are luxuries. They must look to their essential competencies, not in terms of inherited riches or abilities, but in terms of flexibility and utility in the future.

Learning from errors will be an important skill for corporations—and for those who lead them. Lack of success is never very nice, but there is no alternative. A solution that might offer itself is to copy those who have so far succeeded. This is a simplistic inductive approach. Just because one company, maybe of a similar size, has succeeded does not guarantee success for others. There may occasionally be short-term ephemeral success, but this inevitably evaporates unless an adaptive approach is then pursued. After all, the global economy is truly complex, dependent on variables that cannot be readily identified.

Companies must also learn to adapt their identities, maybe occasionally to be shocked at where the market is taking them. There must be a readiness to engage in corporate self-denial. Success in either the past or the present is good and laudable: It is what should drive companies and their employees. But it has a nasty similarity to mercury and will slip very easily from the hands of those who become too complacent or who try to hold on to it for too long and in the same posture. I mentioned early the anticompany structures introduced by Jack Welch at GE. No company should be afraid of taking bold steps. This may mean a complete restructuring and re-engineering. It may also be nothing less than a painful rebirth. But these will often be necessary. Just because something has never been tried in the past should not be an obstacle to its adoption in the future. This has been central to human development.

Beyond Hierarchy

All traditional organizations consciously or unconsciously mirror the military. There is a clear chain of command based on hierarchy, deference to one's superiors, and condescension to inferiors. Nowadays, companies usually don't insist on uniforms, apart from for junior clerical staff, but they maintain the military trappings by employing job titles ending in "officer." The hierarchy is reflected in the company's headquarters. The CEO's office, and maybe the boardroom, are on the top floor, from where there is naturally the best view and from where the city traffic is all but inaudible. This reflects the perceived need of the chief to command the heights and to have a good view over the surrounding territory.

This model emphasizes control, especially by a small group, or maybe by one figure. He may like to think that he has his finger on the pulse, that one word can command obedience and fulfillment. The organism inevitably responds sluggishly. For one thing, the system is too large. There is too much internal inertia and friction. It will probably move, but only in response to simple imperative messages from "the top." So, unless the senior-management echelons are fully cognizant of the need for action, the organization is liable to be overtaken by events.

In an environment where response has to be innovative and speedy, a situation in which all initiatives must circulate, flowing first for approval to the top before being granted approval, is wasteful and ineffective. The pyramid has to be discarded.

Many companies ape this system even though they know they shouldn't. It is as if they can't help it developing. The need to innovate still rubs against notions (maybe unspoken but no less powerful) such as loyalty and unquestioning obedience. There may also be lack of trust. Many companies have internalized a lot of routine, day-to-day activities. They have their own R&D department, marketing department, and so on in which the overall pyramidal structure of the organization is replicated. There is a long-standing belief that the best people to carry out jobs for the organization are those who are on its payroll. They are the ones upon whom the most trust can be placed. Their loyalty can be counted on, and so, hopefully, can their ability to do the job. Subcontractors may be used, and they may be very good, but at the end of the day, their position is akin to that of a mercenary alongside a professional soldier.

Let's briefly examine some of the best and most forward-looking companies in today's world, those that seem truly to possess a different set of corporate chromosomes. Two of them are American, and they are both involved in IT, though at different levels. Perhaps coincidentally, they were both established in the same year: 1984 (BG1).

Cisco Systems is a provider of routers and other internal equipment vital to the smooth functioning of the Internet. It is to the company's credit that most Internet users don't know the name that readily. It does its job in the background. A lot of its work involves traditional research and development of products, testing, manufacturing, and delivery to purchasers. But so much of the work of each department is carried out by subcontractors, or others whose relationship with Cisco Systems (while close) is less than that of payroll members. All these various branches of the organization come together to provide a seamless interface. The Cisco business structure differs fundamentally from Michael Porter's concept of a value chain. This implies seriality and sequence of operations, whereas Cisco relies on what could be best described as a three-dimensional value matrix.

Dell Computers has grown to be one of the largest and most successful computer manufacturers in the world. It has integrated the Internet into the ordering and customizing of computers, allowing home users to order and specify systems and software from the comfort of their own home, thereby cutting out the intermediate costs of dealers and warehousing. Inventory costs can also be kept down.

Also consider General Electric and how it has found new ways of viewing the organization. For a long time, much lip service has been paid to a company's human value, its intellectual capital. But little was done to capitalize on this. GE, in particular, sought to look again at its employees to see what they, as individual skill possessors, could contribute either individually or collectively to the company. GE has sought to promote its employees' retention of their individuality. It has not attempted to browbeat employees into an undifferentiated mass of operatives, each one imbued with a collective company culture.

In conclusion, the successful company in the global, borderless economy must have an intuitive feeling and sympathy with it. General Electric's core competency remains engineering, but it has embraced IT with passion and is one of the world's single biggest users of computers and other IT solutions. Technology cannot be seen as an add-on to corporate structures, thinking, and decision-making. It must be at the corporation's heart.

Many establishments will have to tread the path that old establishments such as GE have treaded over the last 20 years. Leading-edge companies today have fundamentally a different corporate structure, as we have seen in the examples of Cisco and Dell. They are the amalgamation of the human systems and cybersystems spread literally all over the world.

Notes

[1] Figures quoted in "Three Cheers for Cheap Talk," *Far Eastern Economic Review*, 22 July 2004, online edition, www.feer.com.

[2] "Present fears are less than horrible imaginings," *Macbeth*, 1.3. 137–138.

10

THE NEXT STAGE

The Regional Future

It would be nice to be able to sit like a talisman or guru and point with prescient precision at those parts of the world that will one day replace the Dalians or the Singapores of today. Futurology is a risky business, and there are so many developments and forces that lie hidden like snakes in the grass but that may burst forth, either ushering in undreamt of prosperity in one region or leading to the destruction of a once rich and striving locality. The latter should happen far less in the future, but as we have hinted, old habits die hard.

Here are some regions that currently have some of the ingredients to attain the level of a prosperous region-state. In each case, I mention what these are, but I also mention aspects that, if not addressed, could slow or completely stymie progress. In particular, the continuity and integrity of the region's leader or leaders is key. Even in the twenty-first century, prosperity comes down to individuals.

Look at Bangalore in India, which is a large and dynamic city of five million but whose leaders have not lost their original vision. Its leadership in the worlds of IT and branding would not have been possible were it not for early pioneers in companies such as Infosys and Wipro. The realization of Infosys co-founder Narayan Murti was that someone had to create wealth to distribute wealth. Today, the former communist activist is a national hero.

Likewise, the advance of Hyderabad as the IT capital of Andhra Pradesh can be attributed (in part, at least) to its charismatic governor, Chandrababu Naidu; its leading-edge company, Satyam; and its founding chairman, Ramalinga Raja. If you visit Satyam in the bustling outskirts of Hyderabad, you will not believe that the company is in India. Its beautiful facilities are spread over rolling hills; there is a swimming pool and a nine-hole golf course.

Little wonder that, in India, many software companies are asking, "If Satyam can do it, why can't we?" Satyam now has 16,000 employees in 300 offices in 45 countries. So, Infosys and Satyam are leading indices of what could come out of India. Bangalore and Hyderabad are the models for other cities, such as Pune and Chennai (formerly known as Madras). Success breeds success. India is still not a rich nation. What is important for its future is that there is enough money to educate children. India and neighboring Pakistan certainly have enough money to develop nuclear bombs and missiles, as well as keep a large military. The warming of relations between the two countries should herald a decrease in defense spending.

The hope of the global economy is that it enables regions to bring in wealth from the rest of the world, rather than robbing their neighbors. This requires the regions to be equipped with well-educated and disciplined people under a visionary leader who can communicate with the rest of the world.

Hainan Island

The People's Republic of China has been like a Petri dish in a laboratory experiment. It has shown the world how region-states can prosper. It is more than probable that new regions will develop here, but it is really impossible to predict with certainty where these will be. Prosperity will seep out from the half-dozen region-states along the East Coast into neighboring areas, such as Jilin and Heilongjiang from Dalian in Liaoning Province. Such an expansion might threaten the viability of existing region-states, which may suffer wage increases and pressures on scarce resources. But it is possible that region-states will respond to this by a process not unlike a cell dividing in nature. As the cell grows in size, another cell nucleus will develop before the formal division takes place.

One potential region to watch is the province of Hainan Island. It lies south of the Chinese province of Guangdong and is set between the Gulf of Tonkin and the South China Sea. It has a population of around eight million people; the vast majority are Chinese-speakers.

Hainan's economy was traditionally based on subsistence agriculture. One eighth of the population is made up of members of ethnic groups such as the Li and the Miao, who still lag far behind other residents of the island in income levels. In the 1950s and 1960s, tens of thousands of Mainland Chinese were drafted onto the island to establish rubber plantations, a campaign that did untold damage to the island's environment.

Even so, Hainan has abundant natural wealth in the form of mineral deposits, such as gold and iron ore. It is also well placed to benefit from the ongoing exploitation of oil and natural gas reserves in the South China Sea. Its natural beauty also attracts visitors, mostly from Hong Kong and mainland China, but increasingly from farther afield. It possesses a semitropical location: It is as near to Southeast Asia as any part of China can be. Its beaches and holiday resorts have the same facilities as those in Malaysia, Thailand, or the Philippines. Sanya, on the island's southern coast, was the venue for the 2003 Miss World beauty pageant, a significant event for both the island and the nation.

In spite of the island's relative proximity to burgeoning Chinese regions, such as Guangzhou and the Pearl River Delta, it has not taken off to the same extent. This is not due to lack of infrastructure. Wei Liucheng, the former chairman of the China National Offshore Oil Corporation, was appointed governor and signalled his intention to act as the island's chief executive officer, attracting investment from China and the rest of the world, and also assisting ventures that are already up and running. The island's openness to the rest of the world is mirrored in the establishment of air routes both to destinations in Southeast Asia and to Europe.

The province's geography as an island makes it uniquely self-contained. Its government is also outward-looking, in the spirit of other leaders of established region-states in China. It may also benefit from its distance from Beijing, from which it is viewed as too remote to warrant any interference.

Petropavlosk-Kamchatsily, Russia

None of these regions I mention should be considered a sure bet for future prosperity. It is impossible to look with certainty into the future. However, all of them have the potential to become foci of prosperity. One of the features of prosperity in the global economy is that an area does not have to be rich to become rich. In the language of economists, it does not need to have lavish or even moderate factor endowment. In the days of the Industrial Revolution and the heady days of manufacturing industry, such factors as mineral wealth and vast resources of commodities, not to mention capital, were essential. If these did not exist, a large reservoir of cheap human labor could offset the lack of the former.

In his discussion of value, Alfred Marshall wrote about situation value. This was added to a piece of land because of its proximity to a large concentration of population with markets and factories. The advent of efficient means of long-distance transport and effective logistics means that situation value is no longer dependant on being on the doorstep of a potential market. In the past, if land was near a railway upon which goods could be transported, this was sufficient to grant it enhanced situation value.

In the borderless global economy, notions of situation value have been radically changed. There are locations on the planet that would dissuade all but the hardiest explorers from settling there, let alone establishing a business. Siberia, the Alaskan and Canadian Arctic, and Greenland come to mind. These areas have a climatic and geographical disadvantage. They are uncomfortably cold, and they are far from busy transport routes.

Imagine a futures or currency trader who dislikes human company. He is a rugged type who has a high discomfort threshold. He has an idea that strikes many people as bizarre and not a little crazy. He wants to set up a brokerage in a small settlement in northern Siberia or even the eastern coast of Greenland. Maybe he doesn't like cold weather but still values solitude, so he opts instead to establish his one-man brokerage on an atoll deep in the middle of the South Pacific. Such a project would make many observers question his mental balance, but it would be possible. His communications needs could be provided, though at a price. In today's world, the World Wide Web enmeshes our planet.

The ideal imaginary and revolutionary man might live in Petropavlosk-Kamchatsily, the capital of Kamchatka. Although it may seem extreme in terms of climate and winter chill, it is actually located south of 55°N, the equivalent of Glasgow in the United Kingdom or Denmark. Its winter temperature is no worse than Kalamazoo, Michigan, and is certainly comparable to Winnipeg, Manitoba. Since Kamchatka is the first city in the world where the sun rises every morning (though not in winter), if you live there, you could attract currency and bond trading from the rest of the world. If you don't fancy the weather, the same thing could work in Tuvalu in Fiji in the South Pacific.

Vancouver and British Columbia

Three distances are used in the travel industry: physical distance, time distance, and price distance. Of the three, a busy businessperson makes decisions on the second: What is the quickest way to travel? Hence, air travel supplanted cars and trains as the standard mode of business travel. Online brokerage firms such as Expedia and Travelocity are changing this. They make the third option far more attractive. For example, a round-trip from Tokyo to Kyushu is more expensive than one from Tokyo to Honolulu. This explains why a multibillion-dollar development called Sea Gaia went bankrupt. It recreated Hawaii in a huge enclosed Ocean Dome. But then discounts reduced the Tokyo-Honolulu round trip to less than $300. The real Hawaii became "closer." Many other theme parks in Japan are now in trouble for similar reasons. It has become cheaper to go to Denmark than Tivoli Park, Okayama; to Holland rather than Hans Ten Vos, Nagasaki; and Los Angeles rather than Universal Studios, Osaka.

Similarly, from an Asian perspective, the greater Vancouver area is increasingly alluring. This is a geographical and commercial extension of the northwest of Washington State. The home of Microsoft and Starbucks (not forgetting Amazon) is on its doorstep. Communications between the two areas are easy. Already some service providers, such as advertising companies, are taking advantage of lower costs in British Columbia because the footprint of satellite broadcasting already covers this area anyway.

The cost of living in British Columbia is as high as it is in Washington State. Taxes are a good deal higher, and the regulatory framework for many branches of business is rigorous. However, there is a new desire on the part of the provincial government to open up to the rest of the world. Not only does the Vancouver area sit astride Seattle, but it also lies on the eastern shore of the Pacific. Of all Canada's provinces, it is the one closest to Asia.

I have had a vacation house in British Columbia for a number of years. My first one was on Vancouver Island. My second was in Whistler Creek (its ski slopes became popular in the 1980s). Then I moved to Blackcomb when Whistler Village moved eastward to become North America's number one ski resort. In essence, I have moved my properties as locals would. And before the 2010 Winter Olympics is held there, it might be a prime time to exit from the resort. The airfare from Tokyo to Vancouver or Whistler is about the same as to Sapporo, and yet the slopes and facilities are world class.

Estonia

Estonia lies on the southern side of the Gulf of Finland from Helsinki. Finland and Estonia are divided by no more than 120km (74 miles). The inhabitants of both countries are ethnically close. Estonian is one of the few languages in Europe related to Finnish, and the two are mutually intelligible. Despite their geographical closeness, the second half of the twentieth century saw a determined attempt to isolate Estonia from its near neighbor. In 1939, as a result of the infamous Molotov-Ribbentrop pact, Estonia (along with its two southern neighbors) was reallocated to the sphere of influence of the Soviet Union. This allowed for the Soviet occupation of the three republics in the following year and the consolidation of Soviet power along the Baltic. Leading politicians, churchmen, and businessmen were either executed or transported to the frozen wastes of Siberia. This process was interrupted when the Nazis invaded the Soviet Union in 1941, but was resumed with increased vigor following the war's end. Tens of thousands of ethnic Russians settlers were drafted into urban areas.

But even in the darkest days of Soviet occupation, Estonians were aware that they were not isolated. Finland was nearby, and in spite of "Finlandization," it was a beacon of Western-style freedom: Finnish radio and television programs could be picked up in the Estonian capital, Tallinn. Estonians always looked to the north and west for their models rather than east to Russia. This process was helped, albeit accidentally, by the policy of the Soviet government that allowed certain items of "decadent" Western literature to be translated into Estonian, on the quite reasonable assumption that not even the most dedicated Russian dissident would learn Estonian to read them. In the 1970s and 1980s, there was silent resistance to the spread of the Russian language. This took the form of increased fluency in English. The advent of *perestroika* gave Estonia and the other Baltic countries an increased hunger to regain independence. Even before Estonia had formally regained independence, private sector business initiatives had been established, including an informal market in agricultural land.

Once Estonia regained its independence, it was natural that it should look to its northern neighbors, Finland and Sweden, for guidance. It was at this time that Finland was itself entering a new period of openness to the outside world and attracting foreign direct investment. As a result, Estonia emulated the Finnish model—not the old Finnish model of big governments and high taxes, but an economy based on innovation and deregulation. Estonia thus was able to establish a low-tax economy. This is still one of Estonia's most permanent assets, along with a considerable reservoir of educated workers who are willing to work for wage levels lower than those of their Finnish colleagues. Estonia has also benefited from the return of emigrants and their descendants from the United States and Canada, many of whom come armed with business and technical know-how.

One of the most pressing problems in Estonia is the status of the large Russian minority, about one-third of its 1.4 million population (including Ukranians and Belarussians). Since independence, they have suffered various levels of discrimination, sometimes being denied access to jobs in the public sector. The response to the Russians, though unfair and unjust, is partly due to the decades of oppression suffered by the Estonians themselves. Some of these Russians are descendants of families resident in the country for over a century who suffered religious persecution during the Soviet era. It is to be hoped that Estonia's integration into the European Community will remove real and potential opportunities for discrimination.

Currently, Estonia's speedy economic recovery is superficial because it is based on tourists from Finland. Tallinn is only 85km (53 miles) south of Helsinki—90 minutes by high-speed hydrofoil. In 2003, Estonia had five million Finnish visitors, equivalent to the entire Finnish population. The Finns visit the beautiful old town in Tallinn, but they spend the bulk of their time and money in the city's plentiful casinos. Whether Estonia can develop itself as a serious industrial region or simply a Nordic Las Vegas is yet to be seen.

The Baltic Corner

The Baltic is not so much a sea as a lake, even though it has a rather thin and unsubstantial outlet to the sea in the Danish Sound. The Baltic is tide-free, and during the winter months, it is frozen hard, allowing intrepid travellers of the past to walk from Helsinki to Stockholm or St. Petersburg.

The Baltic has a long history as a trading area. In preindustrial days, the lands along its shores were rich sources of timber, wheat, and furs. In the medieval period, the Baltic came to be dominated by a group of German trading cities, the Hansa, who established the first commercial infrastructures in towns such as Riga, Memel (modern Klaipeda), and Tallinn. The role of the German Hansa was taken over by the Swedes, but German influence was never entirely erased. Until 1918, much of the southeastern corner of the Baltic, the area stretching from the city of Danzig (modern Gdansk) toward Lithuania and Latvia, was part of the German province of East Prussia.

The twentieth century witnessed destruction and expulsion of the area's inhabitants. In the era of the Cold War, it was very much set in the Soviet sphere of influence, housing Soviet naval bases and other paraphernalia of mass conflict.

The fall of Communism and the break-up of the Soviet Union saw the emergence of a political checkerboard. Poland was joined as an independent state by Lithuania and Latvia, while the hinterland of the old city of Konigsberg, now known as Kaliningrad, became a rather incongruous enclave of the Russian federation and was excluded from the expanded 25 member EU.

The coastal strip between Gdansk and Riga and its immediate hinterland has the potential to become a prosperous region-state in the global economy. It is already home to many businesses, especially German, Danish, and Swedish, while business process outsourcing operations have been established in the Gdansk area, though Poland has stronger relationships with the United States and France. It is learning that the rest of the world can bring prosperity, as it did in the era of the Hanseatic League.

The Baltic Three will develop individually and jointly. Individually, the ties are clear. For Lithuania, they are with Denmark and Germany. For Latvia, they are with Sweden and, for Estonia, with Finland. Its southernmost member, Kaliningrad, is sandwiched between Poland and Lithuania and will not escape from the EU-ization of the Baltic region at large.

The Kaliningrad enclave was formerly the territory surrounding the Prussian city of Konigsberg, a prosperous urban center with a varied cultural life and a renowned university. Konigsberg was the home of such intellectual luminaries as philosopher Immanuel Kant and mathematic Leonhard Euler. At the end of World War II, Konigsberg was in ruins, and its German inhabitants were expelled by the Red Army. The city was renamed Kaliningrad, for the honorary president of the Soviet Union during Stalin's rule. The area's population was replaced by Russian migrants. Even when the other Baltic States regained independence, Kaliningrad stuck fast to its Russian identity. There were consistent rumors of German investment—even talk of a new multilane highway running from Berlin and Gdansk—but German interests in the area were rebuffed by the area's local rulers and their allies in the Kremlin, who feared that they were preludes to claims for property restitution. As a result, Kaliningrad sits like a relic, a Cold War theme park with rusting industrial machinery, shabbily built apartment blocks, and pipes leaking raw sewerage into watercourses. If the visa situation is improved, the area has potential for tourism development, but swimming in the water along the coast is still not advisable. Kaliningrad has earned a number of superlatives. For example, it has the highest rate of HIV/AIDS infections in Russia. The omnipresent and many-headed mafia is a large presence here, growing rich on anything illegal, from people trafficking to amber smuggling.

The area has great strategic significance in economic terms, having a pivotal position between much of Eastern Europe and the Near East on one hand, and Scandinavia on the other.

Ho Chi Minh City, Vietnam

Ho Chi Minh, the former Saigon, suffered all the vicissitudes of the Vietnam War. Once this ended, it was the unwelcome recipient of much official "attention" from the northern victors. Of all the areas in the now-united Vietnam, it was the place that was viewed as having been most infected with the "vices" of capitalism. So, along with the name change, there occurred an attempt to wipe out the city's freewheeling past. This was only partially successful.

In 1986, under the far-off influence of its newly installed reform-minded mentors in Moscow, Vietnam introduced a policy called *Doi Moi* (renovation). At first, this was cautious because many die-hard ideologues had to be weaned away from opposition. In the 1990s, it blossomed through the establishment of joint ventures with non-Vietnamese firms and the tolerance of domestic private enterprise. In Ho Chi Minh City, the free market seeds, which had lain dormant for two decades, did not take long to sprout again. Taiwan became the largest investor in Vietnam, followed by Korea, Japan, Singapore, and Thailand during the 1990s. However, after 1998, when Zhu Rongji's reforms impacted China, Taiwan's attention shifted from Vietnam. Other ASEAN countries followed suit. Vietnam has now learned that its major competitor for foreign investment is China and that it has to offer something better than China to attract money.

So far, Ho Chi Minh City has not taken advantage of its location in the center of Asian markets. To its north and northeast lie China and Japan, while to its west and southwest sit Malaysia and Thailand. Vietnam is already attempting to penetrate the business process out-sourcing world, though this is hampered by a lack of fluency in English (or any other major language, for that matter). Some people used to speak foreign languages fluently in the days when the country played host to the French and, subsequently, the American armies. After the victory of the Viet Cong, linguistic skills in English were eyed with suspicion and were rarely advertised, though now the formerly concealed liability has been turned into an asset. Although memories of American involvement in Vietnam are frequently painful, this has not dissuaded American direct investment.

Vietnam is politically stable. Although it is attempting to improve communications facilities, this is still very slow. Internet and mobile phone usage is low, a reflection of the lack of sufficient infrastructure. Vietnam is also a one-party state, and while this has not hampered the efforts of the People's Republic of China to embrace the rest of the world, many businessmen, both foreign and domestic, complain of bureaucratic obstacles as well as corrupt politicians. Even so, Vietnam has a very diligent workforce, prepared to work for wage lev-els half the level of most regions in China. Many corporations treat Vietnam as a hedging strategy against China. Should anything happen in China—such as floating RMB—Vietnam is an attractive alternative.

The country as a whole suffers from two main problems: lack of infrastructure and overly centralized decision making. Vietnam's ports, including that at Ho Chi Minh, are dilapidated in comparison to those elsewhere in Southeast Asia. Ho Chi Minh is not capable of handling large volumes, so the port often becomes clogged with shipping, either unloading raw materials or exporting products.

Vietnam's ports are also incapable of working around the clock, partly because of labor regulations. This might not be a problem for manufacturers such as Nike, whose manufacturing partners have invested extensively in the outskirts of Ho Chi Minh. They make a product that is not perishable. It is not important that the product be delivered quickly to a target market. While sea transport of materials and products is difficult, use of the country's land bridge is even more problematic. The road and rail system in Vietnam is very run down. These are pressing problems, but it is possible that, in time, they could be overcome. The state of Vietnamese ports might be improved by advice and assistance from companies such as the privatized Singapore Port Authority.

Vietnam is still a communist country whose communist party holds a monopoly of political power. There is not even a willingness to pay lip service to transparency and openness. In the spring of 2004, the government announced that it was no longer interested in financial assistance from the International Monetary Fund because the latter had demanded to inspect some aspects of Vietnam's national accounting system.

The political dispensation current in Vietnam is not dissimilar to that of the People's Republic of China, but where the latter has embraced not only capitalism, but also a decentralization of decision making, the Vietnamese Communist authorities are still unwilling to allow important decisions to escape a closed circle. This need not continue forever. Internal battles might well result in the victory of more reformist elements. Events in the People's Republic, with which the Vietnamese communists have not had unbroken and friendly relations, may have a bearing, for if those in Vietnam's ruling elite see that decentralization of decision making does not lead to a loss of power and privilege, but rather to a growth in commercial opportunities, they may be more ready to adopt Chinese models. Vietnam is eager to open more to the outside world, especially through membership of the World Trade Organization. Infrastructural problems can be overcome with sufficient investment, but this must come from the rest of the world. Until Vietnam's government is ready to adopt a far more decentralized, federal governance structure, this is unlikely to happen. However, with one charismatic leader, a city such as Ho Chi Minh could change quickly, especially as Vietnam has all the ingredients to succeed in the global marketplace.

Khabarovsk, Maritime (Primorye) Province and Sakhalin Island, Russia

This is a vast, underpopulated area. It has for centuries attracted explorers looking for precious minerals. During the rule of the Russian tsars, Sakhalin was a place of incarceration for political prisoners, and this tendency to use the area as a human dumping ground continued into the Soviet period.

Khabarovsk province lies immediately to the north of China. During the Cold War era, this was an area of conflict and occasional outbreaks of violence. Now movement between China and Russia is much easier, and every day thousands of Chinese traders cross the border to cities such as Khabarovsk to sell merchandise.

In terms of infrastructure, the mainland area is traversed by the Trans Siberian Railway, giving overland access to Europe. Access is also aided by the Amur River, which makes cities like Khabarovsk accessible to ocean-going vessels. There is also a deep-water port at Vladivostok, the capital of the Maritime (Primorye) province of Russia. Sakhalin Island is separated from Japan's Hokkaido Island by less then 50km (31 miles) of sea and is now one of the dynamic areas in Siberia because of successful oil and gas exploration.

For decades, this area, lying on the doorstep of East Asia, was isolated from the outside world by the suspicions of the Cold War. Much of the area's technical infrastructure needs significant investment and improvement. But the area now has a chance to see how looking to the rest of the world can bring an improvement in living standards.

Moscow will have to adopt a hands-off policy to let these regions and subregions interact freely with the rest of the world. Currently, it is still like China in the early 1990s, and all the critical decisions are made centrally. A federal structure with the concept of autonomous regions will invite capital and technology from all over Asia. Once this happens, most of the key cities are within a few hours' flying time of Tokyo, Osaka, Sapporo, Seoul, and elsewhere, and East Siberia could become an area of dynamic growth.

São Paulo, Brazil

São Paulo and environs, a vast teeming megalopolis, seems to encapsulate the whole of Brazil in one locality: fabulous opulence and grinding poverty. São Paulo has traditionally been the financial center of Brazil. It was the power base for the country's coffee growers, and many of the country's rulers have come from the province.

In the 1990s and early years of the twenty-first century, the São Paulo region seemed to take off from the rest of Brazil, enjoying growth rates far ahead of the national average. Part of this has been due to its success in attracting new IT businesses, as well as call centers and back office facilities for companies dealing not only with Brazil, but also with Portugal.

Brazilian provinces are reasonably autonomous already. The problem has been the instability of Brazilian politics and the economy.

São Paulo and its neighbor, Parana, can deal directly with the rest of the world, particularly with North America, Europe, and Japan, not to mention Argentina and Chile. However, politicians in the capital, Brasilia, always try to play the balancing act, first with the Paulistas' old rival, Rio de Janeiro, and second with less developed northeastern (Amazon) regions. If they can finally decouple the São Paulo region from the tight control of the center, the region-state will enter the OECD in no time. One of the triggers could be the formation of a common currency among the Mercosur members or even acceptance of the U.S. dollar as the common currency of the Americas. When this happens, São Paulo will not suffer the volatility of the Brazilian national currency. Traditionally, the real and the previous currency, the cruzeiro, have fluctuated (mostly downward) so much that trading with Brazil contained a higher-than-average risk for global companies. But the intrinsic competitiveness of the region, together with its natural and human resources, is quite high, and it could be the first to demonstrate that there is no reason why Latin America cannot compete with the Asian regions vying for global investors.

Kyushu, Japan

The Japanese island of Kyushu could be a very successful region-state if Japan were to break up into 10 or 11 doshu. A doshu, like Hokkaido or Kyushu, is a larger region consisting of several prefectures. In the citizen's movement I organized in 1989, called Heisei Ishin, I proposed that Japan formally adopt a federal republic governance structure consisting of 11 doshu. Kyushu is the southeastern island consisting of seven prefectures, excluding the islands of Okinawa, which is, in my proposal, an autonomous doshu with 1.25 million people.

Kyushu is surrounded by the Yellow Sea on its west, the East China Sea to the south, the Pacific Ocean and the Japanese Inland Sea on its east, and the Sea of Japan on its north shores. It has a population of 13.5 million, and its GDP in 2003 exceeded $500 billion. If it were a country, its economic size would be ranked among the top 15 in the world—about the same size as Brazil and Korea. It is called the Silicon Island because companies such as NEC, Toshiba, Oki, and Sony have large-scale founderies there. In recent years, all key Japanese automobile companies expanded their production capacities in Kyushu.

Instead of looking east (toward Tokyo), if Kyushu looked west toward China, north to Korea, and south to Taiwan, it could be an ideal location for multinational corporations to put engineering support operations looking after factories in East Asia. Right now, Kyushu does not have such a function because air traffic is divided among the seven small prefectures, mostly catering to domestic passengers going to Tokyo and Osaka. A hub-and-spoke airport in Tosu, the logistical center of Kyushu, would make it possible to become a real East Asian mecca, not only for businesspeople, but also for tourists. Kyushu has many volcanoes, hot springs, and hundreds of beautiful small islands with fresh vegetables and fish. Decentralized Japan would produce a number of prosperous regions such as Kyushu and Hokkaido. What is more, they would not have to be dependant on the distribution of Tokyo's taxpayers.

What we have seen in Hainan, British Columbia, the Baltic corner, Ho Chi Minh City, Siberia, São Paulo, and Kyushu is nothing but a small example of the global potential. If these regions are blessed with a group of people who have the right vision, and if the center understands the key factors of success in the twenty-first century, which is to let the regions interact with the rest of the world, then not only these regions, but a lot more will come to play on the global stage.

The formula for success is not too complicated. What is complex is the need to unlearn the legacies of the nation-state and acquire new skills to work with global business.

From the investor's point of view, the list of attractive regions is getting longer. Getting onto the short list is the key. This is possible only when the region can demonstrate its *raison d'être* in one word. What does it have to offer on the global stage? What is different about it? Like global brands, such as Coca-Cola, IBM, Nike, and Disney, a region has to be recognized, at least among investors, with its forte writ large clearly distinguishable from the rest of the competition.

11

POSTSCRIPT

Reopening the Mind of the Strategist

I wrote *The Mind of the Strategist* in 1975. It was later translated and published in English in 1982. Many people have asked me to revise it to bring it up-to-date. Its Japanese version is still selling in its original form in Japan. I like to keep it in its original form because it was written when I was 29 to 31 years old, and it reflects my thinking and observations in those days.

Although a lot of the comments on strategic thinking and the approaches and tools I proposed in the book are still useful, the very definition of strategy using three C's is no longer valid. Using the three C's, I defined a good strategy as one developed to meet customers' needs in a way to best utilize a company's relative advantage over competition on a sustainable basis.

The problem is that, on today's global stage, we can no longer define competitors, the company, and customers in a straightforward way. For example, you saw in Chapter 9, "The Futures Market," that a competitor of Kodak is no longer Fuji or Agfa. In fact, Kodak cannot even define what Kodak is anymore. If it wants to be in digital cameras, is it willing to go into the mobile-phone business? If it wants to keep the laboratories, is it going into memory chips and ink-jet printers? When and where is it competing, and on what grounds?

Answering these questions is the very fundamental process of strategy development for a company such as Kodak. But it is not a problem unique to Kodak. Think about Dell. Whereas it was competing with IBM and Gateway in the 1990s, it now seems that its biggest competitor is actually HP. Dell's entry into printers suggests that it is quite conscious of this and vice versa. However, if Dell *is* a CRM-based direct-sales company, it should not be limited to PCs and printers. It could expand into digital consumer electronics and office automation equipment without too much modification of its existing systems. In fact, Dell does not have to manufacture goods in its own factories, as it has done in the past. It can link up, as Cisco does, with any number of EMSs and add a broad range of product lines. In the end, Dell could become the world's first company to produce electronic gadgets that are tailor-made to a customer's specification, as its computers are at present. For a company such as Dell, the scope of the business domain *is* the scope and ambition of its strategy. It is less dependent on competitors, but more on the customer-company interface. As long as Dell keeps direct lines of communication with millions of customers, there is not much room for competitors to come in.

For a company such as Sony, it is also difficult to define customers and competitors. Microsoft has become Sony's biggest competitor for its PlayStation 2 (PS2) because the latter has the potential to become a PC in the living room. Microsoft is not going to be satisfied with simply being the champion of the desktop. It probably wants to be champion (or provider of the ubiquitous operating system) of everything, including home, mobile, and office appliances and equipment.

However, the personal computer is also a platform for games. Sony's first job is to sort out, within its own corporate activities, what it needs to develop internally to keep its current position in games. It tries to produce its own engines (in a joint venture with Toshiba), an OS for games, and games themselves. This is not sustainable when they are spread over mobile phones (with Ericsson), PCs, flat-panel TVs, High-Density Discs (HDD), cameras, and Blue-Ray DVD and broadcasting equipment, not to mention traditional audio-video equipment, while maintaining movies and record companies. Each of these businesses is undergoing a sweeping sea-change individually and collectively. So, defining the company, for Sony, is at the crux of the strategy, without which it is not possible to define competition or customers.

Most companies are faced with more or less similar situations to Sony and Dell. As we move further into the twenty-first century, and as we try to climb up onto the global stage, it is clear that the very definition of the three C's (company, competition, and customers) becomes challenging, and strategy is developed first in trying to clearly define them. In the 1980s, strategy was developed to define the relationship among the three C's, but now strategy is about defining *each* of them and then trying to define their relationships in a dynamic, time-sequenced manner.

This process leads to another problem. That is, when you want to define yourself (your company), you need to think through your core skills and define other skills you can outsource. You can define customers and competition as either residents of isolated islands or inhabitants of the combined and emerging continents. Because this process depends largely on who does it, it is person specific.

Because we are dealing with the invisible continent in the borderless cyberjungle, the business domain you carve out is person specific. So, instead of the traditional definition of strategy development, using Ohmae's three C's, Porter's value chains, or Barnard's resource-based emphasis, we need to accept that it really depends on how the strategist sees it and carves out his business domain as his battle ground.

Beyond the Daydream

There is a very good phrase in Japanese, *kosoryoku*. This is what you need in developing strategy. *Kosoryoku* is something like "vision," but it also has the notion of "concept" and "imagination." However, unlike imagination, which sometimes has the overtones of daydreaming, *kosoryoku* is an ability to see what is invisible and to shape the amorphous. It is the ability to come up with a vision that is necessary and, at the same time, implement it until it succeeds. It is a product of imagination based on realistic understanding of what the shape of the oncoming world is and, pragmatically, the areas of business that you can capture successfully because you have the means of realizing the vision.

When you have described your vision, fully utilizing your imagination (realistically, as *kosoryoku* demands it to be), you can spell out your strategy. When you have the strategy, you can develop a business plan that spells out human and capital resource allocation, and a time frame for implementing the plans. It is therefore extremely important that you do not apply the traditional templates in the early stage of strategy development. You need to be quite open-minded about the business domain in which you will fight your battles, and how far and how fast you want to occupy the domain. This mental process is a clear departure from the traditional business school type of teaching of strategy development.

To develop this type of talent, we need to nurture future business leaders in the same way we develop world-class athletes and artists. We need to start early, exposing them to good instructors and coaches. A lot of give and take will help the man or the woman to shape the vision of the world to come. It is not possible to draw a picture of this universe, but we know it and how fast it is moving and developing. It is like describing the shape of a large cloud in the sky, blown off by strong wind. Yet we know its shape and where it is because we see it and sense it. Although it is not entirely possible to describe it in a static way, a world-class entrepreneur can describe it and can even capture a large chunk of it, converting it into raindrops or profit.

I hope this book helped you develop some feel for the new global economy, the coming shape of the geopolitical maps of the future, the key levers corporations can pull, and the dynamic business domains we can tap. Now it is your turn to climb up onto the global stage and perform.

INDEX

A

ABB, 217
abstracting, BPO of, 161
accounting services, BPO of, 163
adaptability. *See* flexibility
advertisements
    newspaper advertisements, 174
    on search engines, 174, 177
Africa, negative effect of nation-states, 88, 92
African Financial Community (CFA), 120
African Union, 120
Agfa, 228, 269
aggregate demand. *See* GDP
agricultural subsidies in Japan, 67-71
Air Campus, 208-209
All Nippon Airways, 179
AM-PM Japan, 179
Amazon, 43, 129, 145, 178, 259
antidumping measures (European Community), 122
AOL, 173, 178
APEC, 119-120
Apple, 43, 231
architects, BPO of, 163
ASEA, 217
ASEAN, 119
Asia. *See also names of specific countries*
    China's economic power in, 100
    rise of nation-states, 85-86

Astra, 217
Astra Zeneca, 217
ATM, as platform, 141
attractiveness (characteristics of region-states), 95
Australia, influence of U.S. dollar on, 57
Autoliv, 219
automobile production statistics, 168
autonomy of China's region-states, 102-103

B

Baltic region (global economy example), 262-263
Bangalore (India) example, 255
banking industry, technological breakthroughs, xx-xxi
Barclays' Bank, 169
Barnum, P. T., 71
Bentsen, Lloyd, 166
Berners-Lee, Timothy, 42
Bezos, Jeff, 129
Bharatiya Janata Party (BJP), 153
Bhattacharjee, Buddhabev, 153
bilateral free trade agreements, 121
bilingualism, 136
bitWallet, 178
BJP (Bharatiya Janata Party), 153
Blix, Hans, 219
Bloomberg, Michael, 7
Bo Xilai, 7-8, 211, 239

trader's paradigm and exchange rates,
66-67
transportation (characteristics of
region-states), 94
Travelocity, 259
Treasury bills and economic models, 448
Treaty of Rome, 115
triadians. *See* cyberites
TTK (Tokyo Tsushin Kogyo), xxi
twentieth century economics versus
global economy models, 45-49

U
UFJ Bank, 234
unemployment and inflation, 62
United Arab Emirates, diversity in, 91
United Kingdom
concerns about BPO, 169
Plaza Accord, 30
United States. *See also* dollar (U.S.)
advantages of federal nations as
region-states, 102
concerns about BPO, 164-170
economic policies, 71-75
Gramm-Rudman Act, 33-35
Plaza Accord, 30-33
power of central government, 194
Universal Studios, 259
UPS, 22, 181, 188
URL addresses, statistics on, 175
USSR. *See* Soviet Union

V
value chains, 180
value-added trade (Japan), 201-202
Van Gend en Loos, 115
Vancouver (British Columbia) example,
259-260
verifying creditworthiness, 180
Vestas, 77
Victoria's Secret, 43
Vietnam, Ho Chi Minh City example,
263-265
virtual single company (VSC), 181
vision and strategy, 271-272
vision for change, 200-201
educational role of government,
206-210
Japan, 201-202
regional strategy, 205-206
roadmap for, 202-205
as trait of good leaders, 240
visiting locations, importance of, xviii
Vodafone, 21, 228
VoIP and telecommunications, 233-235
Volcker, Paul, 32
Volvo, 217
VSC (virtual single company), 181

W
Waterford Glass, 108
wealth distribution by governments
bureaucracy, 198-199
downsizing government, 199-200
taxation, 196-197
Wei Liucheng, 257
Welch, Jack, 236, 244, 251
Wendt, Henry, xix
West Germany, Plaza Accord, 30
Whelan, Bill, 4-5
Whitman, Meg, 43
will to succeed of region-states, 114-115
William Demant, 77
Windows operating system
rise of, 35-37
as technological platform, 131
WiPro, 23, 152, 256
Worldcom, 225
Wriston, Walter, xx
Wu, David, 135

X-Z
x-BPO (cross-border outsourcing). *See*
BPO (business process
outsourcing)
Xia Deren, 9

Yahoo!, 173-174, 178, 244
Yamanouchi, 221
yen, value in relation to dollar (U.S.),
30-33
Yugoslavia, negative effect of
nation-states, 88

Zara, 182
Zhu Rongji, 4, 7, 19, 36-39, 75, 103,
211-212, 264
Zumwinkel, Claus, 188

In five days, even Darwin would be shocked at how you've changed.

The Fortune at the Bottom of the Pyramid
Eradicating Poverty Through Profits
BY C. K. PRÁHALAD

The world's most exciting, fastest-growing new market? It's where you least expect it: *at the bottom of the pyramid.* Collectively, the world's billions of poor people have immense entrepreneurial capabilities and buying power. You can learn how to serve them and help millions of the world's poorest people escape poverty.

It is being done—*profitably.* Whether you're a business leader or an anti-poverty activist, business guru Prahalad shows why you can't afford to ignore "Bottom of the Pyramid" (BOP) markets.

ISBN 9780131877290, 2006, 304 pp., $17.99 USA, $20.99 CAN

Capitalism at the Crossroads
The Unlimited Business Opportunities in Solving the World's Most Difficult Problems
BY STUART L. HART

"Professor Hart is on the leading edge of making sustainability an understandable and useful framework for building business value."
                    – Chad Holliday, Chairman and CEO, DuPont

Capitalism is at a crossroads, facing international terrorism, worldwide environmental change, and an accelerating backlash against globalization. Your company is at a crossroads, too: Finding new strategies for profitable growth is now more challenging than it has ever been. Both sets of problems are intimately linked: The best way to recharge growth is to pursue strategies that also solve today's most crucial social and environmental problems. In this book, you'll learn how to identify sustainable products and technologies that can drive new growth; how to market profitably to four billion people who have been bypassed or damaged by globalization; how to build effective new bridges with stakeholders; and much more.

ISBN 9780131439870, 2005, 288 pp., $29.99 USA, $33.99 CAN